ADVENTURES IN WONDERLAND

BY PAUL CHARLES

2023 First Edition
Published by Hot Press Books, 100 Capel Street Dublin D01 C9P4, Ireland.
Website: hotpress.com
shop.hotpress.com
Copyright © Paul Charles
Art Director and Cover Design: Eimear O'Connor
Production Manager: Mairin Sheehy
Edited by Niall Stokes

Printed by TBC

ISBN Hardback – NUMBER
ISBN Paperback – NUMBER
ISBN Ebook – NUMBER
A CIP record for this title is available from the British Library

Photographs are from the Hot Press Photo Archive and from Paul Charles personal collection. Every effort has been made to trace the copyright holders of any additional photographs in this book but one or two were unreachable. We would be grateful if photographers concerned would contact us.

ACKNOWLEDGEMENTS

I have told the stories in *Adventures in Wonderland* as I remember them. Did they all happen exactly that way? As I was writing, I recalled the interview the then surviving three Beatles did on-camera for The Beatles' *Anthology* documentary series. Paul, George and Ringo were discussing (if memory serves me!) The Beatles' final gig. After a bit of to-ing and fro-ing (not to mention three separate differences of opinion) George said something along the lines of: "Well there you have it. We were certainly all there, yet even we can't agree on what actually happened."

With that in mind for *Adventures in Wonderland* I used PC Theory #64

$$M = \frac{R+D-C}{2}$$

M = method; R = results; D = diary entries and C = circumstances. Why over 2? That, you have to figure out for yourselves!

This utterly reliable formula notwithstanding, Paul Brady and I disagree over when we met Bob Dylan backstage. Paul is convinced it happened backstage at Wembley. I am equally convinced that I never was backstage at Wembley for Dylan and that it happened at Slane Castle, Ireland in 1984...

So... moving swiftly along, I want to say a huge thanks to:

Niall Stokes who shows by example that editing is not a job so much as a work of art; production manager Máirín Sheehy, art director Eimear O'Connor and the rest of the *Hot Press* team; Christina Czarnik for her invaluable research work, typing up my handwritten notes (sometimes, even I cannot read my own writing), all the while keeping the sails aloft on the good ship Asgard; Kathleen and Anne, for always being there; the Flynns, the Toals and the McKeowns, who consistently demonstrate the worth – and the joy – of family life; the songwriters, musicians, road crew, stage crew, managers, promoters, promoter's reps, and agents who have escaped being written about here; Nick Lowe for being... Nick Lowe; Pete Wilson, Peter Aiken and Mark Markie – first call men one and all; Paul Fenn my business partner in all things Asgard, for offering me the desk and phone in 1976 and for sharing an office with me ever since – but most of all for being the ideal agent we can all look up to; Vinci McCusker my song-writing partner and life-saver; Fraser Kennedy, Richard Wootton, Pat Savage, Jake Riveria, Gary Mills, Frank Gallagher, Ivan Martin, Lindsey Holmes and Mike "Coach" Sexton, for always being wise; Michael Eavis for being the best dairy farmer in the UK but also for, in his spare time, running the biggest, most successful and best festival in the world – a true inspiration; Andrew Charles MM for never ever disappointing me; and, most of all, Catherine for joining me in a marriage which has proven to be the greatest of all *Adventures in Wonderland*.

Note: Throughout *Adventures in Wonderland*, 'Song Titles' are in single quote marks. *Album Titles, Film Titles (etc.)* are in italics. Everything else is a jumble!

CONTENTS

CONTENTS

INTRODUCTION

Right at the outset, I feel I should confess to you that every single day of my life since I was 14, I have been indulging in a very addictive drug. I can still vividly remember my first fix. It was early in 1963. I ran into my mother's kitchen and as usual she had the radio on. She was a fan of Frank Sinatra and Tony Bennett, but she absolutely swooned over Emile Ford. Emile and his group, The Checkmates, had enjoyed the first No.1 single of the 1960s with 'What Do You Want To Make Those Eyes At Me For', and their second single, 'I'd Love To Get You On a Slow Boat to China' – another firm favourite of my mum's – peaked at No. 3. Yes, Emile Ford was most definitely my mum's preference in music.

Until then, music had always been just a backdrop for me. If it was good, I enjoyed it. If I didn't enjoy it, well then I found it easy to ignore. But on this particular day, I was ambushed by a sound coming from the big speaker of our Bush valve radio. There was something at once hypnotic and urgent about it. It was a wild release of endorphins I was experiencing, in our wee house on Beechland Road, Magherafelt, in Mid-Ulster, Northern Ireland. I had no idea, of course, that tens of thousands of people the length and breadth of Great Britain and Ireland, were simultaneously responding in precisely the same way.

The music was being made by four young lads from Liverpool who called themselves The Beatles, with a little help from their producer and soon to be friend, George Martin. In those precious seconds, listening to 'Please, Please Me' for the first time, my world had been transformed from the grainy black and white of our small TV set, to the full, splendid Technicolor of the cinema. Or that was what it felt like. It is not so much that The Beatles changed my life with what became their first, transformative global hit, more that they turned on the internal multi-coloured lights that would guide me onto my life path.

'Please, Please Me' was a taster of extraordinary things to come. It can never be stressed enough just how happy the sound The Beatles created made you feel. Equally important was how good this sound made you feel about yourself. I had never experienced anything close to that special feeling before in my life. I was immediately converted.

Given the opportunity, every child strives to discover something they feel completely comfortable doing, and might even excel at. It might involve skate-boarding, cycling, learning about science, building lego cities; or being a singer, a poet, a painter, a carpenter, a sailor or even a candlestick maker. We are all searching for whatever affords us the reason to be able to stand up in front of our best mates, our friends, our families and our peers and feel a sense of our own worth. Sometimes we choose the skill; sometimes it feels like the skill chooses us. Some become so good in their chosen field that we can genuinely describe them as being important. Sometimes word of their notoriety might travel beyond their hometown to the rest of the country, the continent, or maybe even the whole darn world. But generally, it starts with whatever it is that allows us to hold our head up high amongst our own group. You might say that we all need a badge to wear. And in that moment listening to The Beatles – totally inadvertently and without any premeditation – I had found mine.

I wasn't gifted with the ability to make music. Certainly not. But I did have the energy and the desire to help people who had the music-making gene, get up on the stage and create a racket. And so this is what I have done, for the past almost-55 years.

That's a long time, and there were more than a few big hits and near misses along the way, as well as hair-raising adventures aplenty. But first and foremost, I was always and am still obsessed with what great artists do – and how they do it. And so, what I want to do now is to share with you some of the adventures I enjoyed, in pursuit of the next fix of my readily available – and thoroughly life-enhancing – drug: *music!* The idea here is not to spend time settling old scores: there's far too much of that already in the world. Instead, I will try to capture the magic of working with artists who are right up there among the best in the world.

Hopefully, by the end, you too will feel that you have had some utterly memorable *Adventures in Wonderland*.

CHAPTER ONE

MY FIRST ADVENTURE IN WONDERLAND

I know it's going to come as a tremendous shock, but the fact is, I can't dance. I should have realised it when I ventured to my first dance back in 1964. It was in Rasharkin in Co. Antrim in Northern Ireland, and the band on stage that night were called The Driftwoods. I do remember they performed a dramatic version of 'She Thinks I Still Care'. Now *there's* a song with a lyric to produce teardrops:

"Just because I asked a friend about her
Just because I spoke her name somewhere
Just because I rang her number by mistake today
She thinks I still care."

There's a film waiting to be made in those 29 words!

And so in that small dancehall in Rasharkin, I was introduced to a new world of musicians, guitars, saxophones, drum-kits, microphones and the magic-eyes of the amplification equipment glistening back at me from the stage. It was all there, up close and personal. I became so preoccupied witnessing music being created live on stage, for the first time, that I completely forgot about everything else.

On the way across to the rural dancehall, my mate Seamus Mitchell had talked me through the whole ritual. My task, if I understood it correctly, was to blag the last dance from my preferred dance partner before anyone else had a chance to step in and steal my thunder. Sadly, as it turned out, steal my whisper might have been more accurate. Not that my friends didn't try to help me. When Seamus spotted how preoccupied – or even lost – I looked, he got his girlfriend to persuade her younger sister, Maureen, to take me on a few circuits of the dance-floor. Maureen very patiently demonstrated the slow, slow, quick-quick, slow, foxtrot routine and when my foxtrot wasn't producing any satisfactory results, she tried the waltz. She talked me through the routine: right foot forward, left foot to side, right foot close; left foot back, right foot to side and left foot close. All of this amateuristic shuffling resulted only in me realising just how intoxicating her perfume was. As I recall it now, she was the first person to laugh at my obvious lack of dancing skills. Her final attempt proved much more successful when a slow-dance set was announced from the stage. "Put your arms around me," Maureen instructed, "hold me close and just walk me slowly around the outside of the dance floor. And please make sure I don't bump into anyone." Now *this* approach was much more enjoyable. I was so relieved – if that's the right word – that this subsequently became my signature dance-step.

I have an excuse for dancing like a rhinoceros. Unlike, say, the previous generation, I didn't – I mean we didn't – have to go to formal dance classes before we were allowed to venture onto the hallowed ballroom floor. We didn't need to perfect the Quick Step, the Waltz or the Foxtrot because they were being rapidly replaced by people "doing their own thing." In our brave new world, you were permitted, encouraged even, to stand with your feet about a foot apart and your arms arced at the elbows as though you were about to embark on the 100 yard sprint. And then, you'd just go for it, free to move in absolutely whatever way you felt like moving.

Everyone could have a go at 'The Twist' and it was a hugely infectious sure-fire, floor-filler when the song or its sequel 'Let's Twist Again' blasted from the speakers. But there were other dance crazes, including the Hucklebuck, the Shake, the Mashed Potato, the Locomotion and the Watusi. The appeal of these routines was that – once the basic notion was understood – you could simply let-yourself-go, as if your limbs were the branches of a tree on a very windy day. Your only real marker, as I'd been instructed by Seamus Mitchell on my inaugural evening, was how long it took you to shimmy up to your dance partner. Shimmy, I discovered, when I looked it up later in the dictionary, was also a dance.

On the flip side, I was gratified to discover that "a dance" meant you were allowed to enjoy the company of your chosen partner for the duration of three whole songs. God help you, however, if the three songs in question were, 'Hey Jude', 'House of The Rising Son', and 'American Pie' and your partner cold-shouldered you from the beginning of the first song, rebuffing your well-rehearsed opening line of, 'Do you come here often?' Further pain and humiliation followed if she speedily responded with a negative to your request for the last dance. It was a tough old world, even then!

I thought that taking up a musical instrument might cure my dancing ailment. To which end, I joined a pipe band. With hindsight, I'm not entirely sure I was motivated by music – or even learning how to dance. No, my school friend, Wesley Kane, encouraged me. Wesley, it has to be said, arrived at school each day as if his mum had rushed out the day before and bought him a brand-new school uniform. From the tip of his perfectly polished shoes to the peak of his perma-cleaned cap, he was always impeccably turned out, while most of the rest of us looked like we had already worn out our new school uniform on the first day. He was what your parents might have called 'a good example'. But I wasn't so sure about that when he suggested that Margaret Hutchinson (think of Brigitte Bardot but with a Mid-Ulster accent) was also going to be joining the band. Straight away, I was in. The Walls' Street Corner Boys claimed that Miss Hutchinson was personally responsible for numerous youths colliding with lampposts. I have no reason to dispute their claim.

My first practice was at the band-room up on the Fair Hill, Magherafelt. The first thing I discovered was a massive pot of tea constantly on the go. I thought, so far so good. Wesley suggested that, on a parade day, you'd also get sandwiches, an apple *and* a Kit Kat thrown in. How could I resist? The Bandmaster, a farmer with weather-beaten hands but immaculately clean fingernails, seemed like a decent man. I became fixated on his fingers as they very precisely worked their way around the black wood, practice-chanter, producing tunes so effortlessly that I was lulled into believing anyone could play this instrument.

A set of bagpipes is a very deceptive contraption. I had always assumed that the piper had to continuously blow into the mouthpiece to produce music. Not so. I discovered that all you had to do was blow until you filled the bag full of air. Then, didn't a wee valve, lodged where the mouthpiece is connected to the bag, shut automatically, storing the air inside and ensuring that it couldn't escape back out through the mouthpiece? When you squeezed the bag, strategically positioned under your arm, the only way for the air to escape was via the reed of your chanter or through the drones sticking out of the top of the bag and resting on your shoulder. This was how you produced the cacophony – sorry, the music. The effect of this carefully considered arrangement was that the piper could take a wee break every now and then before drawing another deep breath and blowing back into the bag.

On that first night at the pipe band practice, the seasoned pipers piped and the new recruits were introduced to the instrument – not, in truth, to the bagpipes themselves but to the practice-chanter. I could never work out if they were worried about the damage we might do to their instruments or vice versa. The only other novice on that occasion was the Bandmaster's new wife. I took her presence as a good sign, guessing that the Bandmaster couldn't get too cross with us if we were slow on the uptake. Wesley figured that with all the private tutoring she'd be getting at home, she'd leave me floundering in her wake by the second or third week. He was right.

Please forgive me if there are any inaccuracies in my description of the workings of the bagpipes. In my defence, I will say for the record that: (a) it was a very long time ago and (b) I kinda lost interest very quickly after Miss Hutchinson's devastating no-show. Yes, sadly, it turned out that the line about the gorgeous Miss Hutchinson turning up and blowing with the rest of the novices was an outrageous fib. I was heartbroken.

To put the final nail in the coffin of my plan to become a bagpipe maestro, it soon became clear to me that my mum made a much better cup of tea anyway.

****

It was around this time that I took a job as a messenger boy in Dawson Bates's Grocery & Hardware store. In return for delivering groceries up and down the steep hills of the town-lands around Magherafelt, I received thirty bob (£1.50 nowadays) a week, for working after school each day and all-day Saturday, and fifty bob (£2.50) a week, during school holidays. This financed my dubious lifestyle choices, including buying the odd album at 32 bob (shillings) and 6 pence; the more frequent purchase of singles at 6 shillings and 8 pence; a pair of black and white hipsters for 24 shillings; and a 10 shilling black polo-neck jumper. This had a thin band of three colours, which ran up the front, off-centre and from waist to shoulder. I really loved that polo-neck jumper, but for some inexplicable reason I seldom wore it. Maybe I was just shy.

The bagpipe experiment having crashed and burned, I thought perhaps I should try to master an instrument more in tune, shall we say, with the sounds I was listening to. Thanks to my endeavours delivering Dawson Bates's groceries, I was in a position to buy myself an acoustic guitar. It was sold to me by the bass guitarist from the Blueboys – *Eddie and The Blueboys* that is. It cost me thirty bob and it was a beautiful, dark-wood, Gibson.

Like most other teenage boys, I was transfixed by The Shadows' Hank B. Marvin's glorious red Stratocaster. I used to get Burns' guitar catalogues by the dozen. I even bought a copy of Bert Weedon's *Play in a Day* manual.

I wasn't alone in being an acolyte of Weedon. John Lennon, Paul McCartney, Mark Knopfler, Eric Clapton, Pete Townsend, Ireland's favourite crooner, Val Doonican and even Hank B. Marvin himself – plus another two million hopefuls – also subscribed to gentleman Bert's miracle music-manual for the masses. I would sit myself down with the guitar, open Bert's book at the 'Bobby Shaftoe' page, and locate a diagram for the chord, C.

C was a bit complicated, but I duly placed the fingers of my left hand on the strings, pressed them down on the fretboard, as directed and strummed. And yes, to my surprise, I could hear some music coming from the instrument. If I had needed to play only that one chord, I would probably have been okay – *maybe* even good enough, with a lot of practice mind you, to one day be able to join The Shadows. My big problem, however, was moving from one chord to the next. There were only two chords in 'Bobby Shaftoe', but I would have to stop mid-strum and use my right hand to place the fingers of my left hand, one by one, in their correct position on the fretboard, for the second chord, which was a G.

The delay would be so long that I'd have forgotten the name of the song I was supposed to be playing by the time I had the alleged G chord in shape.

I started to think about Mr Bobby Shaftoe. Who was this man? Why had someone written a song about him? And why was Bert Weedon still playing the song? For the record, there seems to be several plausible answers. One theory was that Robert Shaftoe had lived in Hollybrook in Co. Wicklow, in Ireland, and died in 1737; I was more intrigued, however, with the sad tale of the Robert Shaftoe, an MP representing County Durham, England (again sometime in the 1730's), who supposedly left a young Bridget Belasyse devastated when he married Anne Duncombe: Bridget died of a broken heart two weeks later. So the moral to that particular story was: be very careful whose heart you break, otherwise people might still be singing about your dastardly behaviour nearly 300 years later.

The art of moving effortlessly from chord to chord – which I found impossible – was what really impressed me about a young man by the name of Vinci McCusker. Vinci's fingers could instinctively find those complicated positions – and he could smoke a cigarette, drink a cup of tea, unwrap *and* eat a Kit Kat, and continue to talk to me, as he did so. Vinci McCusker's fingers reminded me of the Bandmaster's. Watching these musicians play was a joy: they both gave the impression of being totally natural on their chosen instruments. Neither of them needed to labour over what people call technique. As if by magic, their fingers would just go to the right places – or that was how it seemed – and each and every note sparkled with crisp exactness. By comparison, my attempts were miserably stifled. I knew very quickly that I wasn't going to make the grade, and so – with a hint of regret – I fell discreetly by the wayside.

I couldn't play, but I wasn't completely deterred. While Vinci McCusker and I were at the local Tech College, we formed a group for the annual Christmas concert. It was around the time Hedgehoppers Anonymous were enjoying their one, and only, flush of success with the hit single, 'It's Good News Week'. We changed "Hedgehoppers" to "Goggles" because we all wore glasses and Goggles Anonymous were born. As the only non-playing member of the band, I was duly elected the manager. I was also the one responsible for trying to routine the group through 'Sloop John B'. Okay, it might have had something to do with the fact I had a copy of the single, and I do remember suggesting to the lead singer that a clothes peg might assist him in reaching the high notes. The good news was that Goggles Anonymous mastered 'Sloop John B'. sufficiently to play it on the night of the concert. The even better news was that the girls screamed loudly, just like they did to The Beatles on the telly. Mind you, in our case that might have been due to the pain we were inflicting, rather than the pleasure we were giving. But it was, as they say, a start.

I was hooked on music now, and started to go to as many dances as possible. It didn't matter how good – or bad – the band was: my feet stayed rooted to the floor. My hips didn't move. Some say my embarrassing lack of dance moves was the reason I waited so long before I married. But I can tell you such claims are pure fiction, because the truth is quite simple: I was waiting to meet Catherine.

I often wonder, however, if the farmer who was my pipe-band tutor and Vinci McCusker hadn't been such brilliant musicians, would I have persevered a bit longer? If I had, I might also have developed a couple of successful dance moves of my own.

Maybe I'd have mastered swaggering on the spot the way pipers in a marching band do, as they mark time, to the beat of the big drum, while playing their pipes. Or, if I'd learned to play the guitar successfully, I could have picked up the Shadows' trademark synchronised three-step-moves.

Had I mastered routines like that, I was convinced even the ultra-cool Miss Hutchinson would have been impressed. But it wasn't to be.

As for Bert Weedon, I've recently taken comfort in the fact there was at least one other person – apart from myself that is – in Bert's two million followers who didn't succeed in mastering the instrument. A quick roll of the snare drum... and... let's hear it for Mr Phil Collins.

And guess what? As testified in the Genesis song, and proven in the accompanying video, Phil Collins can't dance either! I'm not sure that this really explains anything, but I decided long ago that as long as I can read, write, watch, talk, walk – and listen – I'll be happy.

Well, at least, most of the time!

CHAPTER TWO

FIRST STEPS IN THE MUSIC BUSINESS – IT'S A KIND OF MAGIC

I had first met Vinci McCusker in September 1964 when I moved from the Intermediate School in Magherafelt, Northern Ireland, fifty yards back towards the town centre, to the Technical College. Vinci was from the neighbouring village of Maghera. At that point I was into Ray Charles, Hank Williams, Otis Redding, The Beatles, The Kinks, Them and Bob Dylan. Vinci was more of a Rolling Stones fan and into R 'n' B in a big way. The major difference, however, was that Vinci played guitar and I didn't. Still, through our shared interest in music – and in the beautiful girls of the Tech College – we became good friends.

The Beatles were making their mark worldwide by that point and their influence stretched even as far as our rural outpost. Long hair, tight trousers and Beatle Boots – or winkle-pickers – were all the rage. Not that long hair was permitted in the Tech back then. But a few of the gang had invented, and were forever fine-tuning, ways to hide their long locks while in school – deceptions that included Brylcream-ing it back into a slick DA and tucking it into their collars and so forth. Come the final bell of the day, we'd be released from captivity: rushing down to Agnews' Café, long-haired locks would be allowed to flow freely again. My fellow students were, as David Crosby so eloquently described it a few decades later, letting their freak flags fly. It was at the Tech that I got both the writing virus and the music business bug.

The exhilarating Christmas adventure with Goggles Anonymous over, Vinci and four of his mates from The Rainey School in Magherafelt – a

Grammar School which had been established by Hugh Rainey in 1713 – formed a group called Blues by Five. There were indeed five of them and they played their version of the blues. Things were much simpler in those days!

Hanging out with Vinci McCusker, I soon discovered the basic requirements for becoming a member of a group: (a) you could sing – that ruled me out; (b) you could play an instrument – not a chance; (c) you owned a drum kit – for a brief moment, I imagined myself giving a set of tom toms a proper hammering, but even if I'd been capable of it, I didn't have the spondulics to invest; or (d) your father had a car and could ferry the band to and from gigs.

Now, in fairness, my dad had a beautiful red Vespa 125 Scooter. It had room for a passenger on the pillion and space in the wheel-guard compartment for a couple rounds of sandwiches, or even a stack of singles. But a whole band on the back? Even my fevered imagination couldn't stretch to that. Things were looking bleak.

In order to continue to hang out with the gang, I had to find something else I could do with The Blues by Five – ideally something which would make me indispensable to the group.

I went to hear Blues by Five at one of their rehearsals. They were excellent musicians, had a great sound, and, out front, they had Paddy Shaw, one of the best singers I've ever witnessed. As a vocalist, he was up there alongside other local favourites, Paul Divito of The Interns, Billy Brown of The Freshmen, Cahir O'Doherty of The Gentry and Van Morrison, who was with Them at the time.

Still, The Blues by Five had a problem. They may have been good, but they weren't doing many gigs. Luckily enough a fine gentleman by the name of Dixie Kerr lived two doors down from me, on Beechland Road. Dixie played saxophone in The Breakaways Showband, which got me thinking.

Relax. The thought of torturing my parents by trying to learn the sax never even entered my head. Instead, I knocked on Dixie's door and asked if he could give The Blues by Five the support slot at some of the dances The Breakaways were playing. In that era, the second band were called the 'relief band' or the 'interval band', because they hit the stage in the middle of the main outfit's set to give them a break – time, that is for a cup of tea, a cigarette and a trip to the toilet.

Dixie being Dixie said, "Why of course." And in that moment, you might say, my fate was sealed. The Blues by Five were delighted at the bookings I'd secured and immediately appointed me as their manager. There was no turning back.

The Blues by Five adventure was a first step into the music business for both Vinci and myself. This was long before there was a phone in every house, and so the Blues by Five business cards I had printed listed the number of the telephone box closest to my house in Beechland. I was 15 years old at the time.

During chemistry classes, I'd design and hand-colour posters for the notice board, located by the front door of the original Technical College building, where my father, Andrew, and my Uncle Harry had attended night classes in their teens. These posters were to announce Blues by Five's up-coming gigs, whether at the Trend Club, or supporting The Breakaways Showband – the local kings of Fair Hill – somewhere exotic like Cookstown Town Hall. Our forward-thinking chemistry teacher, Miss Crowley, wasn't bothered: she applied the sound logic that if you didn't want to be taught, well then, she didn't want to waste her time teaching you. She was happy to leave students completely to their own devices, as long as they had the decency to attend the classes and keep quiet. That suited me down to the ground.

Blues by Five were named after a 1957 Miles Davis Quintet track 'Blues By Five' from their album, *Lookin' With The Miles Davis Quintet*. The line-up on that record was a staggering one:

> Miles Davis (trumpet)
> John Coltrane (tenor sax)
> Reg Garland (piano)
> Paul Chambers (bass)
> Philly Joe Jones (drums)

Their Co. Derry counterparts were:

> Paddy Shaw (vocals)
> Vinci McCusker (rhythm guitar & vocals)

Terence McKee (lead guitar)

Ian Best (bass)

Miles "Tinhead" McKee   (drums)

Geographically the two bands were continents apart – and musically, they were even further. Blues by Five specialised in soul music, a bit of R 'n' B and some blues. Their live set was based on material from Them's second album, *Them Again*, plus songs from Otis Redding, Wilson Pickett, Ray Charles and more songs from a compilation called, *Ireland's Greatest Sounds*. That album featured an incredible group called The Alleykatz, whose track had these unforgettable opening lines:

"I'm your friendly Undertaker, baby

Let me take you for a ride."

No wonder I wanted to jump onboard the good ship rock 'n' roll!

And so I spent the next couple of years multi-tasking: finishing my exams, working part-time delivering groceries for Dawson Bates and managing Blues by Five. In those days, managing meant securing gigs for the group and I set about it with grim determination. I'd hitch a lift to the various ballrooms and visit the owner in person. I'd scour the *Belfast Telegraph* and discover the names of all the Belfast clubs: places like Club Rado, the home of Them, Taste and the Interns; Sammy Houston's Club, Clarke's – the exciting Pound Club was to come later.

My father had progressed from his red Vespa 125 Scooter to an Austin A40 car, and so I got the use of the Vespa. This meant that hitching rides became a thing of the past. I also attached a Blues by Five day-glow-strip-flier to the front, and to the rear, of the scooter for the vitally important 'street level' promotion. Stardom beckoned.

"We can't pay you £10," the Head Teacher of a school in Maghera declared when he wanted to book a band for an annual school hop.

"How about nine quid then?" I suggested, which was six times our regular fee.

The headmaster jumped at my offer, thinking he'd got a bargain. It was a lesson well learned: from then on, I'd always aim to find out what the promoter was prepared to put on the table before I even started to negotiate. We were more than happy with £9, which is the equivalent of

£160 today. The band did seven songs that night which meant that we earned over a quid a song.

We played the Trend Club in Magherafelt a lot and eventually I took to promoting a few shows there including an amazing night with The Interns. They were, as it turned out, very worthy of their reputation as Northern Ireland's top group. They were a very exciting band, with a big sound and oodles of confidence. I vividly recall the hairs on the back of my neck standing up as I watched them, a sure sign that what you're witnessing is the real deal. The Interns were that and more.

In contrast, Blues by Five suffered from the simple fact we were all growing up and needed to think about making our longer-term career choices. Paddy Shaw decided that he was heading off to continue his studies to become a teacher. Miles, Terence and Ian were on a similar path. Vinci was the only member of The Blues by Five who wanted to be a full-time musician. I'd gained the necessary qualifications to pursue my ambition of becoming a draughtsman, en route to eventually being a civil engineer. I'd always figured if you are going to be an engineer you might as well be civil. And so, I headed off to London in September 1967. I got a job in a drawing office in Chessington, right next to the Zoo, spending two nights and one day a week at Twickenham College of Technology.

Of course, my decision to fly the coop wasn't just to do with studying. I had also left Magherafelt and headed to London so that I'd be able to see The Beatles. Or so I thought. At the time, news was painfully slow to make it to Magherafelt. It turned out that the biggest band in the world had played their last ever live gig in August the previous year! Not to worry, sure weren't there loads of other groups to see and hear? There were indeed. Pretty soon I was a regular at The Marquee Club and writing a weekly music column for Belfast's *City Week* which eventually became *Thursday Magazine*. In for a penny, in for a pound. I was becoming an addict.

The London I arrived in was, indeed, swinging. Hair was long, skirts were short, and clothes came in vibrant colours. I felt like I was stepping off the train in Euston Station straight onto a fast-moving platform. It was all hustle and bustle, nods and winks, cockney accents and gales of laughter. It was more Del Boy and Rodney than the Bootsie and Snudge

I was used to back home. I stopped in my tracks to marvel at the sights and sounds; for me, it was just like watching a movie. In addition to the pleasing, make-you-smile colours of the clothes, there were men straight out of a Magritte painting, sauntering around in their pinstriped suits, wearing bowler hats and carrying umbrellas. It turned out some of these pinstriped men worked in the music business. But standing still on the platform in Euston was impossible for more than a couple of minutes, as the crowds surged around me, eventually carrying me forward, as if on an irresistible wave. You have to remember that, until then, the biggest street action I'd been used to in Magherafelt, would have been the synchronised head-turning of the Walls's Street Corner Boys as Margaret Hutchinson crossed the Diamond.

I was even less prepared for the sights and sounds when darkness fell. At sundown the smog appeared from nowhere. Walking around in the gloaming, as I loved to do, made me feel like I might be travelling down the eerily lit Rue Morgue Avenue. On occasion, I'd experience a sudden chill up the spine and a fear that I was about to come across traces of Jack The Ripper's handiwork. In Magherafelt, you could see the stars to the extent you'd use them as a guide and illuminator for stepping out with your chosen one. In London, the smog would not only make your breathing more difficult, it would steal the light from the sky. It was an altogether eerier effect.

Vinci McCusker started to visit London and would always crash at my flat in Wimbledon. He'd work late into the night on a bunch of songs he was writing for a group he was thinking of forming back in Belfast. I still remember those songs – 'Decision', 'Garden Lady' and 'Olde Tyme Future' among them. Vinci's main concern was that they might be a bit too progressive for the Irish Market. I thought they were brilliant.

So, we hatched a plan. Vinci would return to Belfast and form his new group. I'd set up a few gigs for them in London and inveigle some managers and record companies to come down to see them. The as-yet-unnamed group would get signed up, go on to fame and fortune and I'd happily wave them onto the plane. Sadly, it didn't happen that way. It was 1971 by the time Fruupp were functioning as a group. And, by default, I became the manager, the agent, the roadie, the sound engineer, the lyricist, the writer of the stories that linked the songs on stage, and... the last one to be paid.

Fruupp were Vinci McCusker, main songwriter, lead guitar and vocals; Peter Farrelly creator of all the wonderful original artwork, bass guitar, flute and lead vocals; Martin Foye, drums; and Stephen Houston, keyboards, oboe and backing vocals. The band toured extensively and I learned a lot working the turf with – and for – the collective. We released four studio albums in three years, but Fruupp never did break the four-minute barrier. Mr Houston disappeared one night following a gig and he was replaced by John Mason on keyboards for the final album, *Modern Masquerades,* released in November 1975. In 1976, they called it a day.

Almost fifty years later, Fruupp are selling more CDs than they ever did back in the day! A clue to this phenomenon might just be the fact that CDs didn't come along until the mid-1980s when Dire Straits became the first artist to sell more CDs than vinyl albums. But it was an adventure that deserves a place in the history books. In 2007, Talib Kweli would sample Fruupp's 'Sheba's Song' – for the track 'Soon The New Day', featuring Norah Jones, on his album *Eardrum*. It went to No.2 in the US Billboard Hot 100, and as the writer of the original lyrics, I got a co-credit on Talib's hit. The beautiful thing about music is that we never can have any idea where it will end up once we send it out there into the great unknown. As the song says, "It's a kind of magic."

CHAPTER THREE

IT WAS FIFTY YEARS AGO TODAY

The Beatles' 'Please Please Me' turned me, and millions of other people, on to music. I became obsessed with both the single and the group. Soon I'd a cheap record player and, a few months later, was also the proud owner of *Please Please Me*, the band's debut LP, released in March 1963. Another six albums, and just four years later, I thought I'd it all figured out when they hit me – and the rest of the world – with what has arguably become the most important album ever released: *Sgt. Pepper's Lonely Hearts' Club Band*

May 1967. I was still living in Northern Ireland but making plans to leave. I'd bought *Sgt. Peppers* the day it was released but hadn't had a chance to listen to it properly, as I chased gigs for Blues by Five. Then, on Saturday evening, a week or so after its release, I went to a party in a church hall in Cookstown, in the heartland of Northern Ireland, in Co. Tyrone.

Cookstown – Johnathan Swift was staying nearby when he wrote Gulliver's Travels – was famous for having one very broad street which ran the whole way through the town. It might have been called Broad Street, but instead it was Loy Street, melting along the way into Chapel Street. The street was so broad that, as legend had it, pedestrians brought a flask of tea and some sandwiches with them so they could take a snack-break halfway across.

The walls and ceiling of the church hall had been covered that night with a mass of colourful posters, streamers and balloons. The music was great and, as they say up in those parts, the craic was ninety. People were talking, laughing, joking and dancing (well, except me). Some were sitting around, drinking and having a good time. And then someone put the *Sergeant Pepper's Lonely Hearts Club Band* album on a record-player, wired up directly to the PA system.

One by one the party-people stopped talking. The noise and bustle died down completely. The entire crowd, it seemed, was being seduced by this beautiful and inspiring music. Happiness was spreading from one person to another with the same power and speed that panic can move through a gathering. It was wonderful to be there. It was certainly a thrill. With each new track everyone was drawn deeper and deeper into the new world that seemed to open up. Our new world. A world created for us by The Beatles. It was like everything they had ever done had been leading up to it. Every note of music they had ever played, every song they had ever composed had been in preparation for this moment: they were Sergeant Pepper's Lonely Hearts Club Band. It didn't matter that – with the benefit of hindsight – people might argue that the *Revolver* album was "better". It didn't matter that I didn't have someone there with me to love and share this with: there was more than enough love in the air. Nothing really mattered apart from the wonderful sounds that filled the speakers. The Beatles had fulfilled their unspoken promise to us. Or that was how it felt, as if we were being initiated into something brand new, something other-worldly, something only those of our generation were ever going to understand. Years later we'd be able to look back and say for sure: this album wasn't a great album because it sold lots of copies. Rather, it sold lots of copies because it was a great album, a breakthrough album, a landmark.

And the thing about the party that night in Cookstown was that we were all into it: sharing the pleasure and sharing the daring of the music. When John Lennon started to sing 'A Day In the Life', I swear I felt shivers run down my spine. My throat went dry. I could feel my nostrils tightening as though tears were going to flow. No one seemed to move a muscle for fear of spoiling the mood. As the last note, the E Major, drifted into silence, everyone was left stunned and speechless. It was like a mass turn-on – but instead of drugs being the source of the buzz, it had been induced by the show The Beatles had wanted, needed, to present to us.

This was the show they knew they could never do on stage as the "mop tops" to their screaming fans. Instead, they gave it to the world in the form of the *Sergeant Pepper's Lonely Hearts Club Band* album. That probably sounds as if I was indulging in some of the stimulants – which managed to make it even as far as Cookstown in those days. I wasn't. I never felt the need to. I could say that you really had to be there, in Cookstown, on that spectacular summer evening, to know what I'm on about. But I'm not sure. Because, what was happening just down the road from Magherafelt on that particular Saturday night was a reflection of something larger. For us, it was one of those perfect moments that rarely happen in your life: as we strained to hear the disappearing E Major that ends the album, there was the most incredible feeling of elation, of euphoria. When all that was left was the crackle of the needle on its final revolution, everyone started to clap. We didn't know what else to do. We clapped and clapped and then clapped some more.

There is no document that I know of bearing witness to what it was like the first time the 1812 Overture was performed. But, I doubt that the audience for what was arguably Tchaikovsky's most popular work felt anything comparable to what I felt listening to The Beatles' brand new meisterwerk that night in Cookstown.

I never, ever experienced that same buzz again. I don't say that with the slightest regret. I am proud, privileged even, to have been there, and to have enjoyed that once in a lifetime experience. I still love the record. But there was something else happening in Cookstown that was unique and unrepeatable: a communal spirit took hold, which came from the music of The Beatles and, in a mysterious way, connected just about everyone who was at the party that special summer evening.

And we were all the better for it. Of that I have no doubt.

Records in December 1967, with Bert in charge of production. From the crude approach taken, we can see exactly how much Lewis Merenstein and his vision added to the artistic success of the work. But Van remained unconvinced. Strings were added without consultation, with only 'Slim Slow Slider' escaping – and Van didn't like it. It may explain why – at the time of writing – 'Sweet Thing' is the only song from *Astral Weeks* that Van has so far permitted to appear on any of his approved compilation albums.

For me, the use of strings works. The arrangements seem flawless: perfect but never, ever predictable and as vital as Robert Kirby's were to Nick Drake's classic *Bryler Layer* album. Overall, *Astral Weeks* – characterised variously as a song cycle, a concept album, and an opera – is like nothing you've ever heard either before or since. The major problem with trying to describe an extraordinary record like this is the fear that someone might read your words and think: "What? The songs don't have verses, choruses, middle eights or hooks. I wouldn't like it." Honestly, to risk that would be the musical crime of the century.

It may not conform in any way to the expectations of conventional songwriting, but like all great works of art, as with the strings, *Astral Weeks* feels like it is perfectly formed. It has a beginning, a middle and an end, each with its dramatic pay-off. There is, of course, a subjective element to how you experience it. During the first two songs, 'Astral Weeks' and 'Beside You', I feel that you are being drawn in and jostled along. You're unsure of your surroundings, but there is no question of feeling that you can relax. Rather, you're continuously on edge, challenged by the poetry and the music, but too excited by the soundscape to be scared off. In 'Sweet Thing', the singer and musicians do allow you to loosen up just a little bit. Then you realise that the combo has just been setting you up to destroy you – destroy you totally, that is – with the immense and magical freewheeling poetry of 'Cyprus Avenue'.

"Afterwards," (or Side 2 in old money) opens with 'The Way Young Lovers Do'. If you've been tempted to come out of the dream, forget it. *"Then we sat on our own star,"* Van sings, *"and dreamed of the way/ That I was for you and you were for me/ And then we danced the night away/ And turned to each other, to say/ 'I love you, I love you'/ The way that young lovers do."*

Next up are the monumental 'Madame George' and the vibes-led beauty of 'Ballerina', with its precisely drawn poetic imagery. 'Slim Slow Slider' is the album closer they searched so diligently for during the final recording session. With hindsight, it feels like they really couldn't have picked any other song to end the record. Van sets up the closing scene perfectly: we are offered a glimpse of the girl, perhaps his girl, perhaps not, *"with her brand new boy and his Cadillac."* As 'Slim Slow Slider' ends abruptly – and the album with it – you're left wondering where she is going and what the future holds, for her, for Van, for all of us. Maybe, if you listen again, there may be hints along the way. And so you do. Or at least I did: again and again.

There are many myths and legends about *Astral Weeks*. Some, it transpires, are factual, some clearly not. It has been rumoured that there is a 40-minute piece, a missing part of this opera, that was recorded at the same time but never released. Perhaps this particular legend grew from the several ultimately unused tracks they attempted on the final session when they were searching for their closing track. Van has dismissed the notion. And either way, the album has always sounded like a completed work to me, although both 'Hey Girl' (from the *Them Again* album, 1966) and 'Into The Mystic' (from *Moondance*, 1970) sound as if they've come from the same writing streak. Interestingly, when Van recently attempted a live version of the album, he included 'Listen To The Lion' (from *St Dominic's Preview*, 1972) in the concert. Meanwhile, Martin Scorsese claimed that the first half of his film *Taxi Driver* was based on *Astral Weeks*. And so it goes.

It's been said that *Astral Weeks* was the biggest-ever selling import album in the UK. But it was also notorious for not selling very many copies in its original incarnation. The album continues to do well in best album polls: indeed, *Astral Weeks* was voted the Best Ever Irish Album in *Hot Press* magazine, Dublin, in 2009. For his part, on at least one occasion, Van suggested that *Astral Weeks* is a total work of fiction, just stories. If it is, then it just might be one of the best collections of short stories ever written. But I have my doubts. Could he have been writing about – or even to – the same person he addressed in the devastatingly powerful and similarly unnerving, 'TB Sheets', from the *Blowin' Your Mind* album, released in 1967? Is there a code to his writing? Don McLean knew in detail the complicated solution to the sublimely crafted, cryptic lyric of his classic song, 'American Pie'. But what are the lyrics to 'Astral Weeks' about? Do they all have a spiritual backdrop or is there a more sensual sub-plot? Did Van create his own code to deal with subtle sexual elements? Around the same time, from a male perspective at least, Jim Morrison was publicly breaking down the sexual barriers of the late 1960s. It could be argued that, while doing so, he found it impossible to retreat from his stance and regain the traditional, hallowed, solid ground. Maybe the process sped the ruination of his already troubled life. Did Van find a more discreet way? Often, in this work and indeed in later works by Van, you get a sense of someone, maybe even the writer, trying desperately to reclaim something or other that's been lost; or perhaps longing to return to another, happier time. The clues are there to suggest we're talking about something as difficult as unscrambling an egg, or, to put it another way, reclaiming lost innocence – whether that of the writer or a third party. A big part of the success of any form of artistic endeavour is creating a space others can inhabit or relate to. We can't expect sign-posts at every turn – and if we do, we're certainly not going to find them in *Astral Weeks*.

In 1979 I was in the very privileged position of beginning to work with Van Morrison as his agent and promoter. There are so many myths about Van, it's ridiculous. I always found him (a) to have an incredible sense of humour and (b) to be an extremely professional individual, the main thing for whom was always to get the job done. I eventually became his quasi-manager: the legendary Pee Wee Ellis was credited with Van's, 'brass arrangements' and I was credited with 'business arrangements'. When I eventually had the opportunity to discuss *Astral Weeks* with him, Van acknowledged its legacy. When first released, the album had enjoyed considerable acclaim and positive reviews, but reviews weren't paying the bills; he had a wife and a young baby daughter to think of, and he was struggling to earn enough money to survive. So, basking in the financially limited kind of glory that surrounded *Astral Weeks* was not his priority. Elsewhere he seemed to downplay the importance of the album. And yet, on occasion, he still confessed his pride in it. The obvious, if unspoken, difficulty must have been: when you create such an incredible work of true genius so early on in your life, artistically speaking, you have set a high bar. That was certainly the case with *Astral Weeks* – though if anyone was up to the challenge it was Van. Just listen to the title track of *Moondance*, the album that followed *Astral Weeks*, in 1970.

In the seven years I worked with Van Morrison, I attended most of his concerts and it was only on very rare occasions that he included tracks from *Astral Weeks* on the song list. As the intros to these masterpieces started you could sense the audience collectively hush and slip back into their seats in disbelief and anticipation, as the band embarked on a journey, one that more often than not left both the artist and the audience gasping for air.

It is clear that there were things about the album that still niggled. In part, it's probably that, for the original album, Van was part of the deal: he was the singer and the writer, but he allowed himself, and his music, to be arranged and produced. Artistically speaking, he never, ever gave anyone else that amount of control again.

Immersing yourself in *Astral Weeks* is, in a way, a bit like experiencing a brush with death. It happens. And you are changed irrevocably by it.

It really is that good.

To be fully aware of how vital the production was to the success of the record, you have to listen to earlier versions Van had attempted on some of previous Bang Records recording sessions. They were nothing like as accomplished or mysterious. They weren't even remotely as good. The scary thing you start to think is: if Van hadn't joined Them... if he hadn't left Them... if Bert Berns hadn't signed him to Bang Records and flown him to America... if Van hadn't gotten away from Bang Records... if Van hadn't needed to tour with a scaled down acoustic-leaning set-up for financial reasons... if he hadn't signed with Warner Bros... if Warner Bros hadn't enlisted Lewis Merenstein... if Merenstein hadn't been so moved by the material... if Merenstein hadn't read all the signposts from Van's now famous 'Catacombs Tapes' (official bootleg)... if he hadn't made the inspired choice of musicians...if... well, it goes on and on, really. Luckily, all of those things did happen, and this breath-taking thing of beauty was realised precisely because, like so many works of true genius, it came so scarily close to not happening.

As a man said all those years ago, *"The beauty and the magic of Astral Weeks, like all things pertaining to love, will last forever."* Who was that masked man?

CHAPTER FIVE

A ROCK 'N' ROLL MAN, THAT DIDN'T NEED A HELPING HAND...

In January 1971, I made my way by tube, bus and shanks' mare from the sedate suburb of Wimbledon in South London to the wilds of Willesden in the North London Borough of Brent. I rarely ventured north of the river in those days, but that was where I had to go, to interview a gentleman by the name of Rod Stewart for *Thursday Magazine,* a weekly Belfast music paper. I was what they called their "London Correspondent".

Rod Stewart was the lead singer with The Faces (nee The Small Faces). He was also an established young solo artist with a burgeoning reputation. Whether he could successfully manage both roles was anybody's guess, but I wanted to find out what the plan was – if indeed he had one.

The Faces story was fascinating. Rod and his mate Ronnie Wood – later of The Rolling Stones – had joined what was their favourite band, after the lead singer Steve Marriot defected to help form the supergroup, Humble Pie, with Peter Frampton – originally dubbed "the face of '68". The Faces were signed to Warner Bros. As a solo artist, Rod was hooked up with Phonogram. It was, you might say, a form of musical bigamy: only Rod Stewart could get away with it.

Released in 1969, Rod's first solo album, *An Old Raincoat Won't Ever Let You Down* – which featured a version of 'Dirty Old Town', a song written by fellow Scotsman Ewan McColl, and made famous by the rambunctious Irish folk group The Dubliners – had been very well received. There was a bluesier twist to the follow-up, *Gasoline Alley.* Both were excellent albums, but they failed to produce big hits. Back then, the third album was regarded as being crucial: sell enough records and your deal would be renewed. Post a dud and you'd be dropped. With that as background, Rod was holed up in Morgan Studios, working on what would become his third solo album, *Every Picture Tells a Story*. My previous two attempts to interview Rod had fallen through. Perhaps the ever helpful Carole in the Warner Bros press office decided that, if she set up the interview in the studio during the recording, he would have nowhere left to hide.

Third time lucky: Rod was there. It was a late night session and everyone – including top session musicians like Mickey Waller on Drums, Pete Sears on keyboards and Sam Mitchell on slide guitar – seemed to be in great form. I don't think I'd ever been in a proper recording studio before, and I was totally and completely blown away by the sound of music blasting through the studio's ginormous speakers. I remember fantasising about getting speakers like them in my bedsit. The only problem was that I'd have no room for any other furniture whatsoever. But I was still tempted: the audio set-up took the music into another dimension entirely.

The song they were working on was 'Maggie May' and I was there when Ray Jackson – who played with a new Tyneside band called Lindisfarne (whose main songwriter Alan Hull, was one of the best emerging UK songwriters of the early '70s) – delivered that magical mandolin part.

In my mind's eye, Ray Jackson was stick-thin and had a massively impressive moustache. I watched, mesmerised, as he "nailed it" to quote someone who'd been twiddling knobs on a control desk that looked as big as a football pitch to me. There was a little frivolity in the recording room while the engineer set up the next track they were going to work on with Ray.

Rod – who was producing the album himself – led me to one of the outer rooms in the studio, to do the interview. Rod was obviously preoccupied with his hair, cut in a spiky post-Mod style that British footballers seemed keen to emulate throughout the '70s, but otherwise he was very together, down to earth, earnest about his career and extremely easy to talk to. I liked him. By the time we returned to the control booth, work had ground to a halt and an eerie atmosphere had descended. Apparently one of the musicians, distracted by the partying, had accidentally sat upon Ray Jackson's mandolin and completely demolished it.

The Geordie was putting on a brave face, insisting that it was neither a great, nor an expensive, instrument. He claimed he had several in reserve as they were always being broken while he was on the road with Lindisfarne. Come to think of it, he was probably telling the truth! He went to the trouble of demonstrating just how shoddily made the instruments were by pulling the skeleton to pieces and removing bits of yellowing foam padding, which had apparently been stuffed into the sound holes in order to help with the acoustics.

I left them waiting for another one of Jackson's mandolins to be delivered to the studio. The finished album contained some brilliant picking on the classic, 'Mandolin Wind' – though there are debates still about who actually played on that track. What I couldn't have known at the time was that I'd been there for the recording of what would become a stone-cold classic, the track that would turn Rod Stewart into a bona fide superstar.

Every Picture Tells A Story was released six months later, in July 1971. In hindsight, it's easy to say that 'Maggie May' – co-written by Rod with Martin Quittenton, a member of a band called Steamhammer, who also played acoustic guitar on the sessions – was the perfect vehicle for Rod Stewart's unique story-telling voice. But the reality is that the record company didn't like the track. In fact they soooo didn't like it – claiming that it "lacked a melody" – that they didn't even want it on the album. Craftily, it turned out, Rod told them he didn't have any other material. The record company openly demonstrated how little faith they had in the song when they stuck it on the B-side of a single that had Rod's version of Tim Hardin's admittedly brilliant 'Reason To Believe' on the A-side. An American DJ flipped the single and started to play 'Maggie May'. There was a phenomenal reaction from listeners – and that was the start of it. 'Maggie May' became the de facto A-side and ended up going to No.1 in both the US and the UK. *Every Picture Tells a Story* also hit the top spot in the charts in the US and the UK and became a smash hit all over the world. Mr Stewart was up and running. Few artists have had a better start than he did, with three back-to-back classic albums. Later in 1971, The Faces released *A Nod Is As Good As a Wink... To a Blind Horse*, which went to No.2 in the UK and No.6 in the US.

Maybe Rod had a plan after all.

CHAPTER SIX

FRUUPP & THE TALE OF
THE WACCY BACCY

Fruupp smoked some of that wacky baccy stuff. At the time, anyone with long hair was inherently seen as being suspicious by the authorities. This was during Fruupp's "getting it together in the country" phase – if it was good enough for Traffic then it was good enough for us – and they had chosen a place near Thurles, in Co.Tipperary, Ireland, to stay. Bad mistake. The Garda College – where every policeman in Ireland is trained – was just ten miles down the road and the recently arrived long-haired weirdos were soon busted by the Irish Drug Squad. The story broke on the front pages. Luckily I had befriended Tony Wilson, who was pop correspondent with *The Evening Herald*. Keen to spare our families any local embarrassment, he kept the musicians names out of the story. But the people who knew the band knew. My parents, of course, were among them. I rang my mum and she was okay. At the end of the call she said, "Your father wants to talk to you."

"Were you smoking any of this auld funny stuff?" my dad asked.

"No, I wasn't, and I never have," I said.

"Okay that's good enough for me," he said and handed the phone back to my mum.

And I wasn't fibbing like a twelve year-old. I hadn't even smoked a cigarette at that point. I still haven't, and it's probably a fair bet that I never will. I don't know why – even working in the business I've worked in all my life – I never felt the need to sample any kind of drug. I don't even like taking medication that's prescribed by a doctor. In fact, I hate taking anything which could potentially alter my natural equilibrium. Honestly, I feel so brilliant about my life and my lot, and how lucky I am to be able to earn a living, on a daily basis, in the way that I do, I never wanted *not* to be able to fully experience it, while the going is good. I'm being serious when I say that if I could think of anything that would make me feel this good, I would seriously recommend it. So I suppose in a roundabout way, I am doing just that, recommending something which I really can swear by: fresh air.

We'd done a Saturday night gig somewhere down the country. I'd rushed back to London on the Sunday to be ready to hit the office early on Monday. No such luck! In the wee hours of Monday morning, the Drug Squad arrived in numbers at Fruupp's Fabulous Farm. In a moment of farce that seems typical of the times, looking at the tiny amount of dope they had – something like one-eighth of a thimble-full was how it was legally described – one of the Drug Squad called the band members a bunch of sissies. I'd never realised that "a thimble" was an acknowledged measure of hashish. Sissies or not, the fraught four were carted off to Portlaoise Prison, which was notorious as the place where members of the various republican paramilitary factions operating in Ireland at the time were incarcerated. Apparently, one member of the band had complained that he felt it was unfair that I hadn't been busted with the rest of them. But that was ridiculous. It wasn't that I hadn't inhaled: I hadn't even gone near a joint.

He must ultimately have realised that it was in his best interests that I had gone back to London because, first thing Monday morning, I was clearing out my bank account so I could get a plane back to Ireland and bail them all out of jail.

Popular wisdom says that every cloud has a silver lining. And, at least in this case, it was true. The main positive by-product of the drugs-bust was that, from that point onwards, Fruupp shows enjoyed a 200% increase in ticket sales, thereby compensating for the hit singles we never had.

****

There were places in England that Fruupp loved playing – Aylesbury

(Friars), Derby, Chelmsford, Southend, Windsor, Slough, Bracknell (those last three comprising the agent Andrew Kilderry's Music Street circuit) and Maidstone. And, of course, Dublin and Belfast in Ireland. In all of these towns and cities, there were key promoters, who were fans and went above and beyond the call of duty to ensure that there were full houses whenever Fruupp turned up.

The Mad Hatter Club, held in the Corn Exchange in Maidstone, Kent, was a standout. Mick – a.k.a. The Mad Hatter and he wore a top hat to prove the point – ran a brilliant club and always looked after both the band and audience very well. After one great gig there, along with trusted roadie John Urry, we were returning to London in our reliable, but terminally slow, equipment-laden, Ford Transit van. The craic was ninety, as it always was after a great gig, and we were merrily grinding through the miles back to south London when one of us spotted a wheel speeding past us, bouncing its way into the hedge on the opposite side of the road. We were all in stitches about this, laughing our socks off. We assumed the wheel must have come from a car travelling behind us. "That's at least one driver that won't be passing us out," someone roared, to another wave of hysterics.

It was at that precise moment that the van felt like it was taking a corner, even though the road stretched out in front of us as far as we could see. Then we felt the van tilt backwards slightly. It was similar to the sensation you get when an aeroplane is just about to leave the runway. And, just like what happens in a plane, the angle grew more acute.

The laughing had stopped.

Holy shit! It was *our* rear wheel that had passed us by.

All of this happened in a matter of seconds or even mili-seconds. We managed to pull-in to the side of the road, swearing furiously. How close had we come to totalling the van? And ourselves with it? We sat there puffing and panting, and shaking our heads in disbelief, before gingerly climbing out and setting off in search of the missing wheel. To get it back on, we had to improvise by stealing a few nuts from the other wheels. A solemn mood prevailed as we crawled back to Peckham.

Seymour Stein, the man behind Sire Records, who signed The Ramones, Talking Heads, Madonna and k.d. lang, loved Fruupp's third album *The*

Prince of Heaven's Eyes. Everything was building nicely. I knew it in my gut then, and I've seen it over and over again since. If you're involved in something with *potential,* you really need to give it every chance of succeeding. How many ex-members of unsuccessful bands are out there, languishing in the world of also-rans? You couldn't even begin to find, never mind count, them. In many cases, they came to a Y in the road and they took the wrong road. How differently might things have worked out, if they had stuck with the programme? Even at the very highest level, more often than not, the collective is stronger than any one member. To put it at its simplest, none of the ex-Beatles ever visited the same stratosphere, either commercially or creatively, as they did as a unit. That was the way I saw it with Fruupp.

We didn't know it at the time, but the keyboard player in the band, Stephen Houston, had other ideas. Naturally, Seymour Stein wanted to see the band live before inking the deal: it's what every good A&R scout would do. We cherry-picked a favourite gig, Farnbourgh Tech, and Seymour booked his flight. Farnbourough was a guaranteed sell-out, with an audience that genuinely loved the band. Bizarrely, it was at just this moment that Stephen – a bit like the Transit wheel on the way back from the Mad Hatter's – decided to unhitch his wagon from Fruupp's. His timing couldn't have been worse. He did a moonlight flit – taking some of the band's vital equipment with him. We were gobsmacked: he was leaving his mates of five years in the lurch, even as the biggest gig in our career was about to happen. But that was it: he was gone. Fruupp performed the show at Farnborough Tech in January 1975 as an under-rehearsed, entirely un-symphonic trio. It blew the deal with Sire out of the water. Neither, of course, did Sire Records sign Stephen Houston to a solo contract.

Nearly fifty years on, I still can't fathom it – although the fact that he became a clergyman soon afterwards might explain something. At the time, it was like being hit with a sledgehammer: when you think of all the hours we'd spent together, the miles covered, and the jokes shared, in the back of a Ford Transit van, it made no sense whatsoever. We had a final bid for success with a fourth album, *Modern Masquerades* – but by then the heart and soul had been ripped out of everyone and we were running on a tank where all that remained were the fumes of the fuel.

I was once asked what I had learned from being a member of an unsuccessful, professional touring outfit, who lived on the road, pretty much solidly for just over four years.

"You really want to know?" I replied, thinking that might just put an end to it.

"Really," I was told.

"Well, let's see now," I started, as if I was about to reveal a state secret. "From all the driving around in the back of a Ford transit van, I soon learned what an array of strange sounds signalled."

I paused for effect.

"Like, for instance, if it felt like you kept hitting a pothole every few yards, it meant your shock-absorbers were gone. If the engine started to splutter and stall, there was some dirt on the spark plug, or in the carburettor. If the van started to tilt from left to right that meant that the right rear-wheel had spun off its axle. The engine spluttering, stalling, starting, stalling, spluttering and finally coming to a complete stop meant one of the band had put diesel into the petrol tank to save money (the extra cash, on that momentous occasion, had gone on 20 Woodbine, a big bag of crisps and some Coca Cola). And then, finally, there was the engine death-rattle, which sounded like we'd just been run over by a military tank. The big end was gone, which was terminal and expensive and therefore marked the beginning of a month during which beans on toast was the only food we could afford."

I'd also learned that the magic cat's eyes, marking the edge of the hard shoulder on a motorway, were placed 100 yards apart and if you were really bored you could time how long it took you to pass 17 and six tenths of these life-savers. From this you could work out, pretty accurately, the speed of your vehicle. But that information was only of any use if your speedometer wasn't working.

****

In my time with Fruupp, I wrote the lyrics for eight of their songs. Seven of these made the albums; the outlier, 'Be Glad', made the live set but was never recorded. I am always intrigued to find out how different songwriters operate. Dave Clark of The DC5 used to walk among the packed crowds at his gigs, eavesdropping on the audience, on the prowl for gems he could work into his lyrics, like "*When we first met I was feeling Glad All Over*" or "*When he left me I was in Bits and Pieces.*" Another well-known songwriter props a book of sayings – or clichés – up on his piano for inspiration. George Harrison and the Traveling Wilburys were in Bob Dylan's studio-garage, where they spotted the words Handle With Care on some storage boxes, and they had the title of their first hit single. The Beatles were happy to use old posters for inspiration. And occasionally they found ideas by trawling through newspapers, sometimes even the *Daily Mirror*.

I'd mostly start off with a clean page and amuse myself on a flight of fancy, maybe even fantasy, which was perfect for a prog rock band. In one instance, in 1975, I followed The Beatles into the pages of the *Daily Mirror* and a story caught my attention. There was a news item about a wild cat's daring escape from the Zoo and how the beast was eventually sedated by a dart. The words came quickly. I thought the lyrics, originally called 'Sheba's Serenade', were too different to the style of songs Vinci McCusker and I had been writing together, so I put it to one side. A short time later, John Mason, the keyboard player who had come in to replace Stephen Houston, was working on a couple of melodies for *Modern Masquerades*. John asked me if I had any lyrics to spare, I showed him 'Sheba's Serenade'. He set to work, and a few days later we had a track. By now, I had changed the title to 'Sheba's Song'. I loved the recording the band did for *Modern Masquerade*, with Peter Farrelly delivering a beautiful vocal and producer Ian McDonald (ex-King Crimson) tying it all together brilliantly.

We were working on another concept album, *Doctor Wilde's Twilight Adventure*, based on a short story of mine called *The Flight of The Dove*. The idea was to use the music of the 1812 Overture. Ambitious? Certainly, but, if you reach for the sky, you might just get the opportunity to tickle the clouds. The band was busy rehearsing at the foot of the Dublin Mountains and the demos were sounding very encouraging. In their spare time they were doing a few gigs around Dublin under the name of The Future Legends Orchestra. But the reality was the momentum we'd enjoyed at the beginning of 1975 wasn't coming back any time soon. The embryonic Punk/New Wave movement was dating prog-oriented music very quickly. The writing was most definitely on the wall and, one by one, we all accepted this. There was a final puff at the Roundhouse Chalk Farm on Sunday 25th Jan, 1976 – one of the support acts was the 101ers who, within months, would change their name to The Clash. And so the Fruupp adventure, which had begun in Belfast in 1971, ended five years, four albums, three singles, two keyboard players and one drugs bust later.

****

Thus it was that, in 2005, a 17-year old rapper trading under the K.Dot handle happened upon 'Sheba's Song'. In the mysterious way that music has of getting inside people's heads, he was hooked. He sampled it, used John's melody and my lyrics, renamed it as 'Hypnotiq' and released it on his *Training Day* mixtape. By 2009, the rapper had decided to use his real name, Kendrick Lamar.

In 2007, a Brooklyn rap artist called Talib Kweli also picked up on the track, changed the name to 'Soon The New Day' – taken from a line in the original chorus – and brought Norah Jones in to sing it. Whereas I hadn't heard a word from K.Dot – he really was a kid at the time – Talib's people contacted me and were gracious with the credits and the publishing. The track was included on his album *Ear Music*, released in 2007 – which debuted at No 2 in The *Billboard* 200 albums chart and sold very well indeed.

Then Norah Jones decided to include 'Soon The New Day' on her collaborations album, called *...Featuring Norah Jones* (2010), which was a Top 30 album in the US, Canada (where it went gold) and in parts of Europe. In 2012, Madlib – who had produced Talib Kweli's record – delivered his own version of 'Soon The New Day'. There's even a 14-minute instrumental treatment of the track, by Madlib, that was debuted on YouTube in 2018. A great hook is a mystery all on its own.

John Mason was ill around the time of the release of 'Soon The New Day' and his share of the royalties was badly needed. Sadly, however, just a few years later, he passed away. There are some wounds that even music can't heal.

CHAPTER SEVEN

JUST LIKE ARTHUR BROWN PREDICTED

The summer of 1976 was so scorching hot we were building body-height pyramids from used Fanta and Coke cans in our small office in Dryden Chambers, just off Oxford Street in London. Dryden Chambers was a Victorian apartment block. One unit where, allegedly, some long-passed member of royalty housed a mistress or two now served as offices to Asgard, the agency I had formed with Paul Fenn. At that time I was living in a two floor apartment – or flat as they were called at the time – in Dulwich in South London and had two members of Fruupp, the band I was managing, and their girlfriends, crashing with me.

One member of the band, liked to sit in on Fruupp's gig-free nights, sip from a can of larger, chain smoke and eat (very daintily, with his pinkie raised, it has to be said) from a non-stop supply of packets of potato crisps – and whisper sweet nothings to his girlfriend. On one such night I retired to my room in the eaves, leaving the rest of them downstairs, but it was so hot I couldn't fall asleep. 39,333 sheep later, I eventually dozed off only to be wakened in the early hours of the morning by a noise on the roof above me. My first thought was, "Wow, the heat wave has broken." From the noise, I thought the rain was bucketing down.

I tried to get back to sleep, assuming that sleep would come easier and deeper. However, as I lay there, rather than feeling a cool draft, it seemed to be getting warmer – a lot warmer. The noise on the roof grew louder and louder, eventually sounding so heavy and potentially dangerous that I had to get up and take a look. I was thinking that I'd never heard rain like this before. I opened the curtains, slid up the window and stuck my head out.

The first thing I noticed was that the streets were still bone dry. Yet I could still hear the rain beating down incessantly on the slates just above me.

I looked to my right and saw a shower of violent flames.

I thought: shit the house next door is on fire. I immediately jumped into a pair of trousers and opened my bedroom door.

Boomph. There were livid flames dancing in front of me. I slammed the door shut as quickly as I could, realising immediately, from the smell, that I had singed my eyebrows, although for some strange reason my moustache (established 1967) remained intact.

I ran to the window, opened it wide but quickly closed it again as my survival instincts kicked in. I sealed the bottom of my bedroom door using a towel I dampened with a full bottle of orangeade.

I returned to the window, opened it again, stuck my head out and considered my options.

I was surprised at how clear my mind was as I spun through the various potential routes of escape. Outside the bedroom door, I could hear the flames wreaking havoc on most of my worldly possessions, including my albums and books, that had been carefully stacked on shelves in the living room.

If I jumped the three floors to the ground I would most likely break both my legs, and there was a good chance I'd do myself a lot more damage than that. But there was at least a chance I would survive. Climbing, or trying to climb, up onto the roof above me was too dangerous: if I slipped I'd most likely go down head first. On top of which, even if I did make it, so furious were the flames up on the roof, I'd probably be toast.

I'd often read what's supposed to happen to you just before you die, but at no point thus far had my short life flashed through my mind. I decided to shout anyway.

"Help!!!"

The first time it sounded strangely feeble. The second time, no doubt spurred on by the sound of the mass destruction taking place a few feet away, I screamed.

"Help, somebody help me, yeah." It actually went through my mind that I had just inadvertently quoted Stevie Winwood. Weirdly, I thought that the single word, 'Help' just might sound too desperate and scare off potential rescuers in the quiet suburb of Dulwich.

"Hello?" I roared, as best I could. "Is anyone there? Hello?"

Time becomes meaningless in a moment like that. All I know is that I spotted someone running out of a house just across the road.

In London, in the mid-Seventies, everyone kept to themselves. I'd lived in that house for at least a year and I hadn't a clue who my next door neighbours were, let alone who the people from as far away as the other side of the road might be. Whereas back in Magherafelt, everyone knew everything about everyone including, but not limited to, their shoe size and how much they were paid every week, if they were lucky enough to have a job.

The man on the street below seemed more distressed than I was. It was a bit like the situation where the look of shock and horror on relatives' faces when you come around after an accident, can be more damaging to you than the accident itself.

"Do you have a ladder?" I shouted.

He answered in the negative.

"Can you bang on a few doors to see who has?"

"Right," he said, ready to spring into action.

"Before you go," I screamed, "could you please ring my doorbell to make sure my flatmates are awake?"

Which he did, banging loudly for good measure, in case the electricity cables were burnt out.

My mind was still working logically. I started to wonder: if the man below did manage to find a ladder, would it be long enough to reach up to my window ledge? If the ladder wasn't long enough was he going to have to go and knock on some more doors and find a longer one? And would the flames have reached me by then?

Someone else ran out onto the street.

"I rang the fire brigade," she called up. "Don't worry you'll be okay!"

I was taking great comfort in her words – but not for long.

"Why don't you jump?" she enquired.

The prospect didn't look any more inviting.

"I think I can afford to wait a wee bit longer," I said, in case she felt I was being ungrateful.

Lo and behold: Vinci McCusker's head popped out of the bay window below me. "Jeez man, don't worry, we'll get you down," he said. It wasn't exactly Randolph Scott and the 7th Cavalry, but maybe this was how all great rescue plans began.

"The flames from the living room are just about to burst into my bedroom," I shouted.

His head disappeared.

Okay, I thought, maybe the panic in my voice scared him off. Or perhaps he has a plan after all.

I heard one half of his window slide shut and the other half opened. He proceeded to climb out onto his window sill, stood up, supporting himself with one arm secured under the closed upper section of the window frame. Now there were two of us about to die.

"Okay, Paul," he started, "what I need you to do is to back out of your window feet first, face to the window."

I listened intently in the hope of hearing a fire brigade, but drew a blank.

"I'll never be able to climb down there," I said

"Lower yourself down as far as you can," he instructed. "You'll need to keep a good grip on the window sill. Then I'll get in position directly below you and I'll tell you when to let go. You'll land on the roof of this bay window here and slide on past my window. As you're going by, I'll catch you and pull you in."

Right, sounds like a good idea. NOT!

Smoke was starting to billow into the room, past the now-scorched towel.

"Come on Paul," Vinci pleaded, "we gotta do it, you'll be okay."

I consciously forced myself not to entertain any flashing images of my youth, but I thought of my mum and my dad. I couldn't help it. Fear had turned into blind terror. My mind tumbled through the alternatives: broken legs; broken neck; broken back; or burned alive while awaiting the arrival of the bright red fire brigade with its huge ladders.

Stomach lurching I thought, "I just can't do what he's asking me to do. I can't."

In spite of myself, I was now putting my feet out through the window. I turned around so that my legs were on the outside and my torso was on the inside, my stomach resting on the ledge of my window.

The flames had started to break into my room. A quick flash here and a quick flash there, like an advance party checking if everything was set up properly for them so that they could proceed to a full invasion.

I gingerly pushed the remainder of my body out of the window gripping the window ledge with all my strength, as if my life depended on it, which of course it did. So far, so good, as my father has a habit of saying when asked how things were going.

By now my knees had reached, and were temporarily resting in the gutter and so I knew that my feet were now visible to Vinci.

At this point, and I kid you not, I wanted Vinci to be, not Randolph Scott, but Burt Lancaster, as the catcher in Trapeze, the movie where Mr Lancaster apparently did all his own stunts.

"Okay man, let go," Vinci pleaded.

I tried and tried but I still couldn't hear the sound of a fire engine in the distance. There were shouts of encouragement from the gathering crowd in the street.

I twisted my head to the left and then to the right and I still couldn't see anyone arriving with a ladder, long or short. But I could hear the flames now flowing freely through my room just inches above my head.

"Come on Paul," Vinci pleaded. I'm not sure why, but he sounded as if he knew what he was doing.

"Okay, I'm letting go," I said

Maybe it was really that I had no choice, or perhaps that my fingers couldn't take any more pain. My grip slipped open and my body hit the slates and started to slide until my waist reached the rain guttering.

I came to a halt, stuck in the ultimate no man's land, still in immediate danger of being burned alive.

The flames were now leaping out the window above me, hungry for fresh oxygen.

"Push yourself, Paul," Vinci coaxed, and I felt his free arm loosely around my ankles. "Come on man, you can do it."

The palms of my hand were flat on the slate top of Vinci's bay window and – as if they had a mind of their own – they pushed, slipping back up over the slates, ripping the skin in the process.

Slowly, very slowly, my body started to move again, to slide down in the general direction of Vinci, but also in the direction of the concrete pathway two and a half floors below. As I slid, one of the brackets supporting the guttering cut into my chest, tearing the skin as I slid over it.

I didn't feel it. When my head reached the gutter, I clawed furiously at it in an attempt to save the skin on my face from also being ripped open.

"Come on Paul, I've got you, you've got to let go of the gutter."

"Okay!"

And I did.

For about one and one half seconds, it felt like I was in free-fall and then I felt Vinci's arm catch me under my arms. It was as if he had found some kind of superhuman strength. He got enough of a grip to pull and tug me in after him, so that we both fell head first through the window and into his room.

I passed out.

When I came to a few minutes later, I was being dragged out of the burning building. It felt like the kind of bad dream you wake up in a panic from and avoid falling asleep in case you are plunged back into it. Except this was for real. The whole place had gone up in smoke but that didn't seem to matter. I was in some kind of automatic mode. One of the neighbours from across the road brought us into their house, plied us with tea and sympathy, and dressed the wound on my chest. We had nowhere else to go, and so they asked if we wanted to stay the rest of the night. On the well-worn couch in their living room, I curled up into a crumpled ball and slept fitfully.

The next day I walked around the still smoking flat in despair, seeing the exact extent of the damage a fire and the three fire brigades that had eventually arrived, had inflicted. I looked out the window and got the shivers, realising just how much Vinci had risked his own life in order to save mine.

How had the fire started? The fire officer advised us that cigarette ash had slipped down between the cushions on a sofa in the living room. At first the ciggy smouldered quietly, he reasoned, but a few hours later the house was ablaze.

The aftermath was weird. I'd lost a collection of LPs and books, all of my clothes, lots of my papers and personal effects, and a roof to sleep under – but I remember walking around London for the next few weeks feeling ecstatic. I was in a kind of daze, almost certainly still suffering from shock, but very thankful nonetheless for the bravery – and the strength – of Vinci McCusker. Without him, I don't think I'd have made it through.

I really don't.

CHAPTER EIGHT

THE BALLAD OF RAGTAG AND BOBTAIL – MY ONE POP AT POP STARDOM

It was a line from Jimi Hendrix's 'Purple Haze' – "*Excuse me while I kiss the sky*" – that got me thinking. What is the weirdest thing I ever did during my time in the music business? There are many possible answers to that question, but – from the early days – one stands out.

I was working with a gentleman by the name of Eddie Kennedy, as publicist for two of his groups, Taste and Anno Domini. I have to admit that I was hopelessly out of my depth. I suspect that Kennedy had only given me the Taste account because he knew he was losing them and figured that, in the meantime, it would be the carrot required to get me to work on the far less promising, Anno Domini. Taste – comprising Rory Gallagher, (guitar, sax and vocals), John Wilson (drums) and Charlie McCracken (bass guitar) – were quite possibly the best live band in the world at that moment, and Rory Gallagher's talent and natural stage presence made him potentially one of the most effective publicity-generating machines in existence. Even John Lennon raved enthusiastically about Rory in an interview he did for *Disc and Music Echo,* a now long-forgotten weekly music paper.

Anno Domini were another matter altogether. They produced a very pleasing Crosby Stills & Nash type sound. Tiger Taylor, their guitarist, was, in his own right, also a force to be reckoned with. I knew him from an earlier incarnation with his own band, Tiger's Tale. The night I saw them, in Belfast, he and the band had performed, note perfect, Bob Dylan's *John Wesley Harding* album, from beginning to end. Tiger's two fellow band members in Anno Domini were Terry Scott (vocals and percussion) and David Mercer (vocals and guitar). David was a fine songwriter, with a gift for beautiful melodies. Anno Domini supported Taste everywhere. In fact Eddie seemed to be unable to get them any other gigs at all, and therein lay a problem. Taste's audience weren't interested in Anno Domini. That left me, as a neophyte publicist, batting on a very sticky wicket. If I invited a journalist to a show, they'd see the crowd react indifferently, before going hyperactive watching Taste. In some ways, it felt like I was living on borrowed time, when Eddie ambushed me. Picture the scene...

A tiny room, in Eddie' Kennedy's suite of offices at Command Studios (currently the home of Waterstone's in Piccadilly). A young music biz operative from Magherafelt in Northern Ireland by the name of Paul, on the telephone, talking to a journalist. It is obvious from the laughter that this is serious stuff. The camera pans in on Paul's face, which is creased with a smile...

Roy Hollingsworth was renowned for the fact that during a legendary interview with Leonard Cohen, they both, disillusioned by the music business and, no doubt inspired by a fine claret, made a pact to give it all up and retire to the country to get it together. I'm not quite sure what scuppered that grand plan, but I think it was for the better. Imagine the litany of brilliant songs that Leonard wouldn't have written if he had followed through on the promise.

Roy was also one of the few journalists who would actually take my calls, on top of which he frequently gave Anno Domini the requested, "wee mention" in the *Melody Maker* whenever he could. On this occasion he was regaling me with some juicy in-house gossip.

Eddie Kennedy was loitering with intent nearby, pretending not to be listening. What can a poor boy do? I strung the call out as long as humanly possible, in the hope that Eddie might take a wee dander elsewhere and leave me alone to work out the finer points of my world domination plan. To no avail. The second I replaced the heavy Bakelite handset back in the saddle, Eddie sauntered into my room.

"So Paul, what are your plans for tomorrow?"

I didn't like the look on his face.

"I was hoping to hop on a flight to LA..." I began and waited for the delayed effect of him nearly choking on his milky coffee, before continuing,

"...but... as the petty cash tin is pretty low..."

He flashed me one of those I-didn't-think-that-was-funny looks, but he maintained a veneer of patience. Something was up. I could tell.

"I'm going to be bound to the desk here and lighting up the hotwires to as many editors as I can on behalf of Anno Domini," I offered, hoping that my verbosity might be enough to get him to f-f-f-fade off back into his own room.

"Ah good, because I've got a wee job for you," he said.

I winced. It sounded ominous.

"Ah... what will you be wearing tomorrow?"

Kennedy didn't normally express an interest in my clothes.

"Sorry?" I asked, thinking I might have misheard him.

"I mean will you be wearing your current outfit?" he said, looking admiringly at my dark blue loon pants, lavender grandad shirt, blue pinstripe waistcoat, and tan corduroy desert boots.

Suppressing a surge of paranoia – what *was* he after? – I made a fuss over checking my diary. "The Royal Variety Performance isn't on for a few weeks, so I suspect, most likely, I will be in my normal attire."

"Great," he said, "and ah, will you be washing your hair?"

Nowadays, I might plead sexual harassment, the way he was looking over his glasses at my mop-top, which – as it happened – was more Italian Monk than The Beatles' *Rubber Soul* look I'd been aiming for. It turned out that Eddie had been building up to this moment for a few days.

In fairness, Eddie was no slouch when it came to working out ways to extract cash from the music business. One of his habits was to encourage artists to use down-time in the studio to record demos as they pursued the song-writing side of their careers, in the hope that something saleable might just materialise. One such session with a co-operative of musicians from various groups, had in fact produced quite a passable master recording, and – most likely unknown to anyone involved – Eddie had secured a record deal for the song with Deram Records, an off-shoot of Decca Records that launched the careers of Cat Stevens, The Moody Blues and Procol Harum, among others. It was also the label on which David Bowie's first, somewhat eccentric, self-titled album was released.

It later emerged that Eddie Kennedy had already been paid for the recordings. He thought the money was safe in his bank account, but then didn't Deram only go and announce that they actually wanted to release the track as a single. Normally this would have been a good thing: in fact most artists would have given their eye-teeth for a release on a rising, hip label like Deram. The problem was that the musicians who had recorded the track were all contracted to other bands and record labels. Which meant that the group on the tape – the group Deram had accepted and paid for – didn't actually exist. So Eddie urgently needed to form a fictitious group and do photographs for press and artwork. This, apparently, was where I came in. For photographic purposes at least, I was to be a member of the group.

As Eddie spoke, I looked around to make sure that he wasn't talking to someone behind me but no: I was to be one of the chosen ones. Given the precarious state of my finances at the time, it was an offer I couldn't possibly refuse.

The following day we gathered on a building site in the West End. I don't remember where my fellow band members had been recruited from, or how they were dragooned into service, but it was a ragtag and bobtail crew. Which, by the way, was my suggestion for the group name, but Eddie thought Ragtag and Bobtail would be more suited to a duo. We each got paid a fiver, signed a release so we could be willingly exploited and two months later an advert with our moody photo appeared in the *Disc and Music Echo*. There was talk about *Top of The Pops* and a world tour... but... you know, I've always thought that Eddie held the group back just so I would stick around and do the press for Anno Domini.

Not that my PR endeavours did them any good. They released one album in 1971, also on the Deram label, which opened with a version of The Byrds' 'So You Wanna Be a Rock 'n' Roll Star' and featured epics like 'Bad Lands of Ardguth', 'Hitchcock Railway', 'Five O'Clock in the Morning' and the title track 'On This New Day'. They were good, going on brilliant, but Tiger Taylor never did become a rock 'n' roll star. The cards just didn't fall that way.

CHAPTER NINE

ATTRACTIVE SAD GIRL ACROSS ROOM DANCING

Paul Fenn was a great agent. In fact he still is. "Sole-booking" was where an agent persuaded a venue or a promoter to allow them to do all of their booking, on an exclusive basis. It was under this sort of arrangement that Paul handled the gig schedules for two incredible, and loveable characters, Alan Smith and Steve Bates aka Big Al & Steve. These two promoters ran gigs in Dagenham Roundhouse; The Red Lion, Leytonstone; Cambridge Corn Exchange and The Kursaal Ballroom, Southend-on-Sea. The agents for the acts Paul booked for this circuit would do what was called a split-commission-deal, whereby they'd share their commission with Paul. If the act was so big that they could refuse to split commission, Big Al and Steve would always pay Paul a Booking Fee. It was an arrangement that worked for everyone, though sole booking has since gone out of fashion.

The Kursaal was an incredible Grade II listed building. It was opened in 1901 as part of one of the world's first purpose-built amusement parks. The venue was gob-smacking on the inside with all sorts of stunning embellishments, but more importantly it was also a very easy place for road crews to find. The minute they hit town, they'd head for the instantly visible, gigantic Vatican-like Dome. The crowd in Southend were great: the best reactions I ever witnessed in the Kursaal would have been for Rory Gallagher. The home boys, Dr Feelgood, always delivered there too.

I tracked Paul Fenn down quite early in Fruupp's career to blag a spot for the band as a support act on his circuit. I think his office was called Paul Fenn International in those days. He changed the name to Asgard when he started to book a club by the same name. It was a brilliant moniker for a booking agency in that Asgard was going to come first, or close to it, in all the agency directories, which seemed vitally important at that time. The meaning made sense too: Asgard was an ancient Nordic word combining *ass* meaning God (100% true) and *gard* meaning enclosure. I always thought that Asgard would be the perfect enclosure, or haven, for musicians. Asgard is also, as linguistic sleuths will have spotted, an acronym for Attractive Sad Girl Across The Room Dancing. What's not to like?

Paul did eventually book Fruupp across all of his venues. The band and myself got on very well with Big Al and Steve in particular, and they'd book Fruupp as often as they could, despite the fact that they were more into outfits like Rory Gallagher and Status Quo. Big Al was forever telling me I should get Fruupp to do some boogie. "The kids will love it, you'll see, then, when they get their audience, they can do their clever stuff." Big Al did love 'The Steam Machine', Fruupp's permanent rockin' encore.

While Fruupp were headlining clubs, they were supporting name acts in the bigger venues. I always felt that how a main act treats their support says a lot about them. Queen, for instance, were always great, very friendly, and highly supportive, not to mention informative. So too were Genesis (with Peter Gabriel), Yes, Barclay James Harvest, Hawkwind, ELO and the fabulous Man band. Supertramp... not so much.

Big Al & Steve (and by extension Paul Fenn) were good to Fruupp. They'd give them first shout on their last minute cancellations – which happened when a band dropped out, through illness or because they'd managed to secure a spot on *Top of The Pops* – and an extra few bob on the nights they were doing well at the box office.

I got on well with Paul: he'd a very dry sense of humour, always leaving me in stitches of laughter while feeling, "I can't believe he really just said that." His humour came mostly from his shyness (it takes one to know one). He didn't have a lot of acts though, so we came up with a way to double his rep list. He offered me the use of a desk and a phone in his office – hey, he even went the whole way and threw in a chair as well. I'd have a base for my Fruupp management duties: I'd book out the band from there and it would go through Asgard.

Asgard then had two acts, Fruupp and Hawkwind. Paul not only booked Hawkwind, but he also promoted their UK shows on the band and manager Doug Smith's behalf. Paul and Doug had one of the best agent/manager relationships I've ever witnessed in that they were always, but always, on the same page. I often wondered did Hawkwind realise just how lucky they were having those two men covering their backs. When I became an agent, in my relationships with managers, I always tried to emulate the way Paul and Doug worked. I'd frequently accompany Paul to Hawkwind's shows to work in the box office, and I'd be paid the equivalent of what Fruupp earned as their early gig fee, for the privilege.

The Asgard office was a small space sublet in Julia Creasey's office above a coffee shop in South Molton Street. It was one room but with a view, and the wonderful aromas of fresh roasting coffee beans wafting up from the street. Julia was a legend in the early UK folk scene. She worked as UK representative for Paul Simon, when he was living in London and gigging as a solo artist. This was just before 'The Sound of Silence', a song he'd recorded with a childhood friend, Arthur Garfunkel, set American radio on fire. The master craftsman songwriter was recalled to New York. Simon and Garfunkel were reborn – and the rest is history.

When we shared Julia's office, she was also managing Al Stewart. I was a big fan of Al's albums *Bedsitter Images* (1967), and *Love Chronicles* (1969), and used to go and see him around the folk clubs: I'd be mesmerised when he'd perform the core of his second album, the 20-minute song the album took its name from. Al used to visit the office once a week: he'd always come in with a different beautiful woman and they'd head off into the sunset hand in hand, and with Al carrying a very fine bottle of red. I'd meet up with Al again in 2001, when I became his agent. Al's manager Steve Chapman, an ex-drummer with Poco, is one of the great ones; so too is my mate, Peter Van Hooke, who I met first when I started to work with Van. Peter used to drum in Van's band and is now a very fine manager for Paul Carrack.

During this period Fruupp were very successful on the island of Ireland campus circuit and I became very friendly with all the social secretaries; people like Ian Wilson at Trinity, Dublin; Peter Mate at New University of Ulster, Coleraine; Ollie Jennings, Galway University; Billy McGrath at

UCD Belfield, Dublin; Elvira Butler at Cork and Gary Mills, Tim Nicholson, Alistair McDowell, Brian Grzymek and John McGrath at Queens University in Belfast. The ever-efficient and always smiling Gary Mills eventually became Asgard Promotions' main man in Ireland. He once ended up playing air-guitar with Meatloaf on one of the shows we were promoting in Antrim Forum: I felt he blew all the other band members off the stage! It was brilliant working with these social secretaries and not just because they were really good at what they did: they knew what it meant to look after the audience and the acts, and they paid their bills.

Due to what are euphemistically called The Troubles in Ireland – which ran from the late 1960s all the way to 1998 – it became very difficult to persuade a lot of UK and USA based acts to visit Ireland, particularly Northern Ireland. During the 1970s in particular, the college social secretaries and Irish promoters alike were having a hard time. When I was over in Belfast I'd spend time in the Student's Union at Queen's University and I'd help out where I could. I'd try to put them in touch with the relevant agents. But, a lot of the time, it was hard to make financial sense of it. If say Queen's University Student's Union contacted an agent to book an act, the students would only be talking about one show. So, when the act factored in a day to get over to Ireland, a show day and then a day to get back, with the additional ferry costs and/or flights, the sums just didn't add up.

However what if someone could put a campus-based circuit together so that acts could be offered a complete Irish tour? I knew the very 'one' to do it and before long we had everyone on board and we were doing as many as two complete tours a week, with Pat Egan and the famous Gernon sisters (Liz and Margo) at Santa Anna promoting the Dublin concerts. The tours were a big success and I figured I'd keep on doing them. During this period I discovered once again that not only was I good at filling date sheets, but I also really enjoyed doing it.

At various times in my career, I'd become a manager, an agent, a promoter, a publicist, a roadie, a lyricist, a columnist, a sound engineer, and an LD (lighting designer.) Sometimes even a sound engineer and an LD simultaneously. Mind you, that got a bit confusing on occasion. I remember trying to get the guitar louder by turning on the red light, an innovation which I don't think even Spinal Tap matched. Don't get me wrong: these roles are all fine, but the job I love the most, by far, is being an agent. Yes, managers, in theory at least, enjoy more control, which also means they have to take more of the blame; and yes, promoters can make more money, but which also means they can lose more money and – this next one is a major, deal-breaking, negative from my point of view – they're no longer allowed to do their own artwork. A roadie? Well there's no downside to being a roadie: they keep the wheels on the wagon, the show on the stage and the sense of humour factor high in the entourage. A lyricist? Well, why struggle to say something in eight verses when someone else will allow you 300 pages to complete the same task.

After much deliberation I resigned from all my Fruupp roles. Part of me didn't want to: we'd all been through so much together (some bad, a lot good) but I knew I had to. I was totally broke. I'd lost all my worldly possessions. I didn't have a place to live. I knew few feelings worse than not being able to go *home* after a hard day's work in the office and play my favourite albums on my fab Hi Fi stereo system. The temptation was there to leave London and return to my parent's house in Magherafelt and start from scratch again. But, I just couldn't bear to have them think of me as a failure, mainly because it would have made me think of myself as a failure. Downtown Radio (Newtownards, Co Down) wanted me to come and work for them. They had gone on air earlier in 1976, and had made me a decent offer to head up their outdoor promotions team. Being made an offer was very uplifting, but it just wasn't me.

Their offer did, however, help me focus on what I really did want to do. I decided I would become an agent full time.

So I guess this realisation was my *from-out-of-the-flames-rises-a-Phoenix* moment.

I would continue to develop my Island of Ireland concert circuit. And I would start to look for artists I could represent as an agent. Paul Fenn and I became official partners in Asgard UK, to cater for the acts we were working on together and eventually – within a year or so – we were full partners in all things Asgard, including our very successful run as concert promoters with Asgard Promotions Limited. Following several years as runners-up, in 1985, we were Rank Theatre's Top UK Promoter, based on ticket sales.

We've shared an office, or an adjoining office, since 1974. Personally, I could boast that we have enjoyed the pleasure of working with our dream representation list. We get on great – yes we have our "discussions", but we've never, ever had an argument. How lucky is that?

CHAPTER TEN

ANOTHER MUSIC IN A
DIFFERENT KITCHEN

As an agent, there are three basic types of new artists who you can represent.

One: the artist who for one reason or another is the buzz in the biz and you have a limited window of opportunity to help them make their mark, and hopefully secure a career on the live circuit.

Two: the one you know is likely to struggle, but has enough about them that you really want to do your best to make it happen.

Three: the artist who you only have to put up on the stage, let an audience see them and the phone will start to ring off the hook.

Many of the artists I've worked with fit in Category 3 – Robert Cray Band; Rainy Boy Sleep; Eric Bibb; Nanci Griffith; Lisa Ekdahl; Hothouse Flowers; The Undertones; Stevie Ray Vaughan; Ani DiFranco The Roches; Iris DeMent and The George Hatcher Band. The Robert Cray Band are a good example of how those naturals grow in stature. From Columbus in Georgia, this real Southern blues man's first London appearance was at Dingwalls, a club with a capacity of 500. A few albums later, Asgard were promoting RCB's brace of 1988 shows in the Hammersmith Odeon (3400 x 2), going on to book them as special guest with Tina Turner on her eight night run at the 10,000 capacity Wembley Arena.

Nanci Griffth's London debut was on Sunday 7th Feb 1988, in the

Acoustic Room in the Mean Fiddler (120 capacity). Princess Margaret's daughter, Sarah Armstrong Jones, was in the venue, which was so packed that three people fainted. The only way was up. By 1994 Asgard were promoting her in London's Royal Albert Hall on a three-night run which saw 15,000 tickets being purchased, every one of them due to the power of the artist's performances on the way up.

The George Hatcher Band, or, as they were affectionately known around the Asgard offices, The Margaret Thatcher Band, were that rare phenomenon, an Anglo-American band. George was from Texas and the remainder of the group were from Birmingham... that is Birmingham, UK and not Birmingham, Alabama. They were a good-time boogie band – or, rather, a great-time boogie band. They were the perfect night's entertainment on the college circuit or in club-land. The word of mouth factor with the GHB band was incredibly high.

George had recorded an album in America with Huey Lewis's band – later to become Clover, they were used by Nick Lowe as the studio band on Elvis' *My Aim is True*; and then, later again, mutated into the hit-making Huey Lewis and The News. On George's album, *Talkin' Turkey*, they were billed as Bluesy Huey Lewis. George was signed by United Artists and set up a base in London as a potential short-cut to launching his career onto the next level. George was lucky, in that Andrew Lauder, his A'n'R man at United Artists, was an all-around good guy. I'd met Andrew a lot on the gigging circuit: we were both always active, checking-out bands. Andrew wanted me to be George Hatcher's agent. I went to a gig, loved them, met George and his manager Bruce Mac Lean: I thought George, Andrew and Bruce made a great team and so I was happy to join the gang. As my first post-Fruupp act, I sensed that GHB would be perfect for the club circuit Fruupp had done so well on. We secured GHB a good run of gigs, but even more importantly, I made sure that every promoter and social secretary I knew, came along to see the band when they played in their area. I also persuaded United Artists to pull a trick I had used successfully with Fruupp and which in turn I had stolen from my good friend Chris O'Donnell, the then co-manager of Thin Lizzy.

In those days, the two main music papers in the UK were *The Melody Maker* and *The New Musical Express*, aka NME. Both had a couple of pages, positioned towards the back, known as the Club Pages, where they carried advert after advert letting people know what was happening, on a very healthy club circuit. The clubs would run their own strip adverts with their unique club logo at the top, listing in bold print that particular week's menu of artists, and, in smaller print, at the bottom of the advert, the forthcoming attractions. The bookers and agents would read these pages religiously each week to see who was playing and how often. Chris O'Donnell came up with the idea of having Thin Lizzy's record company, Decca, pay for the band's adverts in these pages on a weekly basis. Within a month or so Thin Lizzy *appeared* to be playing absolutely everywhere on the club circuit. Decca would ape the club adverts, not include their own logo or any record release details, so no one was any the wiser. If Thin Lizzy were having a quiet week, with only one or two gigs, then Chris would have Decca duplicate – or even triplicate – the adverts, with a different look. Thin Lizzy had so many gigs in the club pages each week, it wouldn't have surprised me if one of the adverts was for a gig in Chris's living room. The effect was that all the club owners just *had* to book this act who were playing absolutely everywhere; the hope too was that the clubbers would buy into it in the same way. It was a win-win situation because Thin Lizzy became a massive club act and their next single, 'Whiskey in The Jar', with Eric Bell's unforgettable guitar riff, topped the singles charts in Ireland and made it to No 6 in the UK charts. Following in Chris' footsteps, we'd used the same trick to great effect with Fruupp, and it worked even better for The George Hatcher Band – the guys in the group were ringing me up, looking for more nights off, as opposed to more gigs. The George Hatcher Band became very popular on the college circuit and appeared on the Reading Festival in 1977 on the same bill as Thin Lizzy. And, as events turned out, they were a very important band for me, though not in the way I might have expected.

One day, Andrew Lauder called and invited me to come around to United Artists to listen to a couple of songs and have a chat. I said okay, sure, and suggested we get together the following week. He said, "Actually, Paul, it's very important. Is there any chance you can come around now?"

So I scooted around to United Artists offices in Mortimer Street, just a five-minute walk from Asgard – three minutes if you're an Ulsterman.

I wondered if George Hatcher had started to record the new album. It seemed a bit too soon to me.

As it turned out, the meeting wasn't about George Hatcher. Andrew said he and United Artists were very impressed with the George Hatcher Band's full date sheet. He had just signed a new band and they couldn't get any shows at all – would I be interested in them? It was kind of urgent, he said, as they were just about to release their first single and UA had discovered they had no shows whatsoever lined up to support it. The single was 'Orgasm Addict' and the band were called Buzzcocks (they'd always insist that there was no "the" in Buzzcocks). It wasn't their debut release: in the DIY spirit of the latter half of the 1970s, they had already released the *Spiral Scratch* EP on their own label, New Hormones. I'd heard a track from the EP on the John Peel Show and been impressed. Andrew played me a couple of new songs including the single and I loved their sound. It wasn't just the band's energy: I heard a brilliant catchy, clever, pop song. I spoke with Richard Boon, their manager. I liked him, too. Not your typical manager, he was an art-school person, who reminded me of Ray Davies and Pete Townshend.

Now, I think of Richard as a hippie who didn't want to change the world so much as change how people imagined the world. Richard was mates with the band and he genuinely cared about them and wanted only the best for his charges. He didn't pretend he knew about the music business. In fact he admitted he didn't, but he wanted to learn. He was refreshingly honest, spoke very quietly and was very funny. He had all the makings of a great manager. And he had built a fantastic team.

Sure, the band had it in spades. Buzzcocks boasted an incredible rhythm section in Steve Garvey (bass) and John Maher (drums). Alongside Steve Diggle (lead guitar and vocals) and Pete Shelley (lead vocals and guitar) they created their very own special punk version of Phil Spector's Wall of Sound. But, really, it was a team thing. There were Pete Shelley's songs; how incredibly tight and powerful the band sounded live; Andrew Lauder's energy; Richard Boon's wit and calmness – and, to round it off, there was the work of Malcolm Garrett, whose powerful visuals and artwork helped to really set the band apart from the majority of the rest of the punk movement that was on the rise at the time.

Richard Boon took a very relaxed approach to the art of negotiating. He came in for a meeting with me one day and said he'd been sent by the band to renegotiate their commission rate. I said that I was more than happy to renegotiate, just as long as it was in an upwards direction. After his nervous laugh subsided, I explained to him that we couldn't change our rates, as we had the same rate for everyone. Henceforth, in this book, this will be known as "TCC" – "The Commission Conversation."

He said that the band had instructed him to sit at my desk until he'd negotiated a better commission rate for them. I said he was welcome to sit there for as long as he wanted to, but I really needed to get on with my work. He said ok. He sat there quietly as I worked away. About an hour or so later, I realised he'd nodded off, so I woke him up and promised not to tell the band that he'd fallen asleep on the job. Funnily enough he never mentioned the commission issue again.

I did like his approach though. I have no time for managers who think screaming and shouting and banging a desk is an acceptable form of negotiation.

****

At first, nobody on what might be called the 'legit' UK gigging circuit had wanted anything to do with the punks, and so they had to go and find their own venues, to create their own circuit. They also had to turn to independent labels like Chiswick Records, Stiff Records, Rough Trade and Beggars Banquet to release their singles. And when that didn't work, the pioneering punk acts released their own records. It was all about getting things done. Making a statement. There was a 'screw you' attitude, aimed at the suits that ran the big record companies: "we can do it ourselves."

That DIY spirit made all the difference. The punks weren't scared of the fact that they didn't qualify as proficient musicians. They'd scrape together equipment, pile in the back of someone's car and head off to do a gig, sometimes for the sheer hell of it. It was an injection of fresh energy into what had in many ways become a tired scene – and the crowds started to show up in numbers. Suddenly it felt like a movement.

I remember, towards the end of 1975, going down to Moran's Hotel, an influential venue in Dublin. The Boomtown Rats were onstage, playing their Dr Feelgood meets the New Wave brand of high-energy music. That was the night I sensed that there really was a new vibe coming along; and that, as far as my prog-rockers, Fruupp, were concerned, our days might just be numbered. Because anyone who had not 'made it' by that stage, was most certainly not going to make it, if the first stirrings of punk gathering momentum were anything to go by.

Under the new rules, people were permitted, expected even, to make it up as they went along. Increasingly, the bands had the confidence to do it – and the audience, who suddenly felt close to musicians again, lapped it up. It was a radically different approach to Fruupp's. Deliver short snappy songs, with the minimum musical embellishment. Get on to your next song immediately. Jump around. Shout. Roar. Curse if you feel like it. Play to the audience. Get in people's faces. And connect. The look was important too: the spiky hair, the bondage gear, the safety pins, the leather jackets. Like all successful music-based movements, the punks were linked, thread by thread, to their own unique DIY fashion. But in truth, it was the sheer energy, conviction, determination – bordering on desperation at times – that signalled that there really was a changing of the guard.

I felt it in my bones: the punks were responsible for the biggest surge of pure creative energy since The Beatles, The Kinks, The Who and The Stones and I wanted to be part of it. And so, at Asgard, we took the movement in our stride. The rep list was growing. We were booking a lot of the great new wave bands that were coming through into gigs in Ireland – Dr Feelgood, Eddie and the Hot Rods, The Adverts, The Ramones, The Clash, Buzzcocks, The Stranglers, The Undertones, The Runaways, Gang of Four, Penetration and The Lurkers among them.

Had it not been for the sheer quality of outfits like The Undertones, The Stranglers, The Clash and Buzzcocks, the movement would likely have fallen flat on its collective face. For me, it was all about the songs, and as a writer, Pete Shelley of Buzzcocks was just incredible. Their first three albums feature classic song after classic song. John O'Neill of The Undertones was another brilliant songwriter, arguably one of Ireland's greatest lyricists. These were the punk bands we wanted to represent – outfits that combined great songs, with clever music and a fresh and exciting approach to lyrics.

As the legendary Ted Carroll at Chiswick Records, a great music man, put it: tags are irrelevant. Call it punk. Call it rock. Call it New Wave. Or call it pop. It was all *music*. Ted had signed Radio Stars, and we took them on not as a punk band, just as a great pop band, capable of writing powerful pop songs, as their Top 40 single 'Dirty Pictures', proved. Ted also had the Hammersmith Gorillas, and we started to work with them. Coming as if from nowhere, they would go out and literally pack venues. I also represented The Count Bishops, The Radiators from Space (soon to become The Radiators), both signed by Chiswick Records; The Lurkers, The Gang of Four, Penetration and The Human League. Ted Carroll was really in the thick of it, a prime punk instigator. Rockin' Ted, as he was sometimes known, had a record stall down at the market in Portobello Road and he used to come into contact with lots of rising young musicians there, asking for 'the classic this' or 'the classic that'. Ted would have all they needed or an idea where to get it. He knew his music and he knew his stock. He would have had the same sense from his record stall clientele, as I experienced that night in Moran's Hotel.

It was down to people like Ted, Andrew, Jake Riviera – who ran Stiff with Dave Robinson and managed Elvis Costello – myself and other like-minded people who were open to change. I'd find a bar manager or landlord who had an upstairs room that hadn't been used for years, or at least since Brinsley Schwarz – managed by the same Dave Robinson – last played there. As the scene developed, an ever-growing legion of social secretaries in colleges, mostly of the same generation as the punks, were keen to book the new bands.

We were lucky enough to have signed the majority of the new bands before the other London agencies were even aware there was a punk movement. At times, I felt like Dr Livingstone scoping out this new circuit. The blatant prejudice against these groups made it frustrating at times. We did a deal with a city-centre venue for The Clash to play in Dublin. The owners of the venue cancelled the sold-out show because they heard The Clash were punks and they didn't want anyone – or anything – of *that* kind in their venue. They pronounced the word "punks" with complete disdain. The super-efficient and ever reliable Ian Wilson, who was President of the Student Union in Trinity College, came to the rescue and successfully staged the show. Within a few months – for the sole reason that punk bands were doing such great business, selling tickets and shifting records – the music industry finally woke up to them.

John Curd at Straight Music was the main national promoter who started to do extended English tours for acts like Dr. Feelgood, The Clash, The Stranglers and Elvis Costello. I always thought John was a brilliant promoter. He would do reasonable deals and always looked after both the acts and the audience. My hunch was that if The Sex Pistols had worked with John Curd they might have survived. Then again, maybe it was always part of Malcolm McLaren's 'masterplan' that they'd have to self-implode to serve the myth.

****

Right from the get-go, John Peel, on his late night BBC radio show, was also a big supporter of punk. The access he gave punk bands to the airwaves was a major part of the success of the new movement. It was a hungry scene and there was an element of 'we're all in this together'. Still, there were stand-out tracks – and equally unforgettable moments. When Good Vibrations, run by Terry Hooley in Belfast, released the debut by The Undertones from Derry, it might have died a death. Instead John Peel played 'Teenage Kicks' and immediately it was finished, he played it again. It was an astonishing piece of radio, immediately putting the band on everyone's radar. The word of mouth was so effective that by the time The Undertones came over to London to do their first gigs, there was an audience waiting for them, with their hearts in their mouths. Even on their first tour, they sold out most of the shows, which was unheard of at the time. As it happened, I didn't need John Peel to alert me. A friend of mine from Queens University had sent me the 'Teenage Kicks' EP. I spent the weekend listening in sheer disbelief at the brilliance of it. That this band lived less than thirty miles from where I had grown up made it all the more startling. My gut feeling is that The Undertones would have been successful in any era. Or to put it another way, if Them had written and recorded 'Teenage Kicks' as the follow up to 'Here Comes The Night', it surely would have gone straight to No.1 and copper-fastened their success. Mind you, if that had happened, Them likely wouldn't have split up and we'd have been deprived of *Astral Weeks*.

As it happens, I first connected with The Undertones when I was in Belfast for a series of Van Morrison comeback shows in 1978 – the first gigs that I had set up for him as an agent and promoter. I figured there was a good chance The Undertones would join the Asgard roster, if only because I could actually understand what they were saying. They explained with great humour that in record company meetings, they'd be stopped on every second word with a 'pardon', 'sorry', or 'what?'. I assumed it would help that we represented Van Morrison. However, it suddenly became very clear why they wanted me to be their agent. "Of course we want to work with you," one of the band confessed, "you represent the Buzzcocks." I refrained from correcting them by pointing out that "there's no 'the' in Buzzcocks."

With punk doing well on the UK and Ireland circuit, I was able to book my punky bands into Holland and Belgium. Very quickly, France was big into punk; some German cities too, but not all of them. I don't remember anybody doing Italy or Spain. And to the east, was the 'communist bloc'. Again, if a band became big in Britain on a gigging and chart level, in the way The Undertones and Buzzcocks did, then you'd immediately book them into Norway, Sweden, Denmark and Finland. I was working again with all the promoters I'd met on my Fruupp adventures. Rock festivals started to want punk acts. The sky, you might have thought, was the limit.

A certain mythology has been advanced over the intervening years that the punk bands weren't really so unprofessional, that behind the scene they were very together and the DIY was all a show. But a lot of the bands – Siouxsie and the Banshees and Joy Division spring to mind – were infamous for it. They'd arrive late at gigs, bizarrely unburdened by equipment. On multi-band bills, they'd blag the use of the other bands' gear. I remember Buzzcocks taking fellow Manchester band, Joy Division, out on a UK tour with them. Being Buzzcocks, they ignored the standard practice of charging the support act (or their record company) a "buy on" for the privilege of doing the tour. Instead, in a move that was a very refreshing punk innovation, Buzzcocks subsidised Joy Division. When their manager Richard Boon saw the state of Joy Division's equipment at the first show he instructed his crew to buy lots of gaffer tape and do whatever they had to do, to ensure that the gear didn't fall apart until, at the very least, the tour was finished.

Thankfully, they got there in the end.

CHAPTER ELEVEN

THE GHOSTS OF WARDOUR STREET

In the mid-1960s I was 15 and living in my native Northern Ireland. As I ran around, managing Blues by Five, the legendary Marquee Club in London was like a beacon, the place we imagined ourselves playing, our nirvana. The Marquee hosted more groups in a week than we saw in the Northern Irish countryside in a year. We had to be satisfied with the rare, treasured opportunities to see local heroes like Taste, The Interns, The Method, Sam Mahood & The Soul Foundation and The Gentry on our trips to Belfast.

By the time I moved to London in 1967, I quickly discovered that The Marquee Club really was slap-bang, in the middle of the then current Cultural Revolution. As soon as I managed to find my way around the Big Smoke, I set my sights on Wardour Street in general, and No. 100, in particular, where The Marquee was located.

So, what was so special about The Marquee Club? Well, it wasn't just a typical large room with four walls that people thronged to, in order to listen to music. The Marquee actually was a "club". It was where like-minded people – 'members' – met in the shadows of the striped, faux tent and canopy, to enjoy a common interest: The Marquee's special blues-based type of music.

The greater the number of duffle-coat-clad members of the audience on any particular night, the purer the music tumbling down from the stage seemed to be. I was so in awe visiting the hallowed venue for the first time that I've forgotten the name of the act that played. But I do remember dark walls that seemed to sweat; the club playing its own signature tune (a version of the 'Woodchopper's Ball' I believe); and the club secretary, Mr John Gee, who announced, with impeccable diction, the forthcoming attractions, before introducing that night's group.

There was also, generously piled by the box office, a giveaway calendar listing the complete programme for the next month. There were application forms to become club members, offering potential participants a club card and a discount on future events. Joining was a no-brainer.

As a fan, I spent many a great night in The Marquee Club shifting from foot to foot, in order to avoid becoming permanently stuck to the beer stained carpet. Taste, The Spencer Davis Group, The Moody Blues, Cheese, Stackridge, Barclay James Harvest, Focus, Jethro Tull, Granny's Intentions, Rare Bird, Elton John, Faces (a total hoot), Genesis (the Peter Gabriel version), Clark-Hutchinson (performing 'Improvisation on a Modal Scale', in all its majestic ten-minute glory) and Ten Years After (who also performed a version of 'The Woodchoppers Ball') all featured.

Even the lesser names were worth seeing. Cheese, for instance, were an incredible band, one of the best to grace the Marquee's compact stage. From Northern Ireland, they featured Roy Abbott (guitar), Nicko Halliwell (keyboards), Charlie McCracken (bass) and John Wilson (drums). I saw them play twice, towards the end oft June 1968, when they delivered a superb, highly original version of The Beatles' 'Strawberry Fields Forever'. The band returned to Belfast, from their Wardour Street triumph, and imploded, with Charlie and Wilsie leaving to join Rory Gallagher in Taste, replacing Eric Kitteringham and Norman Damery respectively. That power trio lasted just two years, before Rory decided to go solo, but they left an indelible mark, with two brilliant LPs and hundreds of shows. As often as possible I caught them in the Marquee Club. And I was there on the majority of the nights Rory played under his own name. Later, in 1986, I became Rory's agent.

The Marquee really was a musical melting pot. The debut of Joe Cocker and the Grease Band, on Tuesday 25th June 1968 – with Cheese as the opening act – might sound like a culinary disaster, but was a total revelation. Joe Cocker's unique and very soulful performance was somewhat akin to witnessing lightning being trapped in a bottle. The

Grease Band featured Henry McCullough, ex- of The People and Eire Apparent, not to mention The Walter Lewis Showband. Another brilliant double-header matched Stud – featuring John Wilson (drums), Charlie McCracken (bass) by then ex- of Taste and Jim Cregan (guitar) ex- of Family – with Anno Domini on November 2nd 1971. Okay, I was their publicist but I loved them all the same. The nights spent there were the highlight of my week.

****

At The Marquee Club, the artist always received 50% of the door-take. I believe this emolument – that really was a keyword, in those days – was eventually increased to 60%. This was before catering clauses became a major part of every act's contract rider, but the Golden Spoon wasn't too far away: I had a weakness for the pancakes with hot butterscotch sauce there and so they became a major part of the Marquee ritual.

The Marquee didn't have an in-House PA system, so everything had to be carted in via the rear entrance in Richmond Mews. They also didn't provide a stage crew to help hump the band's gear. Fruupp were the first band I booked into The Marquee Club, on 23 July 1971, for what was the first of 10 appearances at the club. That's when I discovered that the musicians themselves, plus our one roadie and myself, as both manager and agent, had to lug it all in, set it up and break down the gear after the show. The humping didn't bother us in the slightest. Vinci and I were equally proud to have our band on stage at the club we'd read – and dreamt – about so much, since the Blues by Five days.

The Club was the foundation stone of what became known as The Marquee Organisation. John Gee left to work at Radio Luxembourg and was replaced by Jack Barrie – and it was Jack who booked the majority of the Punk and New Wave bands I was represented as an agent in the final decades of the '70s: Radio Stars; Buzzcocks; The Undertones; Tubeway Army, The Radiators from Space; The Human League; Sniff 'n' The Tears; The Boyfriends; Tenpole Tudor; Penetration; 999; Thomas Dolby; The Count Bishops; Tom Robinson; The Hammersmith Gorillas: The Lurkers and the Gang of Four. All of the above acts took their turn to step out onto the stage of London's world famous, Marquee Club. The first time was a moment that meant a lot to each and every one of them.

Tubeway Army played the Marquee in February 1978. Looks apart, they were neither punk nor new wave, but Gary Numan guided his sci-fi influenced, synthesizer-led band to the top of the singles charts with 'Are 'Friends' Electric?' (the fourth biggest-selling UK single of 1978) and to No.1 in the album charts with *Replicas* (1979).

Jack Barrie also continued booking some of the old guard from me, artists like Skid Row, The George Hatcher Band, Racing Cars, Motorhead and The Boyfriends. I even made the occasional trip to the club to see artists I didn't represent – including the best non-punk band to come out of the punk/new-wave era, Dire Straits.

The Marquee's brave booking policy also extended to The Marquee Organisation's annual Reading Festival. We agents would have our separate annual lunches with Jack where, after the social proceedings were dispensed with, he'd say, while shuffling to find a more comfortable position in his chair, "Okay Paul, who do you have for me for this year's Reading?" These annual lunches were held in an upstairs room in the nearby St Moritz Restaurant, of exposed brick, with dangling cowbells. This was totally okay by me. The St Moritz Filet Madagascar with potato gratin was so amazing that I can still recall the taste.

Elaine in The Marquee Organisation's office kept us agents up to date with all the comings and goings at the club. She frequently referred to us as her 'boys' and she would show us the safest place to stand in the new bar, stage right, to ensure we weren't going to be permanently attached to the carpet. She'd also try to ensure the correct spelling of Fruupp's name would appear in The Marquee adverts and listings and not Frup, Fruup or even Frupp. Tactically, it was a weakness: I had to keep telling people, it was FRUUPP.

The lesson I quickly learned was: be careful with the actual names of the acts you choose to represent. An outfit like Gnidrolog must have had a lot more than four spellings of their name to contend with.

Elaine would also make sure all "her boys" were properly accredited on the Reading Festival weekend. I remember one rainy festival, I spent a few extremely enlightening hours in the backstage bar being entertained by

Mr Nick Lowe (the Bard of Brentford and key member of Brinsley Schwarz and Rockpile). It was the first time I'd met Nick, although I'd often seen him on stage with the Brinsleys, as they were affectionately known. A few years later I became Nick's agent and have remained so ever since. Talking about decent blokes, one year, for some reason I can't recall – I'd probably been stood up – I ended up hanging out at the artist's entrance at Reading. There I was, standing around with both arms the same length, when someone tapped me on the shoulder. It was Phil Collins.

Phil was the drummer with Genesis (with and without Peter Gabriel) and his band were the main act of the day. They were also a band that Fruupp had frequently supported on the circuit and so we chatted for ages about how it was going and the trials and tribulations of being involved in a prog rock band. That done, eventually, he "walked me in" – a euphemism for someone who has a pass, getting someone who hasn't, into an event.

On one special evening in 1971, Elaine secured me a couple of tickets for the Led Zeppelin stop-off at the Marquee, on their "back to the clubs" tour. The place was packed to the rafters, and Led Zep were in flying form. But there were other even more legendary nights. The box office record for the Marquee had been set by The Jimi Hendrix Experience, who had apparently sold 1,500 tickets for a venue that had an official capacity of just over 700. Taste, as legend goes, topped that by another couple of hundred. How they all fitted in, I'll never know. Thankfully the fire officer seems to have stayed at home on that particular night.

I've never seen a better live band than Taste. Rory had learned early in his career that the secret to a great gig is not playing to the audience, but playing with them.

As Rory duck-walked across the stage, you felt that, if he'd wanted to, he could have levitated, and continued his six-string magic, an appropriate six inches above the heads of the audience. He was a master craftsman. But he was also a musical shaman, a high-wire artist, a sorcerer. If someone told me that photographic evidence had finally been uncovered, confirming that Rory did indeed levitate mid-solo on that incomparable night at the Marquee when he broke all records, then I'd believe it. That combination of time, place and artist was perfect. Taste 'live at The Marquee' is right up there as a contender for the best rock 'n' roll gig ever.

CHAPTER TWELVE

HERE COMES THE KNIGHT

Van Morrison released *A Period of Transition* in 1978. Around the same time, he started working with the renowned UK promoter, Harvey Goldsmith, who became his manager. By then, Asgard was representing a lot of great artists and I had been working with Harvey to promote some Buzzcocks' shows. I blagged an invite from him to go to a showcase Van was doing in London at the Maunkberry Resturant & Club on the 15th June, 1977, with Dr John, Peter Van Hooke, Mick Ronson and Mo Foster in his band, to launch the album. It was the first time I had seen Van live since his famous Rainbow appearance in July 1973, part of which was included on the *It's Too Late To Stop Now* album, which remains one of the best live albums ever released. Van sang his heart out at the showcase – but no other dates had been lined up.

I spoke to Harvey. "Look," I said, "Van hasn't played in Belfast since the Them days. Is there any chance I can book him to do some concerts in Ireland?" Eventually Harvey came back to me, reporting that Van seemed very responsive to the idea. We kept on having discussions. I put together a potential tour for Van to play Dublin, Belfast and Cork. My offers were high, because I knew how well the dates would do. I was waiting for confirmation when Harvey's office dropped a bombshell: they were no longer representing Van Morrison.

I rang up Moira Bellas, a friend at Warners, Van's record company, and inquired if Van had appointed a new manager yet. "As a matter of fact he has," Moira reported. His new manager was also a promoter, the American legend, Bill Graham. I blagged Mr Graham's number from Moira and called him. I told Bill about the Irish Tour I'd been discussing with Harvey. He was very charming, but in essence said that Van couldn't possibly just do an Irish tour: it wouldn't make commercial sense. "Okay," I replied, "in that case I'll promote the UK dates as well." I gulped for oxygen. I was chancing my arm. At that moment, I'd never promoted a concert in the UK, apart from a sole gig featuring Genesis (with Peter Gabriel) – and Fruupp as the opening act – in Merton (Wimbledon) Town Hall on Friday 1 September 1972. Bill Graham said he'd be happy to see a routing and some numbers. I gulped again.

A couple of hours later, Mick Brigden from BGP (Bill Graham Presents) rang me. "Look," he explained, "we have other promoters we work with in the UK, namely Mel Bush and MAM, so we feel it would be proper to also allow these promoters to table an offer." Mick was an Englishman, who'd gone to America with the supergroup, Humble Pie, and never came home. He was a clever fellow. Although he was potentially giving me bad news, he had put such a positive spin on it that I didn't feel bad until about half an hour later, when the implication had finally sunk in..

I put my offer together. It was ambitious. Paul Fenn and I discussed it at length and as always he backed me 100%. On paper, it seemed risky, but Paul said that if I was confident about the numbers, we should go for it. I submitted the offer to Mick Brigden. I felt good about our prospects. The majority of people I knew were already on to the second or third copy of *Astral Weeks*. Now this may have said more about me and the people I mixed with, than it did about the UK ticket-buying public. But I didn't think so. I was bullish.

A few evenings later Mick rang to say my offer was by far the best, but they needed to send it to Van for approval. The following night, Mick rang to say Van had given the tour the green light. It later became apparent the confirmation had nothing whatsoever to do with the size of the offer.

In the *City Week/ Thursday Magazine* days, I'd regularly written pieces on Van and his music. Once I carried a live review of Demick & Armstrong, performing a beautiful song called 'Friday's Child', which Herbie (Armstrong) had introduced as a Van Morrison original. In my review I commented on the quality of the song and asked anyone who knew where

I could find a copy, to please give me a shout. This, of course, was long before the days of the world wide web. The following week a package arrived at the *City Week* offices and the mystery was solved, albeit in a convoluted way. In the package I found a copy of a Them single, on the Major Minor label, with 'Gloria' on the A-side and 'Friday's Child' on the B-side. As rock historians will know, 'Gloria' started life as the original B-side to 'Baby Please Don't Go', the first of two UK Top ten singles Them released on Decca Records (1964). The A-side was a cover of a Big Joe Williams song by way of John Lee Hooker. Two years later when 'Gloria' had started to gain a lot of attention (a Top Ten hit in the USA for the Shadows of The Night, it was also covered by The Doors and Jimi Hendrix), Them's manager Phil Solomon re-released the song with 'Friday's Child' as the B-side, on his own label, Major Minor Records. I'd bought Them's other Major Minor release, *The Story of Them Parts 1 and 2*, but I'd been totally unaware of the 'Gloria' reissue – and had never heard 'Friday's Child' on record. Accompanying the single was a very charming letter from Van's mum, Violet Morrison (a powerhouse singer herself). The letter – thanking me for all the Van write-ups – was one only a proud mum could have written. She'd also mentioned the *City Week* articles to Van and so, the way Mick Brigden told it, when Van saw my name it clicked. He'd instructed Mick that if the offer was acceptable on a business level, he was okay to do the tour with Asgard Promotions.

During 1979, we put twenty-two UK and Irish shows – using images from the previous year's 'Wavelength' album in the artwork – on sale and they sold out in a jiffy. One competitor had offered a tour with The Venue – Richard Branson's 600-capacity club opposite Victoria Station – as the London show. A second one had offered one show in the Dominion Theatre (2,069 capacity). We'd offered three nights at The Hammersmith Odeon, which at 3,400 a night, required us to sell 10,200 tickets. Luckily for all concerned, Asgard, BGP and Van had made the right call.

The excitement each night on the tour was unbelievable. The anticipation of the audience was absolutely overwhelming and the surge of emotion as Van Morrison walked onto the stage took my breath away on each and every one of those twenty-two shows, all of which I attended. But you know what was even more incredible? At every stop on the tour,

Van and the band rose to the occasion and played a blistering set.

Van was clearly enjoying himself – and when the singer was enjoying the tour, the rest of the band were in heaven when they saw him smile. During the Irish leg, Van played the Whitla Hall in Belfast on Tuesday 20th and Wednesday 21st February 1979, and, after the second show we drove down to Dublin, arriving at the Shelbourne Hotel in the early hours of the morning. I was just about to fall asleep when my phone rang. It was Van. "Do you fancy a cup of coffee?" he said. I thought it was churlish to suggest my preference was a good old cup of tea. After doing the box office settlement in Belfast a few hours previously, the thought occurred that I might even break the bank and order a few sticks of shortbread as well. We met in the lounge of the once grand hotel and a kind night-porter delivered our coffee, tea and shortbread.

Van was very happy with the way the tour was going.

"Do you also book shows in Holland?" he asked.

"Yes we do."

"And Germany, Belgium and France?"

''Yes, we book tours everywhere, well everywhere apart from the USA and Canada where we work through various sub-agents," I replied, hoping I knew where this was going.

"Could you set up some dates for me in Holland and Belgium?"

''Why yes of course,'' I replied.

And that was how I became Van's agent for the following seven years.

Forty-three years later, my most lasting memory of the *Wavelength* tour is driving back on the coach to London after the final gig – the City Hall Newcastle on Monday 19th March 1979 – with Van and the band and their tour manager Stephen Pillster. In the early hours of the morning, Van walked up and down the aisle of the coach, an acoustic guitar slung on, and acting as a human jukebox. He played every request thrown at him, and more besides. Hank Williams, The Beatles, The Beach Boys, Dylan, Muddy Waters, Lead Belly, John Lee Hooker, plus every country music classic known – and on and on for the 280 miles – never once struggling over a chord or a lyric. For the record, Van did a much better live version of 'Sloop John B' than Goggles Anonymous ever did.

CHAPTER THIRTEEN

DISCOVERING THE CORRECT WAVELENGTH

As an agent you can put your tours together, hope for the best and take your commission. Rain or shine, you get the same percentage. On the other hand, as a promoter you always need the sun to shine. Personally I've always felt an agent has to do more than just book the shows. I like to plan ahead. Work out a strategy. Where do you want your artist to be in three tours time? Then map out how you're going to get there.

Van Morrison's first tour sold out very quickly, confirming what I had assumed: that he had a very solid fan base. That can never be taken as a given. If you're not careful, the next tour the audience numbers may drop a wee bit and on the next tour again a wee bit more. Realistically Van Morrison was no longer going to have regular hit singles and TV was not his ideal medium. His most recent albums were selling okay, but not great. Where did that leave us? I had to try to figure that out.

In addition to selling out, the first Van tour we promoted had been phenomenally successful in terms of audience reaction and critical acclaim. As I was contemplating the next move, that was a big plus. I saw the possibility that we might build on that, to extend his audience, if we created something different, something special. The hope is always to create a virtuous circle: the bigger the live audience, the more his albums would sell; the more albums he sold, the more his tickets would sell; and the more tickets he sold, the more secure his later career would be. The more I thought about it, the more I realised that Van already had something special, very special. He had his live show.

Van was delivering the goods on stage big time. It was my job to deliver the goods off-stage. The conundrum was a familiar one: when an artist comes to town, there's a bit of fuss in advance, a bit of a buzz on the night, reviews afterwards and before you know it the media are on to the next act who is about to roll into town. So my plan for Van was to bring him to London, not for one or two nights but to do an extended run.

We'd been doing a lot of very successful shows in the Dominion Theatre. The manager at the time, Bill Weir, was particularly helpful and his staff made the artists and crews feel very welcome. So we booked Van for a four-night run in the Dominion Theatre in 1982. On the same tour we also did a week in the Gaiety Theatre in Dublin. These shows were tied into the release of Van's classic *Beautiful Vision* album. We spent heavily on advertising, taking full page adverts in *Time Out* instead of the usual quarter pages. In *The Sunday Times,* and similar daily publications, instead of the usual 8, 10 or 12 cm, double column, we increased our adverts to quarter pages. I know it might sound incredibly simplistic now, but at the time most adverts appeared to me to be a mishmash rehashing of record company artwork, with the venue and date just plonked haphazardly on top. I always thought that it was a good idea to leave as much empty space as possible in an advert or on a poster. I figured humans are more attracted if there's less visual pollution. Now, with these bigger ads, we could test those theories.

We had the Dominion box office monitor where the sales were coming from: *Time Out*, *The Sunday Times* and *The Evening Standard* produced the best results in London and *The Sunday Times* for the regional sales. With a four night run, we had four times the budget to spend on advertising. We also started a new look in concert advertising by minimising the content and thereby creating breathing space. The idea was not to try to be clever but to be classy. In addition to the paid-for marketing, the sheer power of the word of mouth on Van's consistently amazing performances was invaluable. The attention he was receiving, spread over several nights meant his shows quite literally became the talk of the town. And as a result of the word of mouth on how amazing Van's concerts were, we'd already started to have substantial interest from abroad.

There was, however, one problem at the Dominion. At the rehearsal

Van started to complain about the severe rake on the stage. In legit old-style theatres, they would always build the stage with a rake so that it sloped from the rear down to the front lip. This was so that members of the audience sitting in the stalls didn't have their view of the actors/musicians cut off at the knees. The resulting rake wasn't a major problem until the artists started noticing it – which is what had happened with Van. So, overnight, we had carpenters come in and build a level island on top of the Dominion stage. The flat wooden platform was big enough for the band and Van to perform on. Thankfully the sloping stage was forgotten about and there were no further discussions on the matter.

For the *Beautiful Vision* tour we used the distinctive Prism & Rainbow artwork from the album sleeve. I even had the legendary Peter Clarke replicate the image using effective lights on the stage. I had always hated the way the venues ruined the mood at the end of a show. I'm talking about those moments when you're still in your own world – a precious personal space – at the end of a show. The artist has taken you to some wonderful places and then, at the end of the encores – sometimes before the artist even had a chance to leave the stage – the house lights are turned on full tilt.

The roadies rush onto the stage and start to noisily pack the gear away as the venue stewards roll down the aisles shooshing you out as quickly as possible. It's as if the venue staff are saying to the audience, "Okay, the show's over, we've taken your money, now get the feck out of here so we can go home." For me, that can completely ruin the impact of what you've seen and heard, and, in fact, become your lasting impression of the evening.

So on the *Beautiful Vision* tour, Van would finish the concerts, we'd hold the house lights down and bring up – for the first time that evening – the lights Peter Clark had created for us. Peter had painstakingly duplicated the album sleeve with rainbow-coloured, columns of light, recreating the prism effect and was using a mirror ball to give the effect of the stars on the sleeve. We'd play the stunning instrumental track, 'Scandinavia', from the album, on the PA system and let the audience come down gently from the high of the concert. There was an extraordinary mood created by the combination of this piece of music and the moody lights. In effect, we prolonged the feeling of bliss. Everyone in the audience remained in their seats for the additional 6 minutes and 41 seconds of this wonderful piece of music.

The first night we did this, a few of the musicians and crew were standing in the wings by the side of the stage, caught in the novelty of the audience not leaving the venue and being allowed to savour the special memories that had been created out in the auditorium.

"What is this shit?" Pee Wee Ellis, Van's saxophonist and musical director, interjected. He clearly didn't mean rubbish – this was musician-jive.

"That's a track from my new album," Van, who – unnoticed by the rest of the band – had also stayed side-stage to view the lights answered, "and that's the sleeve of my new album."

"Genius, brilliant idea, Van," Pee Wee gushed, as an anti-P45 device.

On the same tour I used a photo I'd taken as a basis for the poster for the week of shows Van did at the Gaiety Theatre in Dublin. I'm not a great photographer, nor even a good one, but I've always worked on the theory that, for every couple of hundred shots you take, at least one of them must turn out okay. This photograph was taken in Gary Mills' backyard, looking across the River Clanrye at sunset with a very dramatic and soulful sky in the background. Phonogram loved it and also used it as the shot on the front of Van's 'Cry For Home' single'.

In 1983, on the *Inarticulate Speech of the Heart* tour, we promoted Van in the Dominion Theatre again, extending the run to seven nights. We also included shows in Brighton, Bournemouth and Oxford and a four-night run in the Grand Opera House, Belfast. The entire tour sold out very quickly with enough demand to have sold at least double the number of nights in each city.

Behind the scenes, we had to fight very hard to get into the Opera House. The politest way to put it is that the Opera House management didn't feel "pop stars" should grace their stage. My argument was that Van Morrison was not a "pop star" but a creative artist, whose talent and success on the worldwide stage was shining a very positive spotlight on Northern Ireland in general and on Belfast in particular. On top of which, the Grand Opera House had recently been given a very expensive refurb on the taxpayers' dime. A lot of those taxpayers were Van Morrison fans and really, when you got right down to it, they had a right to see the city's most famous son on the stage of *their* Opera House.

Common sense prevailed and Van took to the stage at the Grand Opera House for four nights in March. Van decided to record those historic Belfast shows and *Live at the Grand Opera House Belfast* was slated for release in 1984. Van agreed it would be a good idea to have a photograph of the iconic building on the sleeve, so we sent a photographer to take shots, months after Van's shows there. I noticed towards the bottom left of the photograph we selected that there was a poster showing a "coming attraction" to the Opera House. I had the Phonogram art department overlay Van's Inarticulate Speech of the Heart tour poster into that space and we were ready to roll.

In 1984, Van returned to the Dominion. This time, we promoted a staggering 11 nights in the venue, selling 23,000 tickets. In truth, excitement about the gigs was running so high that he could easily have played for a month and there'd still have been people chasing tickets..

Using Van's phenomenal performances as the equivalent of "hit singles" was working very effectively. His live audiences were building and his albums were selling more, and charting higher. He enjoyed a very successful run from *Wavelength,* through *Into The Music, Common One, Beautiful Vision* and *Inarticulate Speech of the Heart*, to *Live at The Grand Opera House Belfast*. The reviews for his shows and albums were all five-star. Van was being awarded silver and gold discs to celebrate these sales. Even the legendary *Astral Weeks* went Gold (100,000 sales in the UK) during this period, sixteen years after its original release date.

There were lots of requests for interviews, which were never Van's favourite pastime. He even went to the trouble of hiring Keith Altham, a very expensive publicist, to say 'no' to all media requests. But the more he said no, the more coveted a Van interview became. As it happened, Van liked Gavin Martin, an excellent journalist with the *NME* and a fellow Belfast man and so he had me set up a lunch for the three of us. Van spent the entire interview – or rather lunch – explaining why he didn't give interviews.

Van had a habit of ringing up at very odd hours of the day and – even more often – night. He was on the west coast of the USA and so daytime there would often be the wee small hours in London. If there were no recording plans on the schedule Van would get bored and he'd ring up and say, "Yeah, you know we haven't done any shows in Holland for a while, could you set up a Dutch tour?" And of course I'd set up a Dutch tour. That was one of the easy ones: Leon Ramakers from Mojo, the Dutch promoter, was one of the best in Europe, and a big fan of Van's and he'd always do an incredible job. So you'd get back from the Dutch tour and the same thing would happen, Van would get bored, ring up, and this time it could be Germany, Italy, Ireland, or... well anywhere really.

One summer, Van was on a long festival tour including several shows in 5,000-ish capacity bull-rings in the South of France. The support act for these shows was a French band called Telephone, who were massive in their home country but couldn't sell a ticket anywhere else. Van was big in France, but so were Telephone and so they had a lot of people turn up just to see them. During Van's performance in Frejus, one of the Telephone fans hurled a bottle at the stage. I was in the audience and I could see it sail through the air, as if in slow motion. Very quickly, I realised that – unless my calculations were way off – it was going to hit Van smack bang on the head, with potentially catastrophic consequences. I put both hands to my face, as if aping Edvard Munch's The Scream: I didn't want to see or hear what happened next. My career was most certainly over. Yes, I agree, it would not have been my fault, but try telling that to the artist! Van was between songs and just as the bottle was arcing beautifully towards his crown, on course to knock him into the middle of next week, I looked out through a gap between my fingers and saw Van stooping to pick up his guitar for the next song. The bottle flew about six inches over the Man's head and crashed into – and smashed all over – Peter Van Hooke's drum kit.

What's six inches between friends, eh? That simple twist of fate is why I was actually allowed to remain in the music business. And what, pray, was in the airborne bottle? Well it wasn't either Lucozade or lager, but it might possibly, at one point, have been either. That, of course, would have been before it was passed through that marvellous filter known as the human body.

****

Van left BGP and moved his base from San Francisco to England. It was around this time that I started to take on more and more managerial duties on his behalf, until I was officially tasked with taking care of his business arrangements. I enjoyed working with Van. He had a great sense of humour. He knew the music business backwards. He was always very fair. He knew how it worked. He was very straight with you. Everything was eminently clear: there was never any confusion over where you stood. He was professional. If he hadn't been an artist, in many ways he would have been the perfect artist's manager. But there was one detail that had escaped him.

In their short career, Van's first hit band Them had released two albums, an EP and about a dozen singles. By the time I was working with Van, I had something like seventeen Them compilation albums in my ever-expanding record collection. All these records had somehow been conjured up using material from the original two albums – *The Angry Young Them* and *Them Again*, an EP called *Them* and various singles – simply because that's all there was. It was a music business variation on the five loaves and two fishes trick – and yet Van had never ever received any royalties whatsoever on these sales. I think I was more upset about this than Van was. He and his lawyer Stan Diamond had tried unsuccessfully over the years to get something out of Decca and had eventually decided it was a waste of time. However, I took my role taking care of "Business Arrangements" rather seriously, and felt that the royalty situation should be addressed. Van gave me the go ahead to see what I could do. I spoke to Decca, they sent me copies of the original contracts and yes, legally, they were completely within their rights, as the band was listed as "un-recouped". They weren't interested in continuing a conversation. And why would they be? End of story.

Well, not quite. Decca was owned by a Dutch company, Polygram and this Dutch Company also owned Phonogram – which was Van's current record company. My contacts at Phonogram kindly put me in touch with their owners in Holland. I explained to them how unfair the situation was.

One of their current high profile artists was being exploited by another of their labels. They had the power to end the situation. They thought about it for a bit – and then that's exactly what they agreed to do. Van began to receive his Them royalties for the first time. In later years he even started to use Them material on his compilation albums.

During my watch, Van played on the same bill as Bob Dylan, on three separate occasions, in London, Dublin and Paris. The London show was at one of the Fleadh festivals in Finsbury Park. I had a few acts on the bill that day, and so I was side-stage watching, as the most famous song and dance man in the world put on a totally mesmerising performance. As I watched, with my mouth open, I felt someone's presence sliding up alongside me. It was Van. I mouthed a quick 'hi', careful not to break Dylan's spell. Van was looking a bit agitated and eventually he nodded in Dylan's direction. "When your man there comes off stage," he said, "tell him I got fed up waiting and had to go." And he was off, just like The Lone Ranger. Apparently Dylan had been planning to invite Van onstage to do a song – most likely either 'Tupelo Honey' or 'It's All Over Now Baby Blue', which Van had done an incredible version of on the *Them Again* album.

Luckily enough, Dylan *didn't* come up to me afterwards to chat about the weather, my latest murder mystery, the gig, or even Van Morrison himself. He was in play-and-wave mode and was whisked straight out the gate, already en route to his next city stopover. I slept well that night. Well, much better than the night when Van was nearly bottled at the Telephone gig. I still dream on occasion about the bottle sailing through the air, except in the dream it hits its target...

****

I studied Van Morrison at close quarters for seven years and I have to say of all the artists I know he is one of the very few who gets so totally lost in the music that he *becomes* the music. The word that he uses to describe this is 'entrainment', which is defined as "the synchronization or alignment of the internal biological clock rhythm, including its phase and period, to external time cues, such as the natural dark-light cycle." The listener, of course, is blissfully unaware of any technicalities. Instead, you're swept up in the feeling of 'rightness' – in the soulful-ness of what's happening in the music. So keen is Van to keep that spirit alive in the moment that he frequently starts to audibly direct his band as to how and where to follow him. On the recorded version of 'Cry For Home', for example, you can hear him exclaim, "One more, one more, open it up, open it up." It's such a precious moment, a joyous insight into how he works artistically.

On the flip side, the reality is that Van can't fake it. He can't mime. He is really not great at rehearsing. I imagine, for Van, rehearsing gets in the way of performing. Even in recording, he doesn't want to do a repeat take. On the *Wavelength* album, the stand-out track to me is 'Hungry For Your Love'. It's also one of the finest tracks of his career. The actual take on the record is Van leading the band through the song for the first and only time. He starts off, not on tape, by giving them the chorus and then a map of the song – not an "it started up in Fife and ended up in tears" (to quote Mike Scott) kind of map – but a sketch of the song. And then they all set off on Take One. I believe the approach is based on the idea that the initial voyage of discovery is the best one, because it's got a spontaneous, uninhibited quality. I know it can be argued that subsequent trips can potentially reveal a new interpretation, a deeper glimpse of beauty. But, where 'Hungry for Your Love' is concerned, it works in the most extraordinary way.

So Van only ever wanted to go into a TV studio, sing a song live – and sing it brilliantly. Then miming came along. So much time was spent making and perfecting records that record companies didn't want to risk what might happen if their artists actually had to play the songs live. Throughout the 1970s, everything on *Top of the Pops* was mimed. So there were unlikely to be any mass protests among musicians when the video age arrived – and they were mimed too.

Videos were more or less essential, if you wanted to have a hit record. With that in mind, I had persuaded Phonogram to finance a video for Van's song 'Cry for Home', released as a single in February 1983, backed with the transcendent 'Summertime in England' (the latter from the album *Common One*, 1980). The record company agreed that 'Cry For Home' was a beautiful song, which had been crafted into a beautiful record: they said 'yes' to stumping up the cash.

The plan was to make the video in Ireland. It'd show an artist (Van) in a nightclub in the early hours of the morning. He'd be far away from home, by himself and writing, maybe to a family member, maybe to a loved one, maybe even just a lyric. A waitress would make her way past Van's table and continue onwards. The waitress in the video was to have been played by a famous, former Miss Ireland, Michelle Rocha, who many years later, in the mid-90s, would marry Van.

On the day of the shoot all was good. The set-up was easy, The director was in the zone. Van, apparently, was happy. We were ready to go with Take One. The familiar call went out: "Quiet on the set."

The intro started. The extras moved around the club. The waitress passed Van's table as "I've been waiting" came out loud and clear on the playback system. The Director looked expectantly at Van. Van continued "waiting" – on camera he appeared to be oblivious to his surroundings. After a minute the Director called "cut!"

"Van, that's where you start miming, you know, where the verse starts."

Van motioned me over and informed me that he can't mime. It's just not in his repertoire.

Until that moment, everyone had assumed he could – including me. We tried setting a mic up beside Van's table, so he could pretend to sing along with the track.

Van doesn't do pretend.

The director explained to Van that this is the way pop videos are made.

In no uncertain terms, the Director is told, "not with Van Morrison it's not."

That was it. We had to abandon the video shoot. Which meant that we had a problem: we'd already spent a large part of the Phonogram budget. So much, in fact, that we didn't have enough money left to even start another shoot.

Desperate times call for desperate action.

I rang up my mate Tony Boland, with whom I'd booked lots of acts onto RTE's *Late Late Show* – Gay Byrne was still in the chair in those days.

"Tony," I said, taking a deep breath, "can I assume if we managed to get Van available for this Saturday's show to sing his new single 'Cry For

Home' you could find us a spot on the show?"

"I can give a very definite *yes* to that one, Paul."

So far so good.

"Tony, would there be any chance that, if we managed to get Van to do the *Late Late Show* this Saturday, RTÉ would grant the full exclusive rights to the performance back to Van so we can use it as a promo-video?"

"I can give a very definite, 'I don't know', to that one, Paul, but let me check."

About 30 minutes later Tony called me back, to say that, in order to secure the appearance by Van, RTÉ would agree, in this one instance, to grant full rights of the clip back to Van. Thus was Phonogram's promo video for 'Cry For Home' saved, along with my ass! The record company had the completed live version – as broadcast the previous Saturday night on *The Late Late Show* – on their desk in London, first thing Monday morning, under budget and on time.

I think the basic idea behind the original approach to the video made sense. Van is a lost soul. It's all there on record to be heard: for confirmation, listen to 'Cry for Home', 'Take Me Back', 'That's What Makes The Irish Heart Beat', 'The Philosopher's Stone', 'These Are The Days', 'Scandinavia' and 'Hey Girl' – just for starters! He's a traveller crying for home while at the same time, *needing* to be displaced and away from home in order to tap into this very rich vein of Caledonia-infused inspiration. He's aware of this. He's an exile. He's always been an exile. He even calls his production company Exile.

This longing, the cry for home, can also – perhaps perversely – be an enjoyable feeling. Out there on the road, you get to experience things you never would have even imagined if you'd stayed at home, married, had a family and dreamed of living happily ever after. Ruminating on this, I'd often wonder if Margaret Hutchinson ended up living happily ever after, or if she too had paid the price, in her case for her beauty.

Is it too big a tariff to pay, involving too big a sacrifice? I'd have to say, in Van's case, from what I saw working for and with him, that he has paid a huge price for his art. But too big a price? Who are we to say? At the same time, I've always felt that 'Cry For Home', covered properly by another artist, could be a *massive* (as they say in Donegal) worldwide hit for someone.

Absolutely everyone who has worked with Van will have a few Van Morrison stories. This one is one of my favourites. Robert Trehern was Van's drummer for quite a while. He was also Nick Lowe's good friend, drummer and co-producer for years. He came from the less-is-more, low-key approach to drumming. His real name was Bobby Irwin. I always thought he should have been knighted, figuring that Sir Robert Trehern would have sounded absolutely perfect. Sadly, he's no longer with us. But he'd been playing in Van's band for ages, when Van announced he was splitting up the current band and taking some time off from touring.

"What are you planning to do?" Bobby asked.

Van replied that he was going to start to make some documentaries and if Robert had any suggestions or ideas for topics he'd love to hear them.

"Oh, I've got a great idea for you," Bobby replied, quick as a flash, "why don't you make a documentary about an out of work drummer?"

CHAPTER FOURTEEN

AN AUDIENCE WITH COLIN DEXTER

I'd met Colin Dexter a few times while wearing my other (crime writing) hat. I was already a big fan of his writing: that is, of *The Inspector Morse* stories. While out on tour, with various acts, we'd while away the autobahn hours on a tour bus watching videos sent by family and friends. One of the ones I received was from an early Inspector Morse story. I wasn't really rushing to view it. When Morse was launched, the reference point for John Thaw was from his crash-bang-wallop cop series *The Sweeney*. Not really my kind of thing and so I (wrongly) figured that Morse would be along the same lines. But on this particular day with an arduous journey ahead, and lean pickings elsewhere, I pitched the episode of Morse as the one we should look at. Well, right from the get go I was hooked. Early in the story, Morse and Lewis, his sidekick, are journeying back to their HQ in Oxford. They have just visited the scene of a crime to view the victim and interview a few local witnesses, On the journey home, they pull in by the side of the road, natter for a bit; get out of the car, walk over to the gate; and lean on the gate (about a metre apart) looking into the field beyond.

So you have this beautiful scene playing out for the camera: Morse's classic maroon SJ6 Jaguar (248 RPA), the yellow of the cornfields, the green of the hedges, the blue of the cloudless sky *and* Barrington Pheloung's soulful, atmospheric music. The camera stayed focussed on the scene. There was no dialogue, just the music and the two Detectives deep in their thoughts, clearly reviewing the facts of the case thus far, while allowing the TV audience to do exactly the same thing.

I thought this was just wonderful and I settled into the comfy tour bus lounge for the next couple of hours – and I was enthralled. After the episode finished I re-ran the earlier cornfield scene and I remember thinking it was really brave television to allow the scene to roll on for that long without any action or dialogue. I wondered if it had been the writer of the original stories (books) or the screen (script) writer or the Director who had been responsible.

We had the following day off in Milan and so I headed to a book shop which had an English language book section and was rewarded for my efforts when I found two paperback copies of Morse stories written by a gentleman by the name of Colin Dexter.

They were both classic who-done-its.

When I returned to London I bought the remaining six Morse stories. I met Mr Dexter a few times at various book events – he was charming and genuinely funny. He was always very gracious with his time and offered lots of writing tips, like... write home often...

Just kidding. He advised me not to worry about a blank page. Faced with one, put two characters down on the page and let them start a conversation. "Don't be scared to follow them," he said. Once you have something, anything, down you can always improve it. Colin would also advise to use short chapters and be careful not to make your pages too dense. "Break it up," he advised, "with paragraphs and sections of reported speech."

I also witnessed a few of his book-store events: he'd often have the audience in stitches. He was capable of being really hilarious. His humour came not from politics, or jokes, or coarseness, but simply from having such a marvellous command of the English language. The majority of his audience wouldn't know in advance what he looked like. He would walk around the store before his spot and he'd say, in passing, to members of the audience, "I've seen this fellow before and he's not all that special. I don't know what all the fuss is about."

At that same time I was also presenting a series of regular shows under the banner of 'Sundays with The Duke', at the Duke of York Theatre in St Martin's Lane: T-Bone Burnett, fresh from his amazing 'Trap Door' EP, David Knopfler (brother of Mark), Paul Brady, Tom Robinson and John

Hiatt had all appeared. I thought it might be nice to watch Colin Dexter do his thing in a theatre rather than in the back of a bookstore. I took the idea to Colin's editor, Maria Rejt, at Macmillan, and she seemed up for my proposal in principle, with a few reservations. Maria put me in touch with Colin and I talked him through the deal. He wondered if anyone would turn up. His main worries were that, as it wasn't in a bookstore, people would have to buy a ticket. He felt if I was confident enough, we should give it a go. "So what do you need from me?" he asked.

"Well now that you've agreed to do it, we need to do a deal and then we can get it on sale," I replied.

"Okay, so how does the deal part work?"

Writers usually do bookstores for free because it helps them sell books: they don't get paid. Since then, the Lit Festival Circuit has emerged and some writers do get rewarded handsomely. But back then that was unheard of.

"Okay", I started, "if this was another show at The Duke, I'd tell the artist the capacity, in this case 640 tickets, multiply that by the ticket price, deduct VAT and the running costs of the show and what's left in the pot is to be divided up between artist – that's you – and the promoter – that's me."

"Okay, what's left in the pot?"

I told him a figure.

"And how do you suggest we divide that up?"

I told him that usually I would give a guarantee against a percentage, so that the artist also participates in the profits from the ticket sales.

"Okay, so what would you offer as a fee?"

I told him a figure.

"Oh no, I couldn't possibly," says he, and he shocked me by suggesting less than half of what I'd offered. This was a completely new experience for me: someone wanting less than they'd been offered.

We agreed a deal.

The performance was billed as "A Conversation with Colin Dexter" and it took place at the Duke of York Theatre on Sunday 11th October, 1992 (two days after his 10th Inspector Morse mystery, *The Way Through The Woods*, was published). The tickets sold extremely well. Colin made extra money on his percentage. He was brilliant, as only he can be. The audience loved him and he met most of them afterwards and spent hours signing books.

There was, ironically, no mystery to it. Just one honourable man, who also happened to be a great entertainer...

(Above): stage The Blues by Five line up left to right in the photograph is: Ian Best (bass guitar); Terence McKee (lead guitar); Miles McKee (drums); Vinci McCusker (lead guitar and vocals); Paddy Shaw (lead vocal) Photo taken in 1966.

(Above): Paul Charles with the founder of Glastonbury festival, Michael Eavis

(Above): Paul Charles Sharon Shannon

(Above): Paul Charles with his wife Catherine

With Robert Plant backstage at Glastonbury Acoustic Stage, looking for his iron and ironing board

The Blue Nile backstage at Bristol Colston Hall on the first night of a UK tour: (front row l-r) PJ Moore, Paul Buchanan, Paul Charles The Agent, Robert Bell

Paul Charles on stage at Dublin Festival 17th July 1983, happy because he has solved two major problems

In London in 1968- the first sighting of the moustache

With Tanita enjoying a drink backstage.

At a book launch for *I Love The Sound Of Breaking Glass, 1997*

London, 2021 about to head off for a daily walk in Regents Park

(l-r) Peter Van Hooke, Max Hole (East West MD), Tanita Tikaram, Paul Charles, Malcolm Dunbar (East West A&R) and Rod Argent (Co-Producer)

Jackson Browne and Paul Charles backstage at a festival in Belgium

John & Yoko Ono Lennon
1 West 72nd Street
New York, NY 10023
USA.   10th October, 1980

Dear John & Yoko,

Re: European Tour

I understand that you are considering touring sometime
next year and would like to introduce ourselves in that
respect.

We promote tours of U.K. and Ireland and act as Agents
throughout the other European territories.   Recent tours
include Van Morrison, Ry Cooder, J.J. Cale, Lou Reed,
Gerry Rafferty, Dire Straits, Roches and Emmylou Harris.

Obviously it would be our pleasure to be the Promoters of
your British dates and I would be prepared to visit New
York to discuss it further with you or your representative.

If you are already committed to a Promoter may I take this
opportunity to wish you every success and happiness with
whatever you do.

Cheers for now,

Paul Charles.

Letter written to John Lennon and Yoko Ono on the 10th of October 19080, inviting John to come and tour with Asgard.

CHAPTER FIFTEEN

MUGGED IN MANHATTAN BLUES

A few years ago, I was mugged in Times Square, in New York – which was, until that moment, one of my favourite cities in the world.

I mean in hindsight I was an ideal target for the muggers. I was in NYC on business, travelling on a budget air-ticket and so I crammed all my meetings into a few mid-week days and then pretty much spent the entire Saturday in the cinema. It was what I liked to do.

So, mid-afternoon, I dandered out into Times Square's hazy day-light, my mind clearly still in the themes of the previous movie. I was wandering aimlessly along New York's buzzing Broadway with 20 or 30 minutes to kill before my next film.

To be honest I hadn't even realised that what I'd walked into was a makeshift tunnel, which had been created by scaffolding spindling overhead, up the front of a block-long building. There were wooden planks (acting as a workman's walk-way) above me, while to my left there were side barriers, solid to shoulder height, protecting pedestrians from the nearby screeching traffic. On the right hand side, the building itself secured the tunnel not only from the outside in but from the inside out – successfully trapping victims in the rat-run.

I was vaguely aware that there were several other humans in the darkened corridor with me. I did notice one particular lad – mid-20s, Caucasian and slim – several feet ahead of me, because he appeared to keep looking back in my direction. Then a string of things happened – and although they all appeared to happen in slow motion I was unable to protect myself in any way whatsoever.

The guy who had been looking back at me, let's call him Noel (as in he was the first), made a speedy dash away from me towards the end of the tunnel. I later realised that he did this to secure the corridor from any pedestrians entering the tunnel from the far end.

Three of his colleagues – they were young – immediately rushed at me. One of them violently shoved me against the building side of the corridor. He jammed his arm against my throat, thereby pinning me to the building, while his two colleagues piled in. One of them kept looking all around him, his head darting this way and that way just like a chicken desperately searching for slim pickings on a stony farmyard. The other assailant literally ripped my pocket from my trousers and the contents – my meagre stash of dollars and cents – dribbled out into his greedy hands. The Ripper and the Chicken then sped off towards Noel, while Chief Mugger himself pulled me away from the wall before heaving me back towards it with such force that I was severely winded and collapsed in a heap on the sidewalk. I think he was disappointed with the takings.

Next a very strange thing happened. A man came up to me and helped me up from the ground. He said, "I'm Clyde, you've just been mugged, but you're okay." He dusted me down, examined my torn pocket. He looked older but dressed younger.. Perfectly groomed hair, freshly shaven, slim build, clothes very clean but looking like they'd been for a spin once too often in the washing machine. He made a major fuss over helping me get my wind and composure back again. Clyde instructed me to stay where I was and advised me that he was going to chase after the muggers to get my money back for me.

He dashed off at a speed of knots after Noel, Ripper, Mugger and Chicken.

By which time a crowd seemed to have materialised from nowhere. They gathered around me and they too were concerned about my well-being. One of them pointed out that the Good Samaritan, a.k.a Clyde, who had helped me up from the ground and rushed off to rescue my dollars and cents, was also, in fact, one of the gang. He had been stopping people behind me from entering the tunnel thereby protecting his fellow Caucasian gang members from the crowd.

Clyde was apparently, like a musician I once knew, a wolf in sheep's clothing. He wasn't concerned for my post-mugging wellbeing. As well as being the rear-guard, his job was to slow me down, disarm me with his friendliness, ensuring I didn't chase after the gang. Not that he needed to have bothered: nothing, but absolutely nothing, was further from my mind.

I headed back to the hotel still very shaken and feeling very sorry for myself. I realised I was on the edge of tears. The thing is that you really don't know how you should feel or how you are meant to react. Obviously being a stranger in a strange land didn't help. Even when I reached the hotel I was unable to shake the feeling: what if they'd had knives? The thought that I might never have made it out of the tunnel of terror was a real one.

Ray Davies was mugged in New Orleans and when the mugger made off with his girlfriend's purse, Ray gave chase and was shot in the leg for his gallantry. Nick Lowe was mugged in Spain. Tanita Tikaram was mugged at the foot of the Spanish steps in Rome. I, and several record company staff and band mates, were with her at the time and again the attack was carried out by a well-organised team. In this instance, several young girls rushed her, begging and lifting their own skirts to hide the fact that one of them was empting Tanita's purse, their actions camouflaged by their skirts and amplified by the shock effect of them not wearing any under-garments. Again, it was a well organised job. Like me, Ray, Nick and Tanita were traumatised by the incidents.

I was meant to join Loudon Wainwright III and Suzzy Roche for dinner that night. I rang them up to tell them what had happened and that I'd like to take a rain check on the meal. I just didn't feel up to it. They wouldn't let me cancel and of course they were correct. A night out with good friends was all I needed to see that absolutely everything wasn't really bad with the world. As it turned out, the company of good friends was the perfect cure for those Mugged in Manhattan Blues.

CHAPTER SIXTEEN

IT'S NOT SO MUCH WHO YOU KNOW, AS WHO KNOWS YOU

One morning I received a call from a young man in the EMI A'n'R department. Roger Ames was his name and he was working with a band called Dexy's Midnight Runners. Dexy's had enjoyed a UK No.1 single with 'Geno', a homage to the powerhouse live soul performer, Geno Washington. I was working with Van Morrison at the time and both Roger and Kevin Rowland – Dexys' main man – were big fans of Van. Roger wanted to know if Van would produce Dexy's second album. Van was touring and recording on and off at the time, and politely declined. Clive Langer and Alan Winstanley were given the gig instead.

Several months later Roger called again. Dexys were progressing well with the album, which would eventually be released as *Too-Rye-Ay*. They were currently working, Roger explained, on a cover of one of Van's songs, 'Jackie Wilson Said' (the first track from Van's, ground-breaking, 1972 album, *St Dominic's Preview*). Roger and Kevin said they'd love Van to sing on Dexys' version. Van and I visited the studio to "check out the situation." We had a suspicion that the idea was about getting attention for the track, rather than what might have been best for it musically. Instinctively, it didn't sit well.

A couple of passes were tried, with Van and Kevin doing a duet on the song. It didn't take Van long to decide he wasn't really adding anything worthwhile to the recording and he retreated from the session.

That wasn't the end of it. Van liked Kevin's spirit and approach. It was, he informed me, the producers who had put him off. So I returned to the studio and invited Kevin to join myself and Van around the corner in the local café for a cup of tea. He extricated himself and the two singers had a great chat.

'Jackie Wilson Said' was Dexys' follow-up to their global smash hit, No.1 single, 'Come On Eileen', and they did TOTP using a large photo of the darts king, Jocky Wilson, as a backdrop. It wasn't the worst joke ever. The single peaked at No. 5 in the UK and sales of *Too-Rye-Aye* benefitted accordingly. The record was a very big hit.

I was travelling in the USA during one of the eight weeks 'Come On Eileen' was No.1 in the UK charts. It would become the biggest selling single of 1982, shifting over a million copies in the UK alone. Roger Ames tracked me down again on my travels. This time he had a different kind of request. He was having a big problem with Dexy's touring plans and wanted to know if I would take the band on as an agent. Well, of course I would. I cut short my USA trip, which really impressed the manager, and got stuck into setting up both a European tour and the band's first visit to the USA.

Make no mistake: Kevin Rowland is a very powerful live performer and he feels that every tour, every concert even, is a very special event and should be celebrated as such. He developed a theme for each tour, as opposed to just performing a selection of songs. In fact, he has successfully continued this approach ever since, reinventing himself on numerous occasions in the interim.

Dexys started that first USA tour the week 'Come on Eileen' hit No. 1 in the States. But here was the big shock: apart from NYC, we hardly sold any tickets. It was a well put together tour in all the proper venues. The promoters were very happy to shell out their hard-earned cash to pay the band's fee because of 'Come On Eileen', which sold a million copies there as well. The problem was that fans didn't equate this mega selling single with the band, Dexy's Midnight Runners. The single, it transpired, was bigger than the band. It was another lesson well learned by the artist, promoters and agent.

****

David Bowie was planning a stadium tour. Dexy's Midnight Runners were mega in France and so the French promoter wanted to add Dexy's as special guests on Bowie's Paris show, scheduled for the Hippodrome d'Auteuil on 8 June 1983. Bowie's office approved Dexy's, I negotiated a generous fee with the promoter, befitting the band's status in France. The show was announced, went on sale and sold squillions. What's a squillion? Well, I believe in this instance slightly above 65,000 would be in the ballpark.

On the day of the show, the Dexys' crew were a bit annoyed at the restrictions imposed on Dexys' equipment set-up by Bowie's gang. Dexys took to the stage on a sunny afternoon and the set was going well. They had a lot of fans in the audience. But not as many as David Bowie. About midway through Dexys' set, something upset Kevin. I didn't know what it was, but he was visibly rattled. He dropped the band down to a quieter vamp and started to talk to the audience using the musicians as a backdrop. "Just because we are here today, doesn't mean we're fans of David Bowie," he confided. And then he compared Bowie – rather unfavourably – to Bryan Ferry.

Uh oh.

The promoter along with Bowie's very together PA, Coco, and Bowie's head of security, Jim Callaghan, tracked me down and started screaming at me.

"Tell him to shut up!"

"Tell him to get off the stage!"

"Tell him WTF!"

Jim Callaghan was the friendliest of the three. I put it down to the fact that his brother, Paddy Callaghan, head of security for Elvis Costello, was a good mate of mine. Jim said, "What's his problem, Paul?" I admitted I didn't know, but that I thought it might have had something to do with their crew squeezing our crew. When Dexys finished the song, the applause this time wasn't as loud.

They started up the next song, which was 'Jackie Wilson Said'. Kevin was staring intensely at the audience. Some of the Bowie fans were clearly growing impatient. Suddenly, Kevin looked like he had just enjoyed a light-bulb moment. I imagined the cogs whirring. "Hang on," he was thinking, or so I assumed, "most of these people are French, so they wouldn't have had a clue as to what I was saying." Kevin crossed the stage to John "Rhino" Edwards, his bass player and a future member of Status Quo. Kevin said something to John. John followed Kevin centre-stage and over to Kevin's vocal microphone. Kevin said something into John's ear and John announced, in perfect French, to the 65,000 plus fans, "Dexys n'aime pas Bowie!"

Oui, they got it this time. And, just to make sure they had, Kevin had John repeat it.

The inevitable booing started. Missiles were thrown at the stage. Finally, Kevin looked like he was happy. He had made his point. Then the band pumped up the volume. The Dexys fans loved it. The Bowie fans quite clearly didn't.

Coco, who'd been carefully calmed down by Jim Callaghan, went up to Mach 10 again. Jim and the promoter were at the end of their tether. "Look," Jim said, "we're going to have to get them off stage before there's a riot."

My agent's brain clicked in. "If that's the case, I have to advise you that the band came here to play their full gig as per contract. If they are frustrated in their endeavour to do so by any member of Mr Bowie's team, Dexys will still be entitled to their full fee."

The promoter immediately agreed that he would honour the contract, "Please Paul, just get them off the stage," he said wearily.

I was about to do so when the Bowie crew turned off the PA system. Kevin realised what was happening and he and the band left the stage meekly, to some serious booing. I feared for the band's safety, not so much from the audience but from the backstage crew. With Jim Callaghan around, however, common sense prevailed. Everyone calmed down and team Bowie clicked into gear with the aim of getting their artist on-stage as quickly as possible.

In situations like that, it's best not to take anything personally. Stay detached. Don't react to someone else's anger, because you'll just bring on your own.

The band received their full fee and when they returned to Paris they played a bigger venue and sold it out very quickly, proving once again that "every crowd has a silver lining." Or something like that.

Looking back on it, I had to ask myself not what I felt about Kevin's behaviour, but how I would have reacted if I had been on the other side. It is never possible to say for sure, but I believe I'd have thought, "We're David Bowie for heaven's sake. They're just Dexy's. In Paris, they can sell 5,000 tickets; we can sell 65,000. This is just a storm in a teacup, which will be long forgotten by the time David walks onto the stage."

Kevin Rowland is a pure artist through and through. He felt it was important, to counter the rudeness of some Bowie fans, by making it clear that Dexy's may have been sharing a stage with Bowie, but they weren't fans. And you'd have to conclude that it was his right to do so. Was it judicious? That's a different question.

I met David Bowie only once. He and his entourage came backstage to meet The Roches at one of their Swiss shows. I have to say I found him to be totally charming. Life is full of strange circles within circles. The best thing to do is to enjoy them while you can...

****

I've often been asked to manage someone I'm already agent for. I'm usually happy to do it – but mostly just until someone I would describe as "a proper manager" comes along. It's my belief that every act needs a full time exclusive 24/7 manager. I know it's not a common view, but I feel that the great managers are the ones who only manage one act.

In my career, I've managed Blues by Five, Fruupp, Radio Stars, Paul Brady, Van Morrison, Gerry Rafferty, Tanita Tikaram, The Waterboys, Ray Davies and... didn't Kevin Rowland only go and ask me to manage Dexys Midnight Runners. I was already their agent and so I accepted the job. Pretty soon it became apparent that the real reason Kevin wanted me to be his manager was that he knew I got on well with his record company, Phonogram. He wanted someone – say for instance me – to tell Phonogram he didn't like the shade of maroon the record company had used to print the sleeve of their forthcoming album, *Don't Stand Me Down* – the band's follow-up to the multi-platinum selling *Too Rye Aye*. Kevin wanted the label to pulp the 400,000 sleeves that had already been printed, and have them re-printed in a different shade of maroon.

I resigned within the week, telling Kevin that he really needed a different kind of manager. The manager before me was a fun gentleman by the name of Paul Burton, Kevin's hairdresser; and the one after me was Kevin's brother.

****

Roger Ames delivered on the promise he'd been showing as a record company man by forming London Records with Colin Bell and Tracey Bennett. Although they worked under an old name – London Records had been the USA name for Decca – London was the first new major UK label to be launched in ages. Tracy had been one of the A'n'R scouts you'd see every night at two or three gigs, checking out the new acts. And Colin Bell was a class act. He knew the big secret of the music business: records do not sell by accident. They sell by getting singles on the radio and in the charts; by getting albums in the press and in the charts; and by getting the artist or band on the road, working, and building their fan-bases. As a result, at London Records, Roger & Co., had a healthy budget and were ready, willing and able to put it behind their artists.

Roger continued to be a big supporter of Asgard and for a while we effectively became their in-house agents, an arrangement where they offered us every new act they took on: artists like Bronski Beat, who immediately morphed into The Communards. They released two albums, *Communards* and *Red*. Both went multi-Platinum in the UK and charted heavily all over Europe. Their No.1 single, 'Don't Leave Me This Way' spent four weeks at the top of the charts and became the biggest-selling single of 1986 in the UK. They toured extensively all over Europe and sold out every show they played. When The Communards disbanded, London Records launched Jimmy Somerville on a very successful solo career. Then there was Shakespeare's Sister (1989), with Irish woman Siobhán Fahey, ex- of Bananarama, sharing the stage with Marcella Detroit: they released two Top Ten albums and their 1992 single, 'Stay', topped the UK charts for a staggering eight weeks. Again, like the majority of their stable-mates, they were a very successful touring act for us until they disbanded in 1993.

London Records was also home to Hothouse Flowers, one of my favourite bunch of people. Liam Ó Maonlai (lead vocals and keyboards) and Fiachna Ó Braonáin (lead guitar and vocals) were childhood friends in an Irish-speaking school in Dublin, who eventually began busking together on the streets of the capital as The Incomparable Benzini Brothers. They were joined by Peter O'Toole (bass guitar and vocals) and continued busking, in 1986 becoming Hothouse Flowers. U2 released Hothouse Flowers' first single, 'Love Don't Work This Way' on their Mother Records label. I heard it on the radio and loved it. The single came to the attention of London Records, who quickly signed the band. They invited me over to see the Flowers do an outdoor show in Dun Laoghaire, the seaside town just outside Dublin which gave Bob Geldof, of The Boomtown Rats, to the world. I couldn't believe the sound of the band. It was a beautiful mixture of Irish, gospel, soul, rock and folk music, hooked around brilliant songs and one of the best vocalists I'd heard in ages. Just like Bob Dylan's former backing outfit, The Band, the Flowers played together like they'd been at it all their lives, which they pretty much had. They didn't need to work at starting the song together, keeping the tempo, and finishing the song at the same time – they had moved beyond all of that, as if it was the most natural thing in the world. They really enjoyed being on stage and making music together. Their performance was so infectious that evening, it made you feel good about yourself. They were the perfect act for an agent. I instinctively knew people would fall in love with them when they saw them live. They were nice people on and off stage too: genuine, the real deal.

London Records released their debut album, *People* in 1988 and it became *the* most successful debut album in Irish history up to that point. It went straight to No.1 in Ireland and eventually climbed to No.2 in the UK. They toured a lot, became a festival favourite playing The Pyramid Stage at Glastonbury in 1989 and received such a phenomenal reaction that Michael Eavis immediately booked them back for the following year. They are still one of Glastonbury Acoustic Stage's favourite acts. Every festival they play, a return booking is on offer. They toured Australia annually and became mega there; the same in Japan.

With Hothouse Flowers I was always on the lookout for head-turning events. I wanted to push them beyond their comfort zone, to play Wembley

Arena. I felt it could be a major career-enhancing statement. London Records were nervous – they felt we should go the safer route and play Hammersmith Odeon and add extra shows as demand required. Roger Ames rang me up to voice his concern. I explained the thinking behind my plan. The Wembley Arena appearance would be a major head-turning night. Hothouse Flowers were one of the hottest live acts on the road and they would be well capable of winning the audience.

"But what if it doesn't sell?" he asked.

"As the promoter, I'll lose a lot of money," I admitted.

Roger laughed... but very nervously.

I went on to explain that this would not just be another night at Wembley. My idea was to create an event, make it a special night, a celebration of the band and their music. I predicted people would come from all over the UK and even Ireland to celebrate this special night with Liam, Fiachna, Peter and the band. The plan was to use the Wembley Arena to give Hothouse Flowers the status of an arena act, without actually being an arena act.

"Okay, okay, I'll buy a ticket," Roger laughed, and he and London Records were on board.

To me Wembley Arena had always been an imposing and uninviting venue. The first time I went there was on the 5th December 1968, to attend an *NME* Poll Winners Concert, when the venue was called The Empire Pool, Wembley. My lasting memory of that show is how cold the place was, like a ginormous bus station on a winter's day. Built in 1934 for the British Empire Games, it felt like the venue was bigger than my hometown of Magherafelt. On stage, The Rolling Stones appeared to be no bigger than insects, small insects at that (and I'm not talking about Beatles!). Marianne Faithful was sitting in the front row, throwing roses at the band, on what was to be their final appearance with founder member, Brian Jones. The sound was atrocious. There was no way we could risk a repeat of any of that.

My plan was to dress the venue completely differently for the Hothouse Flowers concert. I wanted to make the audience feel welcome, warm and as if they were coming to see the Hothouse Flowers and not just attending another "Wembley" Concert. The venue were very cooperative and helpful, allowing us to give the night a real Irish flavour.

On the walk-up to the venue, we installed huge, colourful banners with the band's circle of life logo, to welcome you. Inside, you felt like you were walking back into the Dandelion Market in Dublin, where U2 played those infamous early gigs, on a beautiful summer's day. We'd invited traditional musicians and trad groups to do their thing at various key locations around the lobby of the venue. Irish arts and crafts organisations came and pitched their wares. We had painters, potters, photographers, poets, all doing their thing. And yes, I do believe there was even a pint or two of Guinness on sale.

Hothouse Flowers at Wembley Arena on 19 December 1990, completely sold out in advance. And when they got there, the audience loved it. By far the most important ingredient, of course, was the Flowers' music. Rising to the occasion, they walked on stage like they were playing in the Olympia Theatre in Dublin and were hit by a wave of love coming at them from the arena. And then they proceeded to tear the place apart. They could have played all night – and knowing the band they probably did, later on, in a bar, hotel lobby, or hotel room, to savour the moment by prolonging the craic.

****

To me, there are few scenes as sad as an empty venue, after a show. I often take the opportunity to have a wee walk around the auditorium reliving the memories. That night, as I did my after-show stroll, I could still hear Liam's soaring, soulful vocals. The echoes of the audience's applause filled my ears. The ghosts of the songs always seem reluctant to give up their glory moments, hanging around for an encore bow. These particular ghosts know that when the roadies and the crew have packed the gear into their flight cases and loaded them onto the waiting trucks, leaving discarded set lists and dressing room signs for the next act in to replace, they'll fade away as the lights are turned off and the doors are securely locked.

But my overwhelming feeling was that Hothouse Flowers had come to Wembley and made it work, in what would ultimately be the only show I'd promote at Wembley Arena. I still prefer venues where the audience can see the whites of the artist's eyes.

A few months later the promoter of an INXS show at Wembley Stadium – capacity 75,000 – contacted me to invite Hothouse Flowers to appear with INXS as very special guests. I quoted the band's fee.

"But that's nearly as much as we're paying INXS," he protested, one imagined, with a forked tongue.

We stuck to our guns and insisted on the Hothouse Flowers' fee. They were very happy to do the show, but they didn't *need* to do it, which is a big advantage when you're negotiating an artist's fee. I got a call from the promoter to say OK. It was a deal. The gig, at Wembley Stadium on 13 July 1991, was a huge success. Once again Hothouse Flowers produced the magic and, in my biased opinion, *totally* stole the show.

On another occasion I proposed the Hothouse Flowers do a few nights at The Royal Albert Hall – but to make it an event, I suggested they do it in the round, performing in the centre of the spectacular auditorium. Once more they rose to the occasion. A vision in white stage-gear, they delivered the goods big time.

Thirty years later, they're still nice people – and Asgard are still their agents. They play like a very tight band of brothers. They travel that way too. Hopefully they'll never ever stop.

CHAPTER SEVENTEEN

RORY GALLAGHER - THE MAN WITH TASTE

A few years ago I read in *The Irish Times* that Jimmy Page had claimed that Led Zeppelin were the best live group in the world... or words to that effect. This is all very subjective, of course, and if I pass comment it's not to contradict Mr Page nor to speak poorly of his group. However it made me feel like sticking up my hand at the back of the class and shouting, "Excuse me Sir, but isn't he forgetting about Taste?"

But let's not jump ahead of ourselves.

Rory Gallagher was the lead guitarist of the Cork based Fontana Showband when he was 15 years old. He went on to form Taste in 1966 (nicking the word from a Guinness beermat), with Eric Kitteringham on bass and Norman Damery on drums.

Taste came to Belfast in the Summer of 1967, and took up a residency in The Maritime Club, the old stomping ground of Van Morrison's Them. Every hipster in Belfast was talking about Taste and how electrifying they were on stage. Rory's name was on everyone's lips. Among the more established showbands in Northern Ireland at the time were Derek and The Sounds, with ex-Them drummer John (Wilsie) Wilson, and bass player Richard (Charlie) McCracken. Wilsie and Charlie went on to form a band called Cheese, but that was toast when they were asked to join Rory in a new Taste line-up in 1968. Soon afterwards, the gang headed permanently to London, winning a prestigious residency at the Marquee Club. I'd go and see Taste there as often as humanly possible. I met Rory for the first time when I interviewed him, for the first of several occasions, for both

City Week and *Thursday Magazine.* It was through Wilsie that I got to know Taste's manager, Eddie Kennedy. Eddie invited me to cover a German tour with Taste, on which they were supported by another Eddie Kennedy-managed band, Anno Domini, who featured a good mate of mine, Tiger Taylor, on guitar.

That tour was a revelation. I got to witness first-hand how phenomenally successful Taste were in Europe and to see, up close and personal, how Rory mesmerised packed houses every single night, no matter what the native language might have been.

Taste were among the pioneers of the UK's Underground Music Scene. Mostly London-based, the scene was broken down into two sections: what was termed Progressive Music and what could be characterised as Blues-based Music. Groups from both camps flew under the pop radar as it were, building up a following around the live circuit, without having hit records. Taste were among the most successful outfits on this scene, which started out in clubs and colleges, eventually leading to concert-hall and festival appearances. All of these groups saw themselves as representing the antithesis of the shallowness of pop music. For them, it was extremely unhip or uncool to release singles.

A further, simple line of demarcation between the "pop groups" and the "underground groups" was that the audience danced to pop groups while they stood, or sat, and watched and listened to the underground groups. When underground groups became really successful on the live circuit, the established, old-school record companies scrabbled around looking for their cheque books. When they signed a band, they'd then try to promote them in the traditional way i.e. led by singles.

Why? Singles required a much smaller investment than an album. Most of the acts went along with it, in effect turning their backs on the underground circuit when it was commercially beneficial to go 'over-ground', as it were. Rory stuck to his guns. There was a legendary Major Minor single 'Blister On The Moon' b/w 'Born On The Right Side of Time', his first ever recording. But that was released *before* it became un-hip to release a single. This was also way, way before it was unhip to be unhip.

****

Rory Gallagher was all about the music. In a live setting, he knew instinctively that the audience is a big part of a performance. He always played *with* the audience rather than, *to* the audience. Attending a Taste gig was a wildly exhilarating experience. From the very first song Rory engaged you, and he never let up, so that you were as exhausted as Wilsie and Charlie were by the end of the set. Well, nearly!

In what was my first shot at writing sleeve notes, I was asked by Eddie Kennedy to sum up my feelings on Taste for the *Live Taste* album sleeve (Polydor 1971). Eddie said I could either have a payment or a credit on the album sleeve for my work. I figured that no matter how much he paid me it'd soon be spent, whereas the credit would last forever. Fifty years later I was right, and he was... richer.

The Robert Stigwood Organisation were agents for Taste. The word-of-mouth reaction to the band was so strong they would double the audience on the second night at any venue and be selling it out and turning people away by their third appearance. My theory was that Taste were primed to be the biggest band in the world. As far as I was concerned, that was guaranteed, a done deal. They were enjoying chart albums; sell-out tours at home and abroad; everybody but everybody was talking about them. Don't take my word for it: Jimi Hendrix and John Lennon are on record saying that Rory was *the* man. Bob Dylan once turned up at a Rory gig in the USA and was about to be turned away from the backstage area by a security person when he was rescued by Rory's brother – and by that time manager – Dónal. The Rolling Stones wanted Rory to join the band when they were replacing Mick Taylor. Taste were the undisputed stars of the legendary Isle of Wight Festival in 1970. They topped the bill at Reading in 1971.The world was in the palm of their collective hand. And then, Rory decided that he couldn't continue. My understanding is that he felt it would be impossible to carry on with the then current manager.

Quite a few of the major bands of that era – Cream, Blind Faith, Traffic, The Jimi Hendrix's Experience – were short-lived. The reality is that groups were being exploited and the lightbulb had started to go on more regularly. But Taste were a more organic outfit. Rory was a world class guitarist. He was also a great songwriter. *On The Boards* is a classic album in any company.

And yet, it also has to be acknowledged that none of the records quite managed to capture the real magic of what Rory and co were creating on stage. I think if Taste had been with a record label who knew how to help them to achieve that particular artistic goal, then things might well have turned out differently. Maybe all Taste really needed was a manager who realised exactly how uniquely talented a band they were. Eddie Kennedy wasn't that man.

Every gig took you on a magical journey. I remember one night, towards the end of Taste's touring days, they did a boogie-influenced piece of music that was about 20 minutes long and completely new to me. After the gig I asked Wilsie what it was called. "New one to us,'" Wilsie admitted, nodding towards Charlie. "The first time we heard it was tonight as we were playing it." I asked Rory the same question when I caught up with him later. "Yeah, it's very new," he said. "It's called, 'I've Bought My Ticket For The Train, But The Luggage Is Going On Ahead'. I believe it was the genesis of a song which would eventually be called 'The Loup'. It really was unbelievable: a brand new song, effectively improvised on the spot by the band, which sounded as flawless as the rest of the set.

When Taste split and Rory was getting his new band together and sorting out his business, I'd ring him up regularly to check on progress for *City Week*. He was always courteous, gave me the time of day and chewed the fat. He re-emerged under his own name and signed to Polydor Records.

Much later on, in 1987, I was lucky enough to become Rory's agent for the world excluding North America and Canada.

****

By the time I started to work with him, Rory Gallagher was a major live draw. He had built a reputation with promoters, festivals and fans alike as one of the aces. As his agent, I can tell you that every single festival on the circuit wanted to book Rory. Every concert he performed was to a full house. His brother Dónal was managing him – the truth being that Dónal Gallagher was the manager Taste should have had. He's a great ideas man and had so much enthusiasm for Rory and his work. Dónal's priority was always what was in Rory's best interests. He was hands on, 24/7, and totally dedicated to the cause. At the beginning of '87, Rory had self-produced a killer album called *Defender* and I put together a deal for it to come out on Demon Records. Rory, Donal and I would meet regularly on their patch in London and we'd discuss touring plans. We'd be well intentioned at the start – well for the first ten minutes or so – and then, led by Rory, we'd get lost in conversations about American crime fiction (on which subject Rory was particularly well read), new artists, new albums by artists the three of us were fans of, or, discussing what Van and/or Dylan were up to musically.

During Rory's time with Asgard we promoted a few concerts with four special guitarists we represented at the time. When I first dreamt up the idea, I promised myself I'd only do it if I managed to get the four first choice guitarists on my wish list: Rory Gallagher, Richard Thompson, David Lindley and Juan Martin. My logic was they were all masters in their own field and the common bond they shared, apart from being Asgard Artists, was they all had a hunger to explore other styles. They all bought into the idea immediately. However they were busy men and it took a while to find a time when all their schedules could be synced for the joint adventure. We promoted concerts under the banner of Guitarists Night, in Cambridge, Guildford and concluded the short run at the Dominion Theatre, London. With mixed bills, there was always a risk that Rory's fans, or Richard Thompson's, might think: "I'll give this a miss because he's only going to do a quarter of the show." Not so. We presented the London show in the Dominion Theatre on 24 March 1984 and it sold incredibly well. They each played their own set and occasionally one or two of the other three would come out and join the featured guitarist for a tune or two. Richard was under the weather with a bad bout of flu but fine trooper he is, he soldiered on. And then they all came on together at the end. It really was a revelation to see how free of ego each of these great musicians was, and how genuinely excited they were to collaborate.

****

There were two very different Rory Gallaghers. Off-stage, he was one of the shyest, politest gentlemen I've ever had the pleasure of meeting; on-stage, however, he transformed into the most extraordinary, extroverted, giant showman and master musician you could ever imagine. I always had the feeling that at some deep level, Rory found things hard. Then again, you couldn't possibly play the blues the way Rory played the blues without being connected to... the blues. I have a feeling the off-stage gentleman was as keen as his adoring fans were to meet the extrovert, who appeared the moment he plugged his beloved Strat into his trusted VOX AC 30.

In my opinion, and in no particular order, Seamus Heaney, George Best, Rory Gallagher, Christy Moore, Brian Friel and Van Morrison are the true great men of modern Ireland.

To Rory Gallagher, performing live was vital; it was life-affirming; it was a way of life. Even as I write this I am conscious that there are people out there who are still missing him deeply.

As it should be.

CHAPTER EIGHTEEN

THE ROCHES – WHY WE ARE HERE

Back in 1979 when Jack Warner and some of his brothers released the beautiful, self-titled, debut album, *The Roches*, being able to make fine music was more than enough.

The Roches were three sisters – Maggie Roche, Terre Roche and Suzzy Roche – from New Jersey, USA. Maggie and Terre sang harmony on 'Was a Summer's Day', a track on Paul Simon's third solo album, *There Goes Rhymin' Simon* (1973), before hooking up with their younger sister Suzzy to form The Roches in 1977.

The Roches were a magical musical act influenced by barber-shop style tight harmonies, Irish melodies, bebop, and Rodgers and Hammerstein. They wrote songs, either solo or in various combinations, about their lives together and apart; sweaty train journeys; cheating husbands; dogs; waitressing; family secrets; trips to Ireland; impossible or improbable relationships; sometimes even an impossible *and* improbable relationship. They didn't fit in, but by not fitting in, they presented the perfect template for all the rest of us, who felt we didn't fit in either. They eventually found a way to fit in by creating – stealing might even be a better word – a space for themselves in a music business that was preoccupied, back then, with rock, disco and punk music. Maggie and Terre and Suzzy were classed as folk, and maybe they were, as in good folk. Certainly, they played acoustic guitars and sang songs about ordinary people. In fairness, they avoided sticking their fingers in their ears when they sang. So maybe they weren't real folk at all. Indeed, they were cute enough to pull the masterstroke of securing Robert Fripp to produce their debut album. A very brave move, in one fell swoop it demonstrated that their horizons were way beyond the perceived limits of folk, or any other contemporary music for that matter.

I still get the impression today listening to *The Roches* – the album – that every second of this sublime, perfect record had been carefully and lovingly created with microscopic precision. Yet, at the same time, it is one of the most soulful albums you will ever have the pleasure of listening to. It hasn't dated a second in the intervening 40 years. Audio Verite it was and, indeed, still is.

Nothing is hidden. Even the breathing of the three sisters sounds in perfect harmony. Robert Fripp's genius production ensured that nothing distracted you from, or got in the way of, the voices. Impossibly sparse, in its own way it was as warm and inviting as The Beatles' 'Here Comes the Sun'. Using guitars and voices – complimented subtly by Tony Levin on bass guitar, Jim Maelen on percussion, Larry Fast as synthesizer programmer and his own exquisite work on electric guitar (and "Fripperies") – Robert Fripp perfected both the voices and the songs.

In their story-telling lyrics, not a single vowel is ever wasted. Their famous harmonies are a melding of Maggie's impish baritone and Terre's angelic high register with Suzzy's expressive, soulful, mid-range pulling it all together. The heart-wrenching blend of the three voices frequently offered an infectious head-turning fourth voice that made you ask: "How the heck did they manage to do that?"

As an agent I had the inside track due to the fact that my friend (and client) Loudon Wainwright III was dating Suzzy Roche. I heard the album before it was released and loved it the same way I loved The Undertones 'Teenage Kicks, EP; Nanci Griffth's, 'There's a Light Beyond These Woods (Mary Margaret)' and Mary Margaret (no relation) O'Hara's debut album, *Miss America*. I couldn't stop playing them.

The next time I was in New York I met up with Loudon and Suzzy and Maggie and Terre at the Lion's Head in the Village. It was all very loose, and – it immediately struck me – immensely entertaining.

The following afternoon the Roches and I met again at Terre's apartment in the buzzy Village, where they were rehearsing. Terre being the host asked me if I'd like a cup of tea.

"I'd love a cup of tea," says I.

"Right so, I'll make you one," says she.

We were chatting away about how I thought they should work in Europe and how we'd set it up. I endeavour, in these early conversations with new acts, to discover the detail of how the artists like to tour. For example: how many shows are they comfortable performing before having a night off? Dire Straits hate to have days off: I believe on one tour they actually played 37 shows without a break-night. Loudon succinctly caught the thinking behind this approach in one of his road songs, 'The Home Stretch':

"If the day off doesn't get you.
Then the bad reviewer does..."

Nights off are not all they're cracked up to be. Yes, if you want to, you can use them to catch a breather. Most artists I know don't want to take a break. It's, "Okay bags in the room and we'll meet you in the bar in 15."

But 37 consecutive days without a break: now that's a lot.

The norm is closer to three consecutive show days and then a break day. But then I needed to know other things like: do they consider a travel day to be a day off (which it's not) or do they like them to be included in the three days on, one day off rule. A successful agent has to tailor the tour to the artist's unique requirements, rather than assuming one format suits all. I'd also explain what we would do for them, where I was suggesting they might play concerts, and our commission. Half an hour passed but there was no sign of my cup of tea.

We were rabbiting away, ten to the dozen. Mostly their questions were based around the theme of, "Yes that's all very nice Paul, but do you think anyone will come to see us?" Every now and then one of them would break into a quizzical smile, which I'd take as a sign of them not picking up on the subtleties of my Ulster accent. So I'd back-track a little, pick up the point again, while ensuring I slowed my delivery down second-time around.

They shared a few of their gigging experiences with me. One of the weirdest performances they had ever given was in the Warner Bros headquarters in Burbank, California, where, for their album launch, they were encouraged to hop up on the table in the conference room and perform a short set for the Warner staff.

An hour passed and all the talking was making my mouth dry, but still there was no sign of the tea. Eventually, about two hours later, I had to leave to get to my next appointment and they needed to get back to their rehearsals, a crucial part of their DNA.

We'd agreed on a time – five months into the future – for their first tour and said our goodbyes. But our goodbyes weren't for long. I was due to meet up with them again that night in the Lion's Head, with Loudon, for a bit more craic.

Over Loudon's regular table in The Lion's head I focused on Terre, wondering what happened to my tea. She was looking at me with an equally perplexed look. A few rounds later she came over and sat down beside me.

"So did you not like my tea?" says she.
"What tea?" says I.
"The one I made for you," says she.
"I thought you'd forgotten it?' says I.

"I left it on the sideboard behind you," says she.

I'd been so engrossed in our chat that I hadn't noticed her setting the cup of tea down behind me. While I was thinking: Terre's forgotten my cup of tea, she had been thinking: he doesn't like my tea.

There must be a lesson in that somewhere, but I haven't quite worked out what it is. Yet.

The odd thing is that the mis-communication actually helped to make a human connection between the group and the agent, and in the early days of such a relationship that's very important. On top of which, that night in the Kings Head, the sisters seemed to think it was absolutely hilarious, which made me like them all the more.

For their first visit to the UK, I booked several cities including concerts in Edinburgh, London and Dublin. In a lot of ways, even though the main Warner Bros office outside the US was based in London, the main concert of the visit would be in Dublin. Ireland has always been a canny backdoor to breaking American (and even English) acts in the UK. Artists like Chris Rea, Nanci Griffith and David Gray immediately spring to mind. The Irish audience was always guaranteed to be open-minded, willing to listen and, if they took to you and your work, they'd embrace you like no other audience in the world. Just ask Garth Brooks.

We promoted them in the Olympia Theatre, Dublin on the first tour in 1979. I still have the poster. For their first visit, at 1,240 capacity, it was certainly ambitious. But in my defence, The Roches really were that good and, as I said, in those different days, being "that good" was always enough. Dublin's music media was in its infancy but key people like Niall Stokes of *Hot Press*, Ian Wilson and Dave Fanning of RTÉ 2fm, the late Chris Roche of Warners Ireland and Tony Boland of *The Late Late Show* were always generous in helping to spread the word about new acts. To cut a long story short, by the time they set foot on the Olympia's celebrated stage in Dublin, the venue was packed to the rafters.

They'd been scared of coming to Ireland, not so much due to The Troubles – though that was the title of a song they'd written about a planned Irish tour, with a different promoter, that hadn't materialised. There had obviously been a miscommunication or a misunderstanding with the PPP (previous prospective promoter) because The Roches thought the promoter's intention was to have them perform in shop windows around the island of Ireland. Spinal Tap would have had nothing on it!

At the Olympia, they took the stage in front of an audience which was in danger of peaking with anticipation from merely seeing them, in person, for the first time.

They sang like a dream:
"*We are Maggie and Terre and Suzzy,*
Maggie and Terre and Suzzy Roche,
We don't give out our ages,
And we don't give out our phone numbers,
Sometimes our voices give out,
But not our ages and phone numbers."

This was the first verse of 'We', the first song on the album and the perfect opening number of their Dublin premiere. The audience was theirs from that song onwards.

The thing that struck me about The Roches that night in Dublin was how absolutely beautiful the voices sounded live; and how always on the button. They were, one and all, first class singers. On top of which Terre Roche is a brilliant guitarist.

They weren't scared of following the individual thread of the evening, or about sending themselves up in front of the audience. If anything they used the stage and the revealing between-song banter as an in-public therapy session. They were not scared of addressing personal issues with each other across the boards once trodden by Charlie Chaplin. Then, just when we thought we started to understand their brilliance, didn't they only turn around and floor all of us with an amazing acapella version of 'The Hallelujah Chorus'. Their show-stopper, in a set full of show-stoppers, was the final part of Handel's Messiah, which had premiered on 13 April 1741 in The Great Music Hall, which had been located on Fishamble Street, Dublin – just three minutes and a few streets away from where The Roches were performing their version. I doubt the original performance could have had anything like the same impact as The Roches: the audience that night nearly lifted the roof off the Olympia.

The Roches launched themselves on a very successful live career in Ireland, UK, Holland and Germany, returning frequently to sell out shows everywhere including amazing concerts in London, in both The Dominion Theatre and Theatre Royal Drury Lane.

They were one of the main acts at the Cambridge Folk Festival in 1981 and their performance shook the festival to its very core. There wasn't one person of the 15,000 on site who hadn't fallen head over heels in love with the music, and, it has to be admitted, the girls, by the end of the weekend.

They had very loyal fans and had a peerless reputation for their live shows. They were a pivotal, influential group for a whole wave of artists including Susanne Vega, The Indigo Girls, Kate Rusby, The Dixie Chicks, Laura Marling and the Be Good Tanyas, amongst many more.

On the recording front, things didn't go so well.

The main problem was that they didn't have a manager. The unfortunate end-result was that, rather than making a mistake, they erred on the side of caution by saying, 'No', to absolutely everything the record label offered.

Warner Bros released debut albums by Dire Straits and Nicolette Larson in the same "window" as they released *The Roches*. Dire Straits and Nicolette's albums quickly gained the tag of being very radio-friendly. Of course, if a committed campaign had been put behind the majestic 'Hammond Song' or the melodically mainstream 'Quitting Time', or even the instantly loveable 'The Train', then The Roches too, in hindsight, could also have been classed as radio-friendly. But when they said, 'No', to everyone, and to every suggestion, all they achieved was to slip down the all-important list of record company priorities.

In their defence, it has to be mentioned that some of the ideas presented to The Roches were pretty bizarre. One of the less bizarre suggestions was to go on a coast-to-coast USA tour as the support act for a mega, heavy-rock, group. Then again, who knows? The blokes in the front row probably would have loved them! Warner Bros were without doubt one of the best artist-friendly labels in the world in those days. The downside to this was that for every project that The Roches turned down, there was an ever growing queue of other artists on the label willing to shout, "Yes!" at the top of their voices, with bells on, and before the label executive even got as far as, "Would you like to…"

They continued to tour regularly, sadly having to interrupt a tour in 1995 when their father died. Later that year they released *Can We Go Home Now* and a couple of years later they indefinitely suspended operations as a group and worked only on individual projects. Suzzy appeared in several movies, wrote a critically acclaimed novel, *Wayward Saints*, did quite a bit of theatre work, and recorded two solo albums and two with Maggie. Then in 2005 after a 12-year break, The Roches released their ninth album, *Moonswept*. Sadly, it was to be their swan-song. They enjoyed, with their brother David, a very successful tour of The USA and Canada. At the end of the tour they announced that they would no longer be touring as a group.

Very sadly on January 21 2017, Maggie Roche died of cancer. She was only 65 years old.

I believe that we are all on this earth first and foremost to try and make it a better place for our fellow humans. As The Roches singing group, Maggie Roche and her sisters most certainly fulfilled their responsibilities to society in that particular department. Would that we all could say the same.

CHAPTER NINETEEN

ALL GOOD THINGS...

When I was living in Wimbledon and managing Fruupp, one of the albums responsible for dragging me through the dark days was Jackson Browne's second album *For Everyman* (1972). I came across Jackson's music via a complicated chain of connections. I was a fan of Graham Nash. He joined up with Stephen Stills and David Crosby, who made a very fine album called *Crosby, Stills & Nash*. Crosby, I discovered, produced Joni Mitchell's first album and as a result of digging a bit further, I read an interview where Joni was singing the praises of Jackson Browne. The first Jackson Browne album I listened to was *For Everyman*.

Jackson was part of the next generation on from Dylan and Paul Simon. He was signed by Asylum Records, thanks to a PA, who retrieved his demo out of the wastepaper basket and insisted David Geffen listen to it again, to be sure his original, negative assessment was correct. It wasn't. Thanks to the PA, Jackson was signed to Geffen's artist-friendly label. A few years previously, he'd have been defined as a 'folkie'. Now, he was signed as a singer-songwriter – a new genre invented by the record labels to pull away somewhat from the beards and beer-bellies of the folk scene. This new gang included Van Morrison (who, of course, would hate any label, including this), Carole King, Gordon Lightfoot, Carly Simon, James Taylor, Joni Mitchell, Neil Young and the aforementioned Graham Nash. Jackson Browne, with his evocative, finely crafted lyrics and big melodies, brought his own unique songwriting approach to the genre.

Jackson had no fear of hard work. With multi-instrumentalist David

Lindley in tow, he toured extensively, building up a very loyal following, with each new album selling better than the one before until his breakthrough record, the classic *The Pretender,* which went to No.5 in the US Billboard Charts in 1976.

During that year, I had planned a trip to NYC, to follow up on a proposed record deal for Fruupp with Seymour Stein's label, Sire Records. I travelled stateside on a Freddie Laker bargain-basement flight – initiates will recall that, over the following few years, Laker alone made it possible for the emerging UK punk acts to successfully tour America. On this flight, the conditions stipulated that I had to stay in NYC for at least a week and a day. Having a few extra days to kill in the Big Apple was a small inconvenience, giving me time to visit a few of the NYC agents I knew. I also made the pilgrimage to my favourite record store, Colony Records, in anticipation of the release of *The Pretender*, which the assistant told me was "due any day." He also told me that Jackson Browne would be in town for four shows in two days at The Palladium that weekend, Oct 13 and 14, 1976.

The shows were sold out, but I went down to the venue on the Friday anyway, and bought a ticket from a scalper. And it was amazing. Jackson Browne had a much tougher sound live than on record and they extended the songs as well, with powerful musical solos and codas. I loved the show so much I blew quite a bit of the PDs I'd set aside for food for the rest of my stay, to purchase tickets from the touts for the remaining three shows. Label-mates, Orleans with their two recent top ten singles 'Dance With Me' and 'Still The One' – both written by journalist-turned-songwriter Johanna Hall and her husband, and band member, John Hall – were the opening act. The second show on Saturday, I seem to remember, ran way, way into Sunday morning.

The follow-up album, *Running On Empty*, released in 1977, did even better, reaching No.3 in the US and staying in the charts for over a year, going on to sell 7 million copies in the US alone, launching Jackson on the 'arena and shed' circuit on which he could attract in excess of 10,000 fans a show.

So when we started Asgard, Jackson Browne's name was on my list of artists I'd love to work with. I tried contacting Jackson Browne's manager for ages but to no avail: story of my life. As luck would have it, on the first tour I promoted with Van Morrison (1979), the tour manager was a gentleman by the name of Stephen Pillster. Pillster – everyone referred to him as Pillster – was a great tour manager and he and I got on "swimmingly" – a word he frequently used. It turned out that, back in LA, Pillster was house-sitting for Peter Golden, who happened to be Jackson Browne's manager. When Pillster returned to LA, he raved to Peter Golden about Van's tour and so the next time I rang his office, Peter Golden took the call. We signed Jackson Browne in 1981, and did our first tour with him during the summer of 1982. I loved his concerts, and went to see as many of them as physically possible.

His overt political activism worked against him. In those days, the music business didn't appreciate songwriters reminding them what was wrong with America, and audiences weren't much better. His once platinum-selling status in the US had dropped to gold. America's loss was Europe's gain. On this side of the Atlantic, his album sales increased – as did demand for his concert tickets.

A few years later I was advised that Jackson had fired his manager. It turned out that Jackson had been offered a spot on the American Live Aid show. Peter Golden had turned it down, allegedly suggesting that Jackson had done more than his fair share of benefits and it was time for someone else to do them. Jackson, the impression was given, wouldn't be doing any more. For an artist who was politically committed, that was a hell of a leap for any manager to make without asking.

Jackson was a bit like Van Morrison and Ray Davies: they all had managers but they still preferred to deal directly with their team. I had quite a few conversations with Jackson about managers and about what he should do next. He was attending the film festival in Cannes with his then girlfriend Daryl Hannah and invited me down to the south of France, to discuss the situation further.

The main candidate for the job was Jackson's long-term, trusted roadie, stage and production manager, Donald Miller a.k.a. Buddha. Buddha and Jackson had been together from before Jackson even had a manager. Doing their early gigs, usually with David Lindley, they had worked out this very successful routine to spook promoters who were trying to take advantage of a manager-less artist. If a promoter tried to short-change

Jackson, Buddha would advise the promoter that he couldn't make the decision to accept less, but would suggest they check with Jackson's (phantom) manager. Within earshot of the promoter, Buddha would pick up the backstage payphone (pre mobile days) and dial a fake number. He would then repeat the promoter's suggestion down the still unconnected line. Buddha would hold the phone away from his ear, clearly suggesting the "manager" was screaming at the other end. "Oh, he's not that bad," Buddha might say, apparently by way of appeasement. He'd put his hand over the mouthpiece of the phone. "He wants to know who you've got coming next?" he'd ask the promoter. Buddha would then repeat the list down the line.

"Sorry, what was that again?" he'd ask the ghost manager.

"When is Tom Petty playing here?" Buddha would ask the promoter. It was usually around this point that the problem would suddenly disappear. No one, it seemed, wanted to get on Tom Petty's bad side.

I thought Buddha would be a perfect manager for Jackson. He really cared about him and wasn't scared of asking questions when he didn't know the answers – always the sign of a wise man. For his part, Jackson liked our hands-on approach to promoting and being an agent. If Buddha became manager, Jackson asked, would we continue to support him? Of course we would. Buddha became the manager and all was good. I continued as agent for everywhere in the world except the US and Canada.

Imagine being such an uber-fan of someone and then getting a chance to work with them! I've had that privilege often. I get asked: "How did a wee lad from Magherafelt get a chance to work with all these great artists?" And my reply is: '"Well, someone has to be their driver, their lawyer, their dentist, their guitar tech, their accountant, their gardener, their electrician, their carpenter, so... why shouldn't the agent be a wee lad from Magherafelt?"

One of the advantages of being an agent is that I got to meet and work with people like Tom Waits, Ray Davies, Van Morrison, Hothouse Flowers, Loudon Wainwright III, Mike Scott, Paul Carrack, Paul Buchanan, Nick Lowe, Lisa Ekdahl and Jackson Browne, amongst others. Are they my friends? Well, maybe some are, some maybe more than others. But the bottom line always has to be that you are not there to be their friend. You are there to be their agent. It's very important not to lose sight of that distinction.

Being there does have its advantages though. In 1992, I was in LA for a business trip and on this occasion Jackson invited me over to Groove Masters, his recording studio in Santa Monica. I'd been there quite a few times: in fact Tanita Tikaram, who I managed, recorded most of her difficult fourth album, *Lovers In The City*, there. But on this particular occasion there was only myself and Jackson in the studio and he played me his forthcoming album, *I'm Alive*, from beginning to end. It was such a beautiful thing that I asked him to play it through again, a couple of times, and he obliged.

It was his meisterwerk, his *Astral Weeks* if you will, and I was acutely aware of the pain the man sitting inches away from me had endured, to make a record that I, and millions of others, would fall in love with. I knew a little bit about his relationship with a famous actress, who had left him for the son of a deceased iconic politician, but you don't ask questions, because it is none of your business.

Everyone needs their space? 100% correct. But on *I'm Alive*, Jackson had set out, in beautifully crafted, heart-wrenching lyrics, perfectly bedded in his best ever set of melodies, all that had happened. No interviews or deep-digging journalistic probing required. As we sat together listening to this wonderful soul-baring music, it was remarkable to see that Jackson seemed to be totally engrossed in listening to his own confessions. Maybe it was all a way of exorcising the demons. Or putting an order on the memories so that they could be labelled and dealt with. The strangest part of the experience was being in the presence of one of my all-time favourite singers, listening to his major work, and discovering that he wasn't a big fan of his own voice. This was a flaw, if it was even a flaw, that he shared with the bespectacled Beatle. That realisation didn't in any way lessen the sheer bliss I was experiencing in Groove Masters Studio that day. It still doesn't today. In fact, I've discovered to my continued pleasure that all Jackson Browne's albums just get better with repeated exposure.

Listening to *I'm Alive*, the saddest realisation was that, no matter how successful artists are, no matter how many tickets or CDs they can sell, no matter the size of their royalty cheques, they still don't have the secret of how to fix a broken heart.

...GOT TO COME TO AN END

When you have worked with an artist – whether it's as a musician, manager, producer or even as an agent booking concerts – that work will always be a fact of your life story. A lot of the time, it is good for musicians who have played together for a few years to go off and play with other artists – as it is for solo artists to work with different musicians. The process can be vital to producing new blood, new ideas, new energy etc. Twenty-nine musicians played with Van Morrison, in his touring band, at various times during my seven-year watch. Some I recommended, some were already there and some were recommended by Van's associates and fellow musicians. That is the way it has tended to work with Van. Some of the chosen ones are asked to go (mostly by not being invited to continue), some move on to experience another, different adventure, while others just drift away.

Why do musicians move on? Some bands positively thrive on new blood. In all, 90 men and women have worked under the umbrella of The Waterboys.

Why do artists leave an agent? It happens for all sorts of different reasons. They acquire new management where there's a favoured agent – a process that has worked to my advantage as much as to my disadvantage. Or maybe the manager marries a new wife, or husband, and a Lumbar Puncture moment happens. Then again some artists want to be as big as Coldplay and blame the agent that they're not. Another agent will offer to do it for less commission, the legendary TCC. Some under-paid – well, in their eyes – member of the artist's management team begrudges the commission the agent is receiving.

Should I keep going? The agent messes up. The artist messes up and needs to find someone to blame. Or heaven forbid, it can be as simple as the agent telling the artist the kind of home truth that they don't particularly want to hear. For example, "We have to address the issue of your dwindling audience." I confess that was a very painful conversation to start. But if you don't do it, you are in the realm of waiting and hoping and thinking and praying.

On other occasions it can, quite simply, just be time for a change.

When an artist wants to leave and go to another agent, I'm totally okay with it.

And you know what: if an artist doesn't want to work with you, you shouldn't want to work with them. Or to put it more selfishly, maybe they don't deserve your services. It was a lesson I learnt from Miss Crowley, my chemistry teacher, at Magherafelt Technical College. If someone didn't want to learn her subject, she didn't make a song and dance about it. Instead, she put all her energy and attention into the students who did want to learn. It's a lesson from my teenage years which has served me well. I say: enjoy your great relationships and put all your oomph into them. They deserve it.

Buddha was gradually relegated to *co*-manager and all was no longer good.

I worked with Jackson Browne for 34 years. I was, and remain, a major fan of his work. I booked or promoted hundreds of concerts for him around the world... and yet in an apparent orchestrated Spinal Tap-type moment it was all over. Fine. That's the way it has to be. Or, as super-agent John Giddings puts it, "if you want loyalty, buy a puppy!"

CHAPTER TWENTY

HEALING SONGS

The opening scene in *The Dust of Death* (2007) – the first in my Inspector Starrett Mystery series – unveiled a crucifixion in a Donegal church. The congregation became an important part of the story. To ensure that I wouldn't upset any of the many churches in Ramelton, I decided to create a fictitious church which I called The Second Federation Church – it was on their premises that the remains of local master carpenter, James Moore, were discovered.

So what faith would my fictitious church be attached to? Again, so that I wouldn't offend anyone I needed the congregation of The Second Federation Church to practice a unique faith, with no similarities to any of the churches in a town whose nickname was the Holy See – and which, at one point, boasted fourteen churches.

I've always been impressed by congregations, or communities, who go out of their way to help and support each other. On one hand, you can pray all day long to a white-haired, bearded man, dressed in white sheets who wanders around above the clouds, in the hope that He might interfere in human affairs just long enough to help you, for example, to write a massive hit song and earn a fortune. Or, on the other hand, you can offer to help your neighbours when they need something done, in the mutual understanding that they might just do the same when you need to save the hay or clean up after flood damage. I think the second approach is far preferable.

This might all sound a bit simplistic but that doesn't worry me. My father was a carpenter. When I was a kid, my parents bought me a junior carpentry set, and I promptly announced to the family that I was going to make a chair. Well, I fluthered around for ages trying to figure out how to build a wooden chair like the ones at the dinner table. I was going for the full Monty: legs, seat, curved back, with strengthening and stabilising supports. The problem was that all of my efforts would end up collapsed in a heap on the floor.

My father encouraged me by asking me how I was getting on and I'd always say I was still working on the creation of the perfect chair. Time passed, and still there was no breakthrough. Eventually, my father came in from work one day a few weeks later, and – on discovering his heir apparent still had nothing to show – he took three pieces of wood and nailed them together in something similar to the shape of an "n", creating a very primitive, yet functional chair. "There's your chair, Paul," he said, "and, until such time as you can do better, this will suffice." His point – a variation on the principle that 'you've got to learn to creep before you can learn to walk' – was well-made.

That lesson was on my mind when I started to build my religion. For me, caring for, protecting and encouraging your family members has always been the most important thing. If we could only learn to love and look after our families properly, then we'd be much better equipped to deal with everyone else in a compassionate way. But humans – or a lot of them at least – seem to need conflict, rather than going along with the greatness of things. So, a family-type support structure had to be a vital ingredient for my religion.

The healing quality of music should never be underestimated. When I was growing up in Magherafelt I remember going to prayer meetings in a wee hall (and in the summertime, when the weather was fine, in a marquee) and being totally turned on by the gospel singing. You know that wonderful sound created by male and female voices together, and the special magic that sparks when the unique harmony of a choir in full flight creates a third voice. I remember the very first time I experienced this chills-down-the-spine sensation like it was yesterday. In fact, I recall turning and looking around the congregation to see where this new voice had come from.

That was my first major "spiritual" experience. It happened again, on occasion, listening to the soulful sound of the voices of the great singers around the Irish ballrooms and clubs at that time: Billy Brown, Paddy Shaw, Van Morrison and Paul Divito always sounded inspirational to me. Meanwhile, on the recording front, I discovered the works of Ray Charles and Otis Redding: both life-changing events.

This thirst for what we think of as spiritual magic was heightened when I was working with Van Morrison and we went up to the Shetland Islands to hear the chanters in the churches. The sound of a burly Scottish gentleman chanting his lines, for the congregation to reply in their sweet soulful harmonies, was just unbelievable. So, when considering the foundations of The Second Federation Church, music was always running through my head: I was thinking of The Beatles, Nick Lowe, Bob Dylan, Jennifer Warnes, Karen Carpenter, Neil Diamond, Van Morrison and so on.

The cent dropped, and everything else fell into place for me one Saturday night when Catherine and I were in our house in Ramelton. The Town Band was heralding the triumphant return of the local football team. There was so much excitement on the street that, had we been in Manchester, we'd easily have imagined Cristiano Ronaldo had scored a double hat-trick for Manchester United. The Town Band was playing Neil Diamond's 'Sweet Caroline'. It was a joyous sound delivered in a passionate, feel-good style. They were, to a boy and girl, beaming from ear to ear in such evident pleasure as they danced along the streets of Ramelton.

I was so inspired that I immediately made them the cornerstone of The Second Federation Church's music, basing the church choir on the Ramelton Town Band. From there, it was a series of very small steps to imagining the choir singing Van's 'Have I told You Lately That I Love You'; Dylan's 'Forever Young'; The Blue Nile's 'Happiness'; Mike Scott's 'Out of All This Blue'; 'Listen' by Christy Moore; 'Here Comes The Sun' by The Beatles; 'You Inspire Me' by Nick Lowe; 'Wonderful World' by Louis Armstrong, 'In The Neighbourhood' by Tom Waits, 'Teach Your Children' – the perfect song for a family and an even better one for the church – by Graham Nash, and then Jackson Browne's 'The Only Child,' with its vital, generous lyric, on the theme of mutual kindness, care and consideration.

This had to be the guiding principle of The Second Federation Church.

Take good care of each other. Is there really anything more important we can do in our lives?

CHAPTER TWENTY-ONE

MR AIM IS TRUE

When I first met Andrew Jakeman he'd recently changed his name to Jake Riviera. He was a debonair, swashbuckling, 'why knock on the door when it's much quicker to walk through the wall?' type. He also had a gentle side and you could completely understand why girls would love him and want to mother him, while mothers would want to warn their daughters to avoid him.

Jake was tour-managing Dr Feelgood at the time, and he was best buddies with Nick Lowe, the future Bard of Brentford and then current bass player, vocalist and chief in-house songwriter with the best pub rock band in the land, Brinsley Schwarz.

A bunch of agents whose offices were located around the buzzing 24/7 Wardour Street, London, West One, would occasionally meet accidentally for lunch in the Star Café, which was on the corner of Brewer Street and Noel Street. The Star Café's burgers were lollipop-stick thin, with a compulsive first bite but left a dire aftertaste. Their string-chips, however, were perfection-on-a-plate and the omelettes weren't bad either, so it was a place for comfort food of sorts. We'd never talk about business at the Star, just music. Jake Riviera would drop in on occasion with Nigel Kerr and Paul Conroy, the agents for Dr Feelgood. Nigel was the responsible agent, and I believe he still is. He was also a dead ringer for Todd Rundgren, so much so that if anyone is planning to do a Bio Pic on Todd, then Nigel is your man. I'm serious. They looked like the twin brother neither ever had.

Nigel was also a great agent, and still is. Paul Conroy was usually going on about a new, impossibly expensive, visual illusion Peter Gabriel was trying to develop for Genesis, who he was the responsible agent for. Paul also was very social, with a great sense of humour in a Chocs-Away-Boys-Own groove. He became one of the good guys at Warner Brothers when Warners needed some good guys. He also was great at organising things. I remember he put together a day trip, by coach, to Brighton for all the agents to go and see Monty Python perform at The Dome. We all met up at the mock Tudor gazebo in Soho Square. Everyone was on time and the trip was a total hoot! The Pythons were too, but I think the agents were funnier – or that was how it felt at the time. In a later life, Paul was the very successful MD of Virgin Records. Jake Riviera and I tried to get an Embassy Records project off the ground with Paul and Virgin. Embassy Records, we figured, would be a safe haven for musicians stranded not so much in a foreign country as a foreign business. Virgin wanted Embassy to sign successful artists – *only* successful artists, that is, which was never going to work. As a result, Embassy became such a safe haven that there was no-one inside apart from us. Well, there was a band from Liverpool, but that's a book in itself.

Jake, of course, formed Stiff Records with Dave Robinson. As early as 1975, Jake had persuaded Dr Feelgood lead singer, Lee Brilleaux, to loan Stiff the £400 required to start the label. At that point in 1975 there were too many sheriffs and not enough desperadoes on the scene. Stiff was exactly what the music business needed – and for the next decade the lunatics had taken over the asylum. By then, Nick Lowe was a very successful record producer. He'd worked with Dr Feelgood, before going on to helm the first ever UK punk single, 'New Rose' by The Damned, released by Stiff in October 1976. One of Nick Lowe's biggest fans was a bit of a train-spotter. A computer programmer, he would regularly hand over cassettes of his own songs, when he'd "accidentally" bump into Nick at gigs. Nick quite liked the computer programmer's cassette and brought it to the attention of Stiff Records. The computer-programmer walked into Stiff as Declan MacManus, received the Jake Riviera whirlwind make-over and walked out a few hours later as the super-cool Elvis Costello. Production-wise, Nick Lowe gave the *My Aim is True* album the edge it needed to avoid the pub rock sound it quite easily could have slipped into.

Nigel Kerr and Nick Leigh helped Jake out with gigs when Elvis eventually took to the road. But Jake wanted to make a statement by not having an agent. From his time with Dr Feelgood he knew how it was done and who all the players were.

By 1977, I was already agent for Nick Lowe, and for his then-partner and soon-to-be-first-wife Carlene Carter, both of whom were also being managed by Jake. I was also promoting shows in Ireland and so I booked Elvis and The Attractions, who were fast becoming a powerhouse live act, thanks in no small way to a band that comprised Steve Nieve (keyboards), Pete Thomas (drums) and Bruce Thomas (bass and champion Morri Spotter). Over the short run of shows in Ireland, I got to know Jake and his team even better. The visit was a big success, particularly the show in Belfast. A week or so later Jake rang me, saying up front that he didn't want an agent for Elvis, *but* could I do him a favour. I was all ears. He wanted Elvis to tour Japan and he asked me if I would set it up for him. He'd pay me full commission, of course, but I wouldn't be the agent.

I was getting the picture.

The Japanese tour I set up with Masahiro Hidaka at Smash Corp was a big deal. A new young Japanese promoter, Masa was a proper music fan; plus, he was very together, paid his money on time and took care of business professionally on and off the road.

When EC & The Attractions returned from Japan, Jake appointed me as their 'honorary' agent for Japan. Since I'd never been an 'honorary' anything before, this was a historic first! Then Jake asked me to set up an Australian tour for them, then a festival leg... until eventually, after another rocking night in Belfast, he said that he wanted me to be Elvis' agent for the world excluding North America and Canada.

Everyone warned me against it. Jake is a bit like Van – he didn't suffer fools gladly. Jake's half-Corgi is where he sits on his hind legs, his paws pumping away as though paddling through water as he barks at you. Then there is full-Corgi, where he just goes straight for the throat. Both moves are legendary in the music business. So I could see why people were worried on my behalf. But we've never had a cross word, and over 40 years later, we're still good friends.

During the course of the Stiff days, Jake and Dave Robinson parted ways.

In the settlement, Jake took Nick Lowe, Elvis Costello & The Attractions, and The Yachts with him and Dave kept the Stiff name and an artist list which included Ian Dury & The Blockheads and Madness. In 1977, Andrew Lauder had set up the Radar label with Martin Davis from Island Records; later, Andrew and his partner Judith Riley, set up their own Silvertone Records – to be celebrated for several reasons not least the fact that they released one of my all time favourite albums, Brendan Croker & The 5 O'Clock Shadows' excellent *Boat Trips In The Bay*.

Having parted company with Stiff, Jake was looking for a new record deal for Elvis and The Attractions. Richard Branson was mega-keen and made a big play to Jake, doing the whole song and dance about how important an artist EC would become, if only Jake would sign him to Virgin Records. Richard claimed Virgin Records believed in Elvis: they knew what needed to be done and they knew how to do it. Jake listened to this pitch for an hour, resisting the inclination to introduce either the full or even the half-Corgi. "Okay", he said eventually, "I'll tell you what I'll do. I'll sign to you right now, here, today, if you can give me the titles of six of Elvis' songs."

Guess what? Elvis Costello signed to Elvis Presley's label, RCA Records. A short while later, Jake formed F-Beat Records with Andrew Lauder. F-Beat Records released Elvis' records in Europe; Elvis signed with Columbia Records for the US.

For reasons that remain unclear, Richard Branson – the same – had the rights back then to do free concerts in Hyde Park. I wanted to do something special with Buzzcocks: their records were shifting serious numbers and their tours were selling out, so a free concert seemed like the perfect thank-you from the band to their fans. I rang Virgin, had a chat, explained my idea and tried to ascertain what the costs might be. They asked me to send a letter. I did and a few days later I received a call from Mr Virgin himself. Richard Branson was very keen. He explained to me that I would need to raise the money for the stage (with roof), lighting, PA, stage crew, security, catering, advertising, after-show clean-up, donation to the Parks, etc., etc. My brain was whirring, trying to figure out how much all of that would cost, and how much I might be able to extract from the record companies of the bands on the bill. I'd already discussed the project with Andrew Lauder, from UA, Buzzcocks' label, and he was up for the idea if we could make the sums work. "And, you'll also have to pay us a facility fee," Richard said, mentioning a figure that nearly made me fall off my chair, which kind of proved I wasn't a real hippie (in contrast to the agents in Jeff Dukes' Gemini, who, allegedly, used to sit on the floor).

The total figure Richard eventually landed on was way above my estimate of the costs. So we were now at double loggerheads. I decided that we'd have to let it go. He claimed the record companies would be happy to cough up the funds for the resultant invaluable promotion. I explained that, in Buzzcocks case, even if the record company did come up with the money, they'd have no money left in the pot to cover the band's upcoming releases. He suggested I get the record company to make it recoupable. I explained that it would take the band years to clear the debt and that I wasn't prepared to saddle them with that burden. And that is why Buzzcocks never appeared at Hyde Park. Elvis Costello did. Eventually.

Elton John was scheduled to headline on 12 July 2013. When he got sick, the promoters pushed Ray Davies – for whom I was agent – to the top of the bill and made it a free show, just like in the good old days. Nick Lowe was on the same bill: just a man and his guitar, he received an incredible reaction. Elvis, also in fine form, followed Nick; and Ray closed the show. It was an excellent day for Asgard artists.

At his own headline shows, Elvis Costello tended to do long sets – in fact, that's probably the biggest understatement in this book. It got to the point where the crew would have sweepstakes each night guessing how long a set he'd play. Legendary stage manager Milo Lewis would invariably win. I started to figure that EC and Milo might be in on it together! I also started to realise why EC did such long sets. You could actually see in his eyes, as he reached the end of a song and the audience burst into applause, that he was thinking, "Oh, you liked that one, did you? Well, okay, in that case you'll surely like this one just as much." But often the audience wouldn't and he'd lose the momentum of the set, and then dig in deep to try and win it back again. But you know what, anyone who worked with Nick Lowe, Steve Nieve and Pete Thomas is totally okay with me. Nick & EC & The Attractions made a few died-in-the-wool, classic albums. That legacy is forever.

Jake Riviera "retired" several years ago from managing the artist he'd very successfully created. A few years later, he passed over the Nick Lowe management reins to his ex-business partner, in what had become known as Two Jakes, Jake Guralnick. Jake R is still a massive fan of music, books, theatre and film. He knows, more than most on those topics. And he has a few secrets to tell. I'd love to read his book, if he can ever be persuaded to write it.

CHAPTER TWENTY-TWO

THE BEATLES, ELVIS, ALBERT & ME

"Tell me this, Paul, did you ever meet The Beatles?" It's a question I'm asked, infrequently, mind you, but still... Given that I'm such a Beatle fanatic (I once had a business card which proudly proclaimed: Author, Agent & Beatle Fan) and the fact that I work in the music business, I have to accept that it's a simple, straightforward, perfectly understandable query.

The answer however is not quite so simple. Let me explain.

Sadly I never saw The Beatles perform live. Nor did I meet them when they were members of The Beatles. I did manage to witness all of them performing in concert as solo artists; and I also managed to meet three of them in the post-Beatles era.

I know this might sound like a dubious confession, but I met Ringo Starr in Monaco. I was at one of those award ceremonies where you win an award for turning up. I was there with Tanita Tikaram, who I was managing at the time. We were hanging around at the run-through when Ringo introduced himself, and said he was going to be in big trouble with his daughter if he didn't manage to get a photograph of himself and Tanita together. He handed me his camera and very politely asked me if I'd take the photograph. Like myself, Tanita is a major Beatles fan and was tickled pink by the request. Later that evening Ringo presented Tanita with her award.

I subsequently met Ringo at a concert at The Royal Albert Hall where he went out of his way to reorganise the seats around him to accommodate the daughter of a friend of mine who was wheelchair bound. He was incredibly charming, thoughtful and discreet.

Talking about amazing drummers, it was Jim Keltner who introduced me to George Harrison backstage at an Elvis Costello concert at The Royal Albert Hall. At that point Jim was recording with George during the day, and performing with Elvis at night, during his six-night stint at the RAH. George was extremely gracious and happy to spend time chatting to a few of us. Jake Riviera, Elvis's manager, asked him why a verse of 'Awaiting On You All', on George's *All Things Must Pass* album, wasn't on the accompanying lyric sheet?

"*While the Pope owns 51% of General Motors,*" the missing lyric runs, "*And the Stock Exchange is the only thing he's qualified to quote us.*"

"I couldn't possibly comment," George said. But it was with a grin.

I saw John Lennon perform live at Twickenham Studios in December 1968. He was there to sing and play guitar with The Dirty Macs (Lennon, Eric Clapton, Mitch Mitchell & Keith Richards) for their one and only sighting at The Rolling Stones' famous Rock 'n' Roll Circus TV special. They played a high octane version of Lennon & McCartney's 'Yer Blues'. I also remember Marianne Faithfull (a future Asgard artist) singing 'Something Better' several times to a backing track with Mick Jagger in dutiful attendance between takes. I don't remember much else except that the audience was dressed in colourful cloaks and witches' hats. Sadly the audience were on a rotating relay system and my group were turfed out, minus our cloaks and hats to make way for the next section of audience, who I believe got to enjoy The Rolling Stones' last ever performance with Brian Jones.

Richard Ogden had acted as publicist for Fruupp. Years later, Richard became Paul McCartney's manager. He called me and said that he was keen to put Paul together with some great young writers – who would I recommend?

"Elvis Costello," I replied without a moment's hesitation, "Paul McCartney has got to write with Elvis Costello. It'll be perfect." It took a few telephone conversations – I suspect that Richard was scared of Jake – but we eventually made arrangements for Mr McCartney and Mr Costello to meet up. This was 1987 and the resultant co-writes included the very

Beatles-ish 'My Brave Face', 'You Want Her Too', 'Don't Be Careless Love' and 'That Day is Done' – all of which made it onto Paul's *Flowers In The Dirt* album; 'Veronica', 'Pads, Paws and Claws', which appeared on Elvis' 'Spike' album; plus 'So Like Candy' and 'Playboy to A Man', which made it onto Elvis' *Mighty Like A Rose* album.

A couple of years later I received another call from Richard Ogden. This time he was looking for somewhere very cool for Paul to play in London – a small club where the former Beatle could do a secret, no pressure, fun gig. I recommended The Mean Fiddler in Harlesden, set up the show for him and several weeks later, on May 10, 1991, Paul McCartney gave a legendary performance to an ecstatic audience, which included me.

I was invited to the MPL Christmas lunch that year by Richard. He sat me beside Neil Aspinall, a school friend of George and Paul, who had been part of The Beatles entourage from the start and who went on to be head of the band's company, Apple Corps. Neil proved to be an excellent storyteller.

Somewhere in the middle of all of this I got to meet my final Beatle. Backstage at an Elvis Costello concert in The Royal Albert Hall, Mr Richard Ogden introduced me to Paul McCartney. The former Beatle was very friendly and charming.

"And what is it you do?" he asked.

"I'm an agent," I replied proudly.

"Now that *is* a very good thing to be," he replied.

And of course he was right. I mean, just think of all the great people you get to meet backstage at The Royal Albert Hall.

CHAPTER TWENTY-THREE

GLASTONBURY – WHAT IS THERE LEFT TO SAY... ABOUT THE CENTRE OF THE UNIVERSE?

In 1981 Michael Eavis rang me up and said he wanted to discuss the possibility of two artists I represented, Van Morrison and Jackson Browne, appearing the following year at his festival, the Glastonbury CND Festival at the Pilton Farm. If anything he appeared totally shocked that I was prepared to stay on the phone and discuss the matter. Apparently he'd been having a very bad run getting agents to take his call.

That sort of thing puzzles me. If someone takes the trouble to ring me, I always try to take the call. If I'm in any doubt, I remember back to the time in 1973, I think it was, when I felt that, if I could get a job writing for the *Record Mirror* my career would be made. I'd ring up the editor of the magazine, the very patient Mr Peter Jones, once a fortnight. He had a beautiful voice – in fact, if he hadn't been an editor he would have made a perfect newsreader. Even as the editor of a grown-up music magazine, he never once made me feel like I was imposing on his time. We'd talk for 15 minutes or so, about everything under the sun including, but not limited to, which groups I'd been to see and what records I'd listened to since we'd last spoken. This went on for about 18 months. I think, in total, I wrote one article for him. It was about Stud. They were brilliant musicians – they really were – but I'd always felt they were doomed, if only because their manifesto was: if you come to see us expecting to hear a version of Taste you're going to be very disappointed. Sadly they were correct. I had a feeling that – like Stud – I was in danger of being trapped in the wrong world, while my life flashed past me. I was obsessed at the time with writing about music and musicians. So I never forgot Peter Jones's manners and patience.

When Michael Eavis rang me up that day, he was equally obsessed with his festival. I felt he was very genuine, totally committed to CND and the other causes he had supported over the years, putting his money (and sometimes his farm) where his mouth was. I told him I was working on plans for both of those artists to tour the following summer so we should keep in touch. He invited me down to the farm to see the lay of the land for myself. He was particularly proud of the massive, permanent, wooden, pyramid stage he had built. He apologised saying that there would be cows under the stage at this time of the year, a condition of the planning permission. I immediately loved the way he solved his problem by thinking outside the box. As in: "Okay the council won't give me planning permission to build a permanent stage on my farm, but they will grant me planning permission to build a cowshed on my land, and, for one weekend of the year, I can use the cowshed as a stage, in all its pyramided glory."

At the beginning of 1982, I visited the farm with some of Jackson Browne's crew, including Ron Perfit, Jackson's unforgettable, and fiercely loyal, multi-tasking tour manager. They were in Europe reconnoitering some cities for their forthcoming summer tour. Michael and Jean, it turned out, were very generous hosts, giving us the full guided tour. I remember climbing a series of internal ladders and platforms to the very peak of the pyramid. The top was a 2 foot Perspex affair, which they used for the laser lights exit, on festival weekend – but on that particular day the watchtower afforded me a spectacular view of Somerset in general and the Eavis's farmland in particular.

Both artists agreed to perform at that year's Glastonbury. The idea was that Van would finish his six-week European tour at Glastonbury, and Jackson would start his seven week tour of Europe the following day, with his first ever appearance at the Glastonbury Festival. For me, it was too golden an opportunity to miss, so I got to spend those 13 weeks on the road with both tours, enjoying some wonderful music, with the Glastonbury performances sandwiched more or less in the middle. Jackson was a big CND supporter and insisted on being paid expenses only for Michael's festival. Jackson and Michael Eavis had a lot in common; they when he opens the gates on Friday morning. Positioned at the main gate, he welcomes the fans onto his land and tells them they're very welcome and he hopes they'll enjoy themselves.

Those 130,000 fans feel they know Michael. I believe they do.

There are no undercurrents or hidden agendas. He says what he means and he means what he says. When he agrees a deal – and this applied even during the very difficult start-up days, when sometimes the ticket sales would be so low the farm was quite literally at risk – he'd never even dream of asking the act for a reduction. His money is always 100% as per contract. No excuses. Just a man who sticks to his word and never asks to be praised for doing so. He's always listening to music. He's always got new music at the ready for his next car journey. All the younger acts love him. When they arrive at The Acoustic Stage, invariably, the first question they ask is, "Do you think Michael will come up to see us?" He spends the entire weekend travelling from stage to stage in his trusted Land Rover.

Over those early years a lot of our acts played my personal favourite, The Acoustic Stage. I remember seeing Brendan Crocker & The 5 O'Clock Shadows perform what was then their new album *Boat Trips In The Bay*, from beginning to end. It was the kind of unique performance that had earned The Acoustic Stage the status of legend.

In 1993, I called the programmer of The Acoustic Stage with a view to starting off the conversation for the next festival. "Sorry, Paul," he announced, "Michael has cancelled The Acoustic Stage. We're finished!"

I immediately rang Michael. He explained that he was sorry but he had to pull the plug on The Acoustic Stage. He told me that each and every year the original programmer had gone over budget – never more so than at the previous festival. In life, as well as on the football pitch, you can only pick up so many yellow cards before they have to give you a red.

"We just can't afford it anymore," Michael offered by way of an apology.

"What was your budget?" I asked him.

When he advised the figure, I said, "Okay, If I can bring it in under that figure will you continue with The Acoustic Stage?"

"Of course, Paul, yes. We love The Acoustic Stage and our preference would be for it to continue."

That was 30 years ago and we've been booking it ever since.

We once booked Damien Rice just so we could hear one of my favourite singers, Lisa Hannigan, sing live. The only problem was by the time we got to the festival weekend, not only had they split up romantically, but she'd also left his band. We had to wait another couple of years for her to arrive with her own band to pack the tent and give us a brilliant performance.

We were very lucky to have booked the following artists before they became big acts. (Please note these are not the positions on the Glastonbury Top 3,000 Acts but the years they first performed.)

2007 Newton Faulkner
2011 Gabrielle Aplin
2011 Fisherman's Friends
2013 Jake Bugg
2013 Zac Brown Band
2014 Kacey Musgraves
2014 James Bay
2014 Hozier
2015 The Shires
2016 Ward Thomas
2017 Lucy Spraggan

Nothing feels as good as witnessing an act packing the spectacular circus tent and getting a great reaction. Nothing feels as bad as how quickly the tent empties after the act leaves the stage. I start wishing (and hoping and praying) that the next act will manage to fill the tent up again. I don't know where they all come from, but the tent always fills up again. I suppose a logical way to look at it would be that there are 130,000 fans on site at Glastonbury each year (and this figure does not include performers, staff, crews, stalls, bars and caterers). Those 130,000 make the site a bigger city than say somewhere like Bath – or indeed Cork, Limerick or Galway. In Bath, on any given weekend, there are concerts, theatres, opera, clubs, raves, silent-discos, cinemas, restaurants, galleries, circuses, each and every one of which can be well attended.

So why not at all the separate stages at Glastonbury? At The Acoustic know. Glastonbury is not a music festival, it is a complete experience." Michael and the Glastonbury team pay a lot of attention to the festival's special events and installations and support artists throughout the year if they are preparing art for the festival.

There was a time when television cameras were conspicuous at Glastonbury by their absence. In 1993, Michael told me that he'd been considering approaches from various television companies about broadcasting live from the event. He had come around to the view that it would be best to let the television cameras on site and so he asked me if I would handle the negotiations. The front-runners were the BBC and Channel 4. On paper there probably was more money available from a commercial station, but the BBC would never have to interrupt a soulful performance with adverts. On top of which, the BBC's producer-in-charge of music, Mark Cooper, was both a music man and a gentleman. Luckily enough, in a recent edition of *Stage* (the entertainment industry newspaper) a boxing promoter had given details of a deal he had struck with the BBC to televise some of his fights. I used that as a template for my negotiations with Mark Cooper.

Boxers want their matches broadcast for the payday. Artists want their performances broadcast essentially for the promotional benefits. So it was tricky. But we did eventually agree a deal and so in June 1994, the BBC moved on-site and have been there every festival since. The BBC have made several approaches over the years – to Michael and to me – to broadcast from the Acoustic Stage. It's my belief that – at smaller stages – cameras and camera crews can come between artists and audiences. It's also my belief that, with a few very rare exceptions, the magic always happens in the tent and not on the screen. Michael has always backed our decision and the Acoustic Stage has remained a camera-free zone.

For an outdoor festival performance, the majority of artists have to tailor their set to avoid playing a slow song at the wrong time. If they're not careful, they risk losing the audience's attention and people disappear off elsewhere, maybe even up to the Acoustic Stage.

Paul Carrack played The Acoustic Stage in 2016 and he rammed the tent and had as many people outside in the field looking in. The reaction was so phenomenal that Michael booked him to come back the following year to appear on the Pyramid Stage, where he enjoyed the same reaction, only this time in front of an additional 100,000 people.

Bruce Springsteen was one of the rare exceptions to the rule about being careful with the structure of your set. Bruce can play a death march in the middle of the set and the power of his performance is so consuming that he holds every single member of the audience in the palm of his hand. Individually, members of the audience feel like Bruce is singing directly to them. One of the few other places I've experienced that feeling is at Christy Moore concerts. It is quite a spiritual realisation.

When U2 played Glastonbury, it appeared to me that they were focusing on, and playing to, their 10,000 core fans directly in front of the stage. Bruce played to the very back of the field and made a lasting impression on 130,000 people. He made the entire audience feel they were all in a wee club having a great night together. With all U2's experience at their massive outdoors shows, I thought they would have done much better. To me Larry, Bono, Adam and the Edge seemed so nervous they never really fully relaxed into their set. What should they have done? It might have worked better if they had focussed on and played to one another – and the audience would have followed, just as they did for Neil Diamond. You got the feeling that some of the audience might have thought it would be uncool to be seen to enjoy Neil Diamond. After the first couple of Neil Diamond's songs, 'Cracklin' Rose' and 'Holly Holy', the audience were thinking, "Feck this being cool malarkey, this Diamond geezer is brilliant!" Mind you a BBC crew sticking their cameras and microphones into U2's shell-shocked faces as they walked off stage wasn't exactly the perfect ending to an imperfect performance.

Other headline acts who made the stage their own included Macca and Coldplay. The Rolling Stones on the other hand suffered from a very poor sound mix. As the man said, "You can't always get what you want..."

CHAPTER TWENTY-FOUR

PUTTING OUT FIRES

The Cornbury Music Festival (Oxfordshire) is another favourite festival of mine. I saw The Beach Boys there in 2019. Now, I've been listening to The Beach Boys since 1964 and even I hadn't realised just how many great songs they have to their name. They played them all at Cornbury – and what was even more surprising was that the audience knew every song and made a fair stab at singing them along with the band. We're talking about fans whose parents hadn't even been born when the original records were released.

In 2008, Paul Simon was booked to headline the festival. Apparently, it was only when Mr Simon arrived on site in his tour bus that he realised he wasn't playing Glastonbury, but the other "nbury" festival. I was at the festival that year with Nick Lowe and Nick delivered his usual crowd-pleasing set – but things seemed a bit strange in the top of the bill's camp backstage. Mr Simon reportedly hid on his bus until show time, and then performed his entire set with his back to the audience.

A couple of years later in 2010, when Jackson Browne was due to play the headline spot at The Cornbury Festival, his deposit didn't arrive as per contract. Late deposits are our early warning alert system that something might be awry with a future show. Contractually, the promoter/festival has to pay a "binder" immediately, but at the very latest, before they announce or advertise the artist in question. Then, six weeks before the festival or concert, the promoter pays the second part of the deposit; and then seven days before the show, the remaining fee is paid. It is a very basic, but effective, protection – no deposit, no artist.

I spoke to the main man at the Cornbury Festival, Hugh Phillimore, a music business legend at organising corporate events and high profile birthday parties. Hugh is ultra-together and efficient and he had the bottle to immediately admit he had a major problem. He was very apologetic. He didn't tell me 'the cheque's in the post'. Or 'our accounts department are on holidays'. Or "gosh did we forget to send it – silly us". Or any of the dozen, or so, excuses Christina Czarnik, my trusted, super-efficient, PA for over thirty years, hears on a weekly basis.

Christina is very together and has the measure of the late-payers. She averts many a looming disaster for Asgard, by heading it off at the pass. But there were no excuses from Hugh. He got straight to the point. "I don't have it," he admitted. He explained that the previous year hadn't been great, box-office wise, and one of his business partners had pulled out.

They say if you are planning to go into the festival business, plan to lose money for the first five years minimum. Then you might start to turn the corner. If you can make back your losses, from the first five years, in the second five years, that's okay. Then, and only then, should you start to think of making a profit. Cornbury Music Festival had the reputation of being a well organised, well run, audience and artist-friendly festival. They were still building their audience. They hadn't yet turned the corner into profit. Hugh wondered if I could wait until the day of the show for the balance of Jackson Browne's fee.

This is a very difficult dilemma for any agent. If I say, 'no,' does that mean that the festival can't go ahead? If the festival collapses will the fans get their money back? Legally they should. A concert ticket is merely a receipt the fan is given for the money they have paid in advance of the show. If the show doesn't happen – i.e. the promoter/artist does not deliver their side of the deal – the ticket-holder is entitled to cash-in their receipt at the point of purchase. The other problem, part of the ugliness of the music business, is that the ticket agent will sometimes refuse to refund the whole price, claiming they are still entitled to their ticket commission. In my opinion, this practice is completely out of order.

As far as Jackson's performance at Cornbury was concerned, if the festival were at risk, it was my responsibility to ensure that the artist did not continue to be listed as appearing at the festival, for fear that, in the meantime, his fans might keep buying tickets to see their preferred artist. If we were prepared to take the risk that Hugh was going to sell enough tickets to pay the act at a later date, we could allow him to continue to sell the tickets. But if he didn't sell enough tickets by the date of the festival, and he couldn't pay the act, there was going to be an even bigger mess. On the flip side, losing a festival fee could potentially have a big impact on the financial viability of the tour. I relayed the scenario on how this would impact the rest of the Jackson Browne tour. Cornbury was to be the final night of Jackson's tour, so it wasn't going to cause any immediate routing problems. But it was a big fee, the loss of which would impact the viability of the tour. I set the phone down fearing that, in all probability, Cornbury wasn't going to happen. Hugh Phillimore is one of the good guys and so – if at all possible I had to find a solution. Time wasn't on my side.

I thought about nothing else for the remainder of that day and most of the night. I came up with several ideas and played them through in my mind to their logical conclusions: comparing the upside to the downside. By the following morning I had narrowed it down to just one idea as to how to keep The Cornbury Music Festival alive.

I rang up my friend Pete Wilson, of the Triple A Entertainment Group. He and his partner Dennis Arnold had put the "Gold" in Harvey Goldsmith Ents before they left to set up their own very successful company, Triple A.

Pete is one of my favourite promoters: he is honest, and he is not scared of actually spending money to help artists sell tickets. And he is always in the office early. Pete and Dennis run a very efficient house with one of the best promoter's stage managers in the world in Jolyon Burnham, plus Jeanne White and Fiona Bailey-Atwood leading the team that keeps the wheels on the wagon back at base in Putney.

"Do you fancy buying into a festival, Pete?" was my opening gambit.

He didn't put the phone down on me: so, so far so good.

I explained the situation to Pete as plainly as Hugh had explained it to me. Pete said he would speak to Dennis.. He rang me back an hour later and said he and Dennis were interested in having an exploratory conversation with Hugh.

I rang Hugh, told him my idea and he was up for it. I put them together and they worked out their deal. By the end of the week Jackson's deposit had arrived from Triple A.

The festival went ahead and Jackson had a very successful final night of his tour.

At the following year's festival, in 2011, Ray Davies topped the bill. Elvis Costello took the honours in 2012. The Cornbury Music Festival has been going strong ever since.

****

As someone who worked for the Cambridge Fire Brigade, Ken Woollard was also very good at putting out fires. But Ken was more, much, much, more than that. He loved folk music so much that, in 1965, he created, with backing from the local Labour Party, the world-renowned Cambridge Folk Festival. Coincidentally a very young Paul Simon appeared at the first festival.

Ken ran the festival until he – very sadly and prematurely – passed away in 1993.

He used the main phone in the fire station to book the artists.

Sometimes you'd be on the phone to him finalising a deal and he'd say "Oops, there's the siren, I gotta go and put out a fire, I'll talk to you later." Sometimes you'd wonder if it was just a brilliant negotiating tactic.

In truth, however, you also knew that Ken was a great festival promoter and organiser. He was into acts new and old. When The Clancy Brothers with Tommy Makem got together for a reunion tour we set up for them in 1985, Ken Woollard was head of the queue wanting to book them. I was very proud of that tour, in that the only act my dad ever took an interest in when I was growing up was The Clancy Brothers. It was his only album in our house-collection. Yes my dad knew all about Van Morrison and Ray Davies and Lonnie Donegan – but the only time he was impressed by one of my artists was when The Clancy Brothers were involved. They played at The Cambridge Folk Festival on 28 July 1985 and warmed the hearts of all in attendance. At the other end of the age-scale, I sent Ken Woollard a cassette featuring four Tanita Tikaram songs before she'd signed her record deal. He rang me back the next day saying he loved her voice and her music and he definitely wanted to book her for that year's festival. He made an offer that was very generous for an unknown artist. It turned out he was well ahead of the pack because, by the time the festival date arrived, she'd signed a record deal with Warner Bros and recorded her first album *Ancient Heart*. On the very day she did her final set at the Cambridge Folk Festival, Sunday 29 July 1988, her first single, 'Good Tradition', entered the UK Top 40 single charts.

I'd always felt that the local council hadn't really looked after Ken properly. In my book he had gifted them a brilliant folk festival, which he successfully ran for all those years. Cambridge Folk Festival, with its unique, stylish posters was easily the most famous folk festival in the world. The festival was turning a handsome profit and Ken was getting a pittance for his efforts. And he was about to be let go.

I spoke to several artists who'd worked with Ken over the years: Christy Moore, Loudon Wainwright III (who had introduced me to Ken), Ralph McTell, Tanita Tikaram and The Bronte Bros. They were, one and all, very fond of him, as was I, and so we agreed to put on a benefit for Ken at The Royal Albert Hall. He was tickled pink. We scheduled it for Thursday 30 June 1994 and it was going to be a big celebration-cum-testimonial night. But, before it could be done, on 19 October 1993, he died. I spoke to him a few days beforehand – he rang me from the road trip he was enjoying up North – and he was as excited as ever about the following year's festival. We were going to meet up on his return. and start to look at acts for the 1994 festival. We were all devastated when we heard the sad news, and agreed that the RAH show with Christy, Loudon, Ralph, Tanita & Bronte Bros would go ahead as a celebration to Ken's life and work and to benefit his wife Joan. It was a highly emotional concert. Tanita was very distracted by a bird flying around the inside of the venue during one of her songs.

None of the rest of us were bothered. We knew it was just Ken, checking in to see how we were all getting on.

CHAPTER TWENTY-FIVE

MUSIC MOST JOYOUS

Record releases were major social and artistic events before I left Ireland in 1967, and that continued for the next decade or so. In the beginning, more than anything else, it might have been to do with having to save up the thirty-two shillings and sixpence required to buy an LP. Later, of course, album launches became massively celebrated cultural events.

Take, for example, the release of *Sgt. Pepper's Lonely Heart Clubs Band* which was the scene-stopping happening of the era. Mind you, the same might have been said of its predecessors, *Rubber Soul* and *Revolver*. Even its follow-up LP, *The Beatles* (aka *The White Album*) and their penultimate opus, *Abbey Road* could be painted in a similar light. But, really, Sgt. Pepper's was the one.

Sometimes the anticipation would be close to unbearable, like with Van Morrison's *Moondance*, the follow up to his critically acclaimed masterpiece, *Astral Weeks* – though very different it was a cracker too. Or Tom Waits' *Rain Dogs,* wherein he turned the whole genre of 'singers who wrote their own songs', totally on its head.

I felt that way about a lot of records, but I don't think it was only me. The Beach Boys' *Pet Sounds*; Bob Dylan's first post-motorcycle accident release *John Wesley Harding*; Crosby, Stills and Nash's eponymous debut; Leonard Cohen's *Songs From a Room*, the follow-up to his groundbreaking debut, *The Songs of Leonard Cohen*; Simon & Garfunkel's *Bridge Over Troubled Water*; Otis Redding's *Otis Blue*; Jackson Browne's *The Pretender* (which seemed to take forever to hit the racks); Dire Straits' *Brothers in Arms*;

Pink Floyd's *Dark Side of the Moon*; *The Traveling Wilburys Volume 1*; Paul Simon's *Graceland*; U2's *The Joshua Tree*; Gerry Rafferty's *City to City*, which was perfectly heralded by the classic single 'Baker Street'. People waited for these records with a high sense of expectation. Of course we might be disappointed. Sometimes we were. But the important thing was that they mattered. Maybe, for a different generation, the latest LP by Beyoncé, Taylor Swift, Lana Del Rey or Fontaines D.C. is awaited with the same sense of expectation. But I am left with the feeling that, with the drip-feeding of status updates, the overnight release of tracks and the general feeling of overload that the instant availability of the entire history of popular music, more or less, on streaming platforms like Spotify creates, has undermined the epoch-making impact that great LPs had in that moment, when so much of this was still new.

In my personal bubble, I'd also be counting Taste's first album, called simply, *Taste*; Rockpile's *Seconds of Pleasure* (they were so incredible live I couldn't wait for their first album: obviously I had to, since there was no alternative, bar a quick visit to the legendary crossroads); The Undertones' self-titled debut; Buzzcocks' *Another Music in a Different Kitchen* and Genesis (with Peter Gabriel)'s *Foxtrot*. There were, of course, other event-albums from artists like The Rolling Stones, The Sex Pistols, Led Zeppelin etc., etc., but even for a complete music nut, there's only so much music with which you can fall head over heels in love!

Artistically speaking, it helped that many of the artists of that era were spurring each other on. Brian Wilson was so inspired on hearing *Rubber Soul* that he went off and wrote and recorded *Pet Sounds*, including two of the most extraordinary tracks in the history of contemporary music, 'God Only Knows' and 'Good Vibrations'; which, in turn, was a wake-up call to The Beatles, motivating them to deliver *Sgt. Pepper's* the following year.

It was what they call a virtuous circle. Well, musically speaking...

****

Before the worldwide web existed, the build-up to album releases was created mostly around press announcements, paid press advertising and the word-of-mouth from advance reviews. The unbearable countdown was sign-posted by sneak preview airplay, a bit of telly and lots of chatter, to the extent that by the time the album was released, the world had cranked itself up to fever-pitch. Radio shows would be tripping over themselves to secure an exclusive. In the case of The Beatles, some stations took to playing the albums in their entirety (and yes, including The Beatles double white album) in the weeks prior to release.

Radio stations had much more impact then. Since there were but a few of them, they each consequently reached a much bigger audience. Back then, the singles chart was much more dynamic and fast-moving. In contrast, the better albums didn't fade away after a couple of weeks, but hung around the higher regions of the charts for something like six to twelve months. A few even managed multiple years in the charts. In fact, albums like *Sgt. Pepper's* and *Abbey Road* by The Beatles, *Rumours* by Fleetwood Mac, and the likes of *Abba's Greatest Hits,* continue to sell in impressive numbers forty to fifty years later.

That was all many decades ago and event-albums like that don't happen anymore… or do they?

Well, I can think of one.

Out of the blue, Bob Dylan dropped a new track on the internet and radio, on March 27, 2020. This streaming-services format of releasing new music is part of the new normal. But the song 'Murder Most Foul' was different, very different.

Then again, Dylan has always been unique. He is one of those rare artists, whose current songs can stand up majestically alongside any of the songs from his earlier albums, a major feat when you consider that any new album would be his thirty-ninth. His first, entitled *Bob Dylan*, was released in 1962. That's all of 60 years ago.

Would a Bob Dylan type of artist get a record deal today? It's a good question. I mean, if he had the same song-writing skills and music, and someone was shopping for a deal for him as an unknown, what would the chances of success be? The simple answer, I believe, is a big zero; he wouldn't be offered a recording contract in the current (music business) climate. In fact, his representatives wouldn't even get a meeting, unless he, the artist, was already socially followed in the millions; prepared to do all the self-promoting; didn't need an advance; and would give up a share of his publishing, merchandising and touring. If he had all of that going for him, as it were, then maybe, just maybe, he'd get a deal. Sadly, that is pretty close to the reality for emerging artists in 2022.

'Murder Most Foul' caused a major stir and shot straight to No. 1 on the *Billboard* chart. Dylan then released a second song, 'I Contain Multitudes', in the same manner. And this was followed, in May, by a third, titled 'False Prophet'.

The word filtered out that Bob Dylan would release an album *Rough and Rowdy Ways* on 19 June 2020. This would be his first album of new material since 2012's *Tempest*.

Three strategically released songs in, it became clear that *Rough and Rowdy Ways* – named after a single released by Jimmie Rodgers in 1929 – was guaranteed to be a No. 1 in the charts had already captured the imagination of music fans. In the week of its release, it went to No.1 in the UK and Ireland, and to No.2 in the US.

The event-album was back!

****

The reviews for *Rough and Rowdy Ways* were all five-star. The album was widely heralded as one of Dylan's finest ever. The (London) *Times* carried their review in the news pages as opposed to the Arts Section. *Uncut Magazine* gave the album a six-page review. I had never seen them – or indeed anyone else – do this before.

On Friday 19 June 2020, the man from Amazon popped my copy of *Rough and Rowdy Ways* through the letterbox. I had that old tingling feeling back. I had to hear it straight away. In full.

The opener, 'I Contain Multitudes', breezed in from absolutely nowhere. It's a perfectly recorded song. You feel Dylan is right there, in your room, telling you his new set of stories. The backing music perfectly compliments the song, never – even for one second – competing with the singer.

"*I'll sing the songs of experience/ like William Blake/ I've no apologies to make,*" Dylan offers as we settle in.

"*I'm just like Anne Frank, like Indiana Jones, and those British bad boys, The Rolling Stones,*" he sings, in a perfect story-telling voice, which has never sounded so good.

"*I'll drink to the man that shares your bed,*" he confesses, a line I couldn't get out of my head even after the end of the song.

Next up is 'False Prophet', a bar-room stomp with gentle hints of John Lee Hooker. Dylan and his band (Bob Dylan – vocals and guitar; Charlie Sexton – guitar; Bob Britt – guitar; Donnie Herron – steel guitar, violin and accordion; Tony Garnier – bass, and, Matt Chamberlain – drums) make this song sound like they've been road-testing it for twenty years before eventually cutting it. It sounds like they take so much joy from playing together. It is all highly infectious.

'My Own Version of You' is smooth and very satisfying, with the band playing barely above a whisper.

By the second time I played 'I've Made Up My Mind To Give Myself To You', I felt like I'd known this song all my life.

'Black Rider' has the band playing at a whisper again, the melody set up chord by single chord. The voice, as ever, is the focus holding it all together.

'Goodbye Jimmy Reed' cranks it back up again. It's a homage – a walking blues, by way of 'Leopard-Skin Pillbox-Hat' – that you never want to end.

'Mother of Muses' is perhaps an ode to his maker, acknowledging all the gifts Dylan has been given. "*I'm travelling light,*" he sings, "*and I'm slowly coming home.*" I am reminded of those great lines from 'Not Dark Yet' (*Time Out of Mind*, 1997): "*I was born here, and I'll die here, against my will.*"

'Crossing The Rubicon' is a bit like Buddy Guy, slowed-up just as the electricity meter runs out. Replete with another amazing vocal performance, it is a towering expression of Dylan's particular genius.

Final track on disc one is 'Key West (Philosopher Pirate)' which gently breezes in, the musicians allowing the song to breathe. I'll say it again: the voice he has spent all these years growing into, is now the perfect story-telling voice. You can clearly hear each and every word and so not a single one is wasted in either the writing or the delivery.

****

The first few dozen times I listened to 'Murder Most Foul' on YouTube

(I believe it's over 5,000,000 plays and counting,) I was worried that the album could turn out to be a support system for this one, monumental song. That anxiety has proven totally unfounded. There is no padding here, no passenger song, no poorer cousin. Every single song earns its place. The record is like the perfectly thought-out show, with several peaks and some lighter shades, before the dramatic pay-off. The production sounds perfect in that this album has not been produced; it has been *recorded*. The performance is at the essence of the production.

The final act, 'Murder Most Foul', at 16 minutes and 59 seconds takes up all of disc 2. It is vivid, dramatic, scary, tragic, sad and – I am going to be bold enough to claim – out-Shakespeare's William Shakespeare. In centuries to come, this will be the go-to document for the times and crimes of the 20th Century. It is, to me, one of *the* factual works of modern times and of Dylan's career.

It's about the 1960s: artists, bands, music; the Kennedys; Vietnam; injustice; civil rights; The Beatles; America; causes; politics, and... corruption. This is the kind of an ultimate corruption where all the baddies bought themselves white hats. If someone had shouted out, "He's behind you," even JFK would ignore the pantomime call. Never for a second would he glance back as he concentrated on the road towards Dealey Plaza, waving to the crowds.

Set against a hypnotic, sensitive, ambient, piano-violin-percussion led backdrop, Dylan recalls his take on the Crime of The Century. "*Take me to the place Tom Dooley was hung*," he sings as he does. It's factual, but so far-fetched you are tempted to treat it as fiction. I've never heard Bob Dylan sound as tender as he does when he sings, "*The Beatles are coming, they're gonna hold your hand*."

As a piece, this works very successfully, in the way that both Norman Mailer's *Executioner's Song* and Truman Capote's *In Cold Blood* worked. You might think that 'Murder Most Foul' should be a book. In fact, it is a book, a mighty book, only this particular troubadour forsook the page for the stage. It sounds like the Judgement Day address before the final sentencing. When the song concludes you are left in shock. No matter how many times you hear 'Murder Most Foul', I guarantee you will feel stunned. You will feel like you need some time alone. Or at least that's been my experience.

I just found it amazing – and reassuring – that an artist could deliver an album as brilliant and as challenging – not to mention enjoyable – as *Rough and Rowdy Ways* in 2020. I suppose, all things considered, I really shouldn't have been surprised that the name on the disc was Bob Dylan.

Rough and Rowdy Ways may well be the event-album to end all event-albums. Then again, maybe not. I hope and pray that there is a new wave of music and musicians coming over the horizon, who can reach for the sky but not just to surrender. In the meantime, I have a new and welcome addition to the event-albums section in my collection. That's the section where you wear out the repeat button.

Now where did I put the number for that hi-fi repair man?

CHAPTER TWENTY-SIX

THE CONSEQUENCES OF THE LACK OF THE ART OF COMPROMISE AKA SAYING NO TO THE ROLLING STONES

Following in the footsteps of the truly inspiring Rory Gallagher at the Macroom, Mountain Dew, Festival, in Co. Cork on June 26 1977 – which I believe was the first major outdoor Irish Rock Festival – we promoted what we called The Dublin Festival 1980. Our one-day event took place at Leixlip Castle on 27 July. The owner of the castle, Desmond Guinness, was an excellent host, a very reasonable man and couldn't do enough to help us. The bill we finalised was: The Police, Q Tips, Squeeze, The Moondogs, John Otway and, the show-stealers on the day, a young U2. The festival was phenomenally successful and The Police regretted taking a higher flat fee rather than a more reasonable fee against a percentage. Equally it has to be admitted that the fee they received was their career best up to that point.

A couple of years after Rory took one small step for all musicians, and a giant leap for the Irish music business, we started to work with Van Morrison as his agents for live work. Van Morrison's manager at that time was a gentleman by the name of Bill Graham – a genuine 24 carat rock 'n' roll legend from San Francisco. I enjoyed my numerous meetings with him. He would walk me around the corridors of his offices to talk me through his memorabilia and entertain me for hours with tales of his Fillmore West and Fillmore East adventures.

I was working very closely with BGP (Bill Graham Presents) in general and Mick Bridgen (as BGP's appointed project manager for Van) in particular. BGP, as well as managing Van Morrison and Santana, amongst others, also presented national and international tours. Mick was aware of the success of our Dublin Festival 1980. Putting these facts together resulted in a call asking if we – Asgard – would be interested in presenting an outdoor show in Dublin with an act they were just getting ready to tour.

I was not immediately in love with the idea. While Dublin Festival 1980 was a success, I'd always preferred music being created on stage in smaller indoor venues. To that end some of the best music I'd ever heard has been at the 2080 capacity venue known as The National Stadium – a boxing hall on South Circular Road, Dublin, where I'd really enjoyed the music of Dire Straits, Carole King, Ry Cooder, JJ Cale, Loudon Wainwright III, Gerry Rafferty, B.B. King, Van Morrison, John Prine, Eric Clapton and Kate and Anna McGarrigle, amongst many others. Each of these magic shows have since become, in their own right, legendary.

However, on some occasions, it was a challenge to persuade the musicians and their crews that the blood still splattered around the dressing room was purely as a result of legit boxing matches rather than fights breaking out backstage between the promoter and the artist at the previous night's concert. At the same time the music coming from the stage made the effort all the more worthwhile. It's funny how some venues acquire a reputation for having a brilliant audience, even though the actual composition of the audience differs drastically from night to night. Examples include The Barrowland in Glasgow, The Royal Albert Hall in London, The Olympia in Paris, The Carre in Amsterdam, The Opera House in Belfast – or indeed The Ulster Hall (before the refurb). These venues share a common factor: that the audience and the artist are both physically and – if the artist has the magic touch – spiritually close to each other.

During the course of our further conversations it turned out that Mick Brigden was referring to a worldwide tour they were about to do with The Rolling Stones. The tour was scheduled for the summer months of 1982. We talked about the idea for ages. I went off to investigate suitable venues. I had to rule out Leixlip, great and all as it had been as a venue for our Dublin Festival 1980: it was just too small for the Stones. On paper the place that attracted me the most was Phoenix Park; we ruled that out too, due to the cost of putting a plant on site and securing a perimeter. I also tried Dalymount Park. The venue representative I spoke to went by the name of George Harrison and I took that to be a great omen. I could also see a brilliant top line for the adverts and posters: "Asgard by arrangement with George Harrison, presents The Rolling Stones." Can you imagine Mick, Charlie, Keith and the boys arriving and seeing that banner? Sadly Dalymount was also too small. In the end all roads led to Slane Castle.

Mick Brigden flew over and we were treated to an excellent lunch in the Castle by Lord Henry Mountcharles. The potato soup we were served is still the best potato soup I've ever tasted. Our gastronomical preference was all well and good, but the big question was: did Lord Mountcharles want to rent out his castle for a rock 'n' roll show? Does Paul McCartney love publicity or, as Christy Moore would say, does a bear poo in the woods? The short answer to all three questions was a big YES: Lord Mountcharles was up for it and with bells on!

Negotiations rumbled on. BGP sent us over their promoter's bible – a point by point, minute by minute guide as to how to promote an outdoor event. I imagine some of the promoters around the world found a good use for the tome: namely, if they wanted to increase their stature from five foot eleven to over the six foot mark they now had the perfect device. Or perhaps they may have considered using the book as toilet paper. In fact toilet paper was one of the hundreds of points listed in the manual.

My memory of the deal was not how much the band cost. In fact what they were proposing reversed the usual promoter/artists roles somewhat. The promoter was to be paid for promoting the show. On the positive side this meant the promoter was not really taking a risk. Mind you having said that I do remember ringing EMI in Dublin to check how many copies the Stones previous record, *Tattoo You*, had sold and discovering that it had sold a measly 741 copies in total in Ireland. Those were the kind of numbers The Undertones were then currently selling each and every day! We, on the other hand, needed to sell 70,000 tickets! But The Rolling Stones were... well... they were The Rolling Stones. We knew they were a big draw. Just how big remained to be proven.

The basis of the deal was that the promoter would pay for all the costs of producing and presenting the show in advance and then on the day of the show at the "settlement" all these costs, plus the promoter's fee, would be deducted from the pot (the box office take) and the balance would be paid over to the artist. There might also have been some kind of deposit to be paid to the artist in advance if only to show willing – and to confirm that the promoter had access to some funds.

However, when it got down to it, we had three major stumbling blocks with BGP.

1. They (BGP & The Rolling Stones) wanted to run the show on a Sunday. Slane is a very small village and I didn't feel it was fair to be inconveniencing the locals on their way to their places of worship.
2. They wanted to charge a uniform ticket price across the entire tour. I felt it was too high for Ireland.
3. They wanted to have one support act on the bill, The J Geils Band. I felt it was vitally important to have some local acts among the supports.

The BGP team including Mick Brigden, had decamped to London and I was summoned to a meeting at the Stones office in Cheyne Walk, Chelsea, at 09.00 am on Wed 25 April to finalise the deal.

They, BGP, wouldn't budge on any of the three key stumbling points. The BGP team had previously explained to me that they learnt in these instances to use Bill Graham as a figurehead. They equated Mr Graham to a bear in a cage. So sometimes when promoters were resisting parts of the deal, also known as, not toeing the line, they'd bring the promoter to see Bill and 'rattle the cage'. If the promoter still wouldn't concede the outstanding points the BGO team would threaten to let Mr Graham out of his cage.

None of the above mattered a damn to me. Quite simply I didn't feel comfortable with the deal on the table and so I walked away from the project.

When I thought about this later I realised why. Whether as a promoter or as an agent, one of the biggest factors in your success is your ability to negotiate. Or, to put it another way, your ability to compromise. In this instance what I neglected to do – in truth what I didn't want to do – was to negotiate with them. I liked Mick Brigden and I liked Bill Graham, but I had no personal investment in the act they were representing. I grew up at a time when you were either a Beatles fan, or you were a Stones fan. Me, well I was a 100% committed Beatles fan. Yes, I enjoyed a few of the Stones singles and some of their album tracks like 'You Got The Silver' and 'You Can't Always Get What You Want', but I didn't really care about them. Consequently I had no desire to make it work outside of my personal comfort zone.

If I had, then I would have clicked in with: "Look, in most of the other places you're going to, there will be taxes coming off your tickets sales, but in Ireland there will be no tax deductions from your ticket price (true at that time) – which means even if we drop the ticket price to a more reasonable level you'll still nett more than in the UK."

I could have followed that up with: "The J Geils Band are great and of course they should be on the bill, but as it's going to be a big audience and it's going to take a long time for the audience to get onto the site, why don't we open the doors early and put someone like Paul Brady Band or Moving Hearts on, or even both, which'll mean that by the time the Stones hit the stage everyone will be in a great mood and ready to rock."

Then I could have hit them with my ace card...

"And as I've compromised with you on those first two points you can surely compromise with me and move the show to a different day of the week. It'll work to your advantage in that you'll be respecting the locals and, on top of which, you'll sell a lot more tickets on a Saturday."

But I didn't. I just couldn't compromise. I couldn't do the deal with them. Maybe if they'd wanted to play somewhere like the Boxing Stadium I would have reacted differently.

As it turned out The Rolling Stones did appear at Slane in 1982. They did invite a local act, one Mick J had a personal relationship with, The Chieftains. And they also added George Thorogood to the bill. The show was ably promoted by Gentleman Jim Aiken, the sun shone and everyone lived happily ever after. Both Jim Aiken and Mick Brigden invited me, but I didn't have the heart for it. I'd seen the Stones live in Hyde Park on the 5 July 1969, two days after Brian Jones died. There were an estimated half a million people there for what was a free show. And what I remember most about the show – apart from Mick's white dress and the Stones letting off lots of white butterflies – was the fact that King Crimson, doing an afternoon spot, blew everyone away.

When I said everyone lived happily ever after, that wasn't strictly true. The next major world tour BGP put together a couple of years later was with Bob Dylan. I've always been a major fan of Dylan. I waited for Mick Brigden to call me about the Dublin show. But the call never came, perfectly demonstrating the downside of ignoring the art of compromise. Jim Aiken got the call. And why wouldn't he? Hadn't he done his usual impeccable job with the Stones at Slane Castle? I went to see the Dylan show at Slane on 8 July 1984 and got to meet the great man at his caravan and shake his hand (but gently). How did that come about? Well, along with Paul Brady, I attended the event as Mick Brigden's guests and when we got there we were told that Dylan was very keen to meet Paul and would like to do so before the show. We were taken backstage and introduced to the great man at the door to his caravan. Dylan wanted Brady to teach him the chords to the Ulsterman's interpretation of 'The Lakes of Pontchartrain'. Brady and Dylan retired to the depths of Bob's caravan and the lesson proceeded.

Now that, right there, was a performance I'd have done anything to witness: Bob Dylan and Paul Brady performing 'The Lakes of Pontchartrain', in a wee caravan backstage at Slane Castle. The only thing which could possibly have made it any better would have been for Lord Mountcharles to have served all of us another bowl of his special potato soup.

CHAPTER TWENTY-SEVEN

THE GENESIS OF THE ABBEY ROAD GRAFFITI: A MYSTERY IN ONE PART

When *Abbey Road* by The Beatles was released, on Friday 26 September 1969, I was dating Ann Burgess. She was my first serious girlfriend in London. It had taken me two years to get over the girl I'd been seeing back home in Ireland. I rushed out to buy the album on release day. I was living in Wimbledon in South London at the time and bought it in Goodness Records up on Wimbledon Bridge. It cost me one pound, twelve shillings and sixpence – about one sixth of my weekly wage.

I took the day off work and used the artificially engineered long weekend to get better acquainted with the songs. I loved them, particularly 'Here Comes The Sun', 'Something' and the section on side two The Beatles had been referring to as "The Long One" during the recording sessions. The album very quickly became a good friend.

The sleeve too was a classic. The Beatles had cheekily (intentionally) omitted their name from the *Rubber Soul* and *Revolver* albums sleeves, which in itself was a major first! But to have neither the title nor the name of the band on the front of the album, well... as Mud Flanagan would say, that was just totally habben-flabben.

I guess the iconic image of the four Beatles walking over the zebra crossing, which bridged the footpaths of Abbey Road, needs little comment. But the shot on the reverse of the sleeve – with an Abbey Road street-sign, tiled into the dirty-cream, brick-wall – was also a fascinating picture. The mysterious girl in a blue mini-skirt rushing through the shot stole the limelight for me. The movement of the girl, obscuring part of the NW8 tiles in the wall, gave the scene life: I felt I was there, outside the studio. I wondered about that girl. Was she a plant? Or did she just happen to be passing at the moment Iain Macmillian pressed the shutter release button? Was she rushing to work, or back to meet her partner? Did she immediately turn left into Alexandra Road? Did she live there? I was intrigued as to what her story might be.

At that time, as a trainee civil engineer, I was practised at using Letraset sheets of lettering: I thought it was a classy way of transferring various fonts onto drawings or plans. Over that first weekend, and without thinking a lot about it, I added the first ever graffiti to the wall outside the Abbey Road studios:

Paul

L

Ann

Of course I'm talking about the *Abbey Road* album sleeve. I used white Letraset letters, placing them at an angle – and to make it even more realistic I used only the left-hand side of the "L" of Paul and the second "N" of Ann, so that it appeared as if the girl in the blue mini-skirt was blocking out part of those letters.

My theory: that was how the graffiti started to appear on the walls outside Abbey Road Studios, or EMI Recording Studios as they were then.

About four or five years later I was sharing a flat with the other members of Fruupp in Peckham, South London. In the very early hours of one morning we returned wearily from a gig only to discover the flat had been broken into – and most of my vinyl albums and lots of my books had been stolen. Amongst the precious items that had been nicked was my unique copy of the *Abbey Road* album with my personalised "Paul L Ann" graffiti.

So I just wanted to say that if you're ever searching for your own golden fleece and come across a fifty year-old copy of *Abbey Road* please flip it over to the back and if you see white Letraset lettering with the legend:

Pau

L

An

with the missing "L" and "N" disappearing behind the leg of the girl in

CHAPTER TWENTY-EIGHT

NORTH AND SOUTH

From my Wimbledon days, when I could only afford a rare few albums, the ones I did purchase became positively totemic. I'd play them endlessly. One such album was titled *The New Humblebums*. The Humblebums were a Scottish folk rock outfit that started with two members, added one to become three and then lost an original member. Which isn't as complicated as it might sound.

Released in September 1969, a great year altogether for albums, *The New Humblebums* was their second LP and featured Billy Connolly and Gerry Rafferty. The album was so titled, because Gerry had replaced Tam Harvey after the first Humblebums album on Transatlantic Records. On paper Billy and Gerry were a weird combination, on stage they were even weirder – but on record it worked big time, mainly down to Gerry's beautiful voice and his evident Beatle influences. I loved the album so much that my mind automatically went to the intro of the next song as the current one was fading. "I'm humble and he's a bum," is how Billy Connolly would introduce the duo as he and Gerry walked on stage. Billy was a wannabe comedian then, who matured into the comedian every comedian wanted to be. Gerry could give Paul McCartney a run of his money in delivering beautiful melodies and first class lyrics.

'Her Father Didn't Like Me Anyway' is such a beautiful, flawlessly written song.

> "*The coat she wore still lies upon the bed*
> *The book I gave her that she never read*

She left without a single word to say
Her father didn't like me anyway..."

This is just the first four lines and already he's broken your heart. Or mine at least. And the film – sorry, song – only gets sadder and more intense from there on. I mean, come on, "The coat she wore still lies upon the bed." He's got you hooked in those first nine words. Why did she leave? And why so hastily that she left her coat and book behind? What might he have done that inspired her to leave? As the lyric progresses you realise that he didn't do anything wrong at all. If "Daddy" had only spent some time talking to him, then none of this might have happened.

I've been listening to the song since 1969 and it still hits the mark every time. Maybe it's become a bit more poignant again since Gerry passed away early in 2011, but it is a song I always loved. The Humblebums disbanded not long after the album was released, because, in Gerry's words, "Billy's introductions were getting longer and funnier and it got to the point that there was no time left in the set for songs." But they remained good friends until Gerry's death.

Gerry's first solo album, released in 1971 was called, *Can I Have My Money Back*. It was another fine collection of Beatles-influenced songs, spiced with his dry sense of humour. He hit the bull's-eye with another classic, 'Mary Skeffington'. Mary goes into her young son's room in the middle of every Saturday night, wakes him up, dresses him warmly and takes him out to walk the streets, before her abusive husband, father of the young boy, returns from the pub. Mother and son continue to walk the streets until the mother is convinced her husband will have fallen asleep in a drunken stupor and so she will have thereby successfully saved her son from abuse. Gerry's mother's maiden name was Skeffington; her Christian name was Mary; and so the song is autobiographical. It was Gerry and his mother Mary, who used to walk the streets of Paisley on a Saturday night.

I first met Gerry Rafferty in 1980. He was touring on the back of the success of 'Baker Street' and the *City to City* album – and I promoted his concerts on the island of Ireland. I found him to be painfully shy – but when you got to know him you'd discover how funny and warm he really was. I got to know him relatively quickly because I got on well with Hugh

Murphy, his record producer, live sound-engineer and best mate. Hugh was a good man. A short time after that tour Hugh set up a meeting between Gerry, himself and myself and Gerry announced he had decided he wanted Asgard to be his agents and promoters. We were with him all the way, right up to the very end.

We'd meet up regularly at the Montcalm Hotel, London, around the back of Marble Arch, or they'd come around to my flat in West Hampstead, a.k.a. East Kilburn, a dozen steps, a skip and a spit from the National Ballroom. We were always talking about dates, tours and concerts. He didn't do very many shows, but he and Hugh always took such great care in putting together wonderful large expensive bands, featuring great musicians. Gerry liked to avoid the bigger venues: he wasn't interested in anything over 2,000 capacity. He was happy to do multiple nights rather than move up to arenas. He always needed to do multiple nights in Ireland. But he wasn't really doing the shows to make money. Sometimes in this business you come across artists who work on the principle that making music is more important than selling it. Gerry Rafferty was one. If you play 2,000 seaters with a big band of top, expensive players and the quality of sound and lights Gerry preferred, well there wouldn't ever be a lot of change left.

Gerry enjoyed the process of putting the band together, the rehearsals, and the comradery of being on the road with his "fellow travellers." The concerts achieved a kind of perfection. You'd close your eyes and it felt like you were listening to Gerry's records on a top Hi Fi system. His vocals never faltered, they were always spot-on. So were the band. So it didn't surprise me that he sold out every single show he did.

Gerry and Hugh were brilliant company. We might start off talking about concerts, but we always ended up playing records. Gerry was a lot like Van Morrison in that he had an encyclopedic knowledge of contemporary music. He and Hugh also loved The Beatles as much as I did. I've always felt that a good yardstick by which to gauge any artist was to find out how big a fan they are of other artists! Gerry was a scholar of the recording process. When he could see you were enjoying a record as much as he was, he'd ask for it to be played again and explain why he thought it was brilliant. He'd declare, sometimes close to tears, how the simplicity of a Beatles song was unbelievable. "'Here There and Everywhere'," he'd explain, "that's just three voices, a guitar and the occasional quiet push from minimal drums."

I swear, he knew every breath they had taken. Gerry would, over the next few years, record a complete album of Beatles covers. Sadly I could never persuade him to release it. "We have to wait until the time is right, Paul," he'd declare. To be honest, I don't think he ever planned to release what was a kind of pet project. Gerry was one of those artists who did not need the confirmation of record sales, or chart positions or box office returns, to prove his worth. He was a true jobbing artist. He felt he was put on this earth to make music, to write it and play it. And that was exactly what he did. How many copies he sold or how much it made was never his priority. I've heard a couple of Gerry's Beatles tracks and they were unbelievably brilliant. His version of 'Because', in particular, was stunning. Gerry had done all the voices and played all the instruments himself.

Gerry and Hugh had treasures in the vaults. Gerry was always writing and recording. Hugh would give me regular reports on their sessions and Gerry was clearly a working man in his prime and at the top of his game. Even the demos they made of Gerry's new songs were equivalent to most people's masters.

They had pretty much worked everything out in the demoing process. Their painstaking approach to making demos came in handy for Gerry when the session-player they hired to play the alto saxophone riff on 'Baker Street' claimed, out of the blue, that he had written the part he played. Gerry produced the original demo for 'Baker Street' which clearly displayed Gerry playing the line in question on guitar. Of course, 'Baker Street' and the riff in question were at the top of quite a few car-manufacturers shopping lists for music for their TV adverts. But Gerry point blank refused to allow any of his music to be used for any adverts, on occasion turning down the massive amounts of money that were being offered.

From what I know of Gerry and Hugh's approach to recording sessions there must be at least a dozen unreleased Gerry Rafferty records waiting to see the light of day. Whenever I meet up with Russell Roberts, Gerry's solicitor, I keep hoping he's going to have one of these gems up his sleeve with my name on it.

he wasn't up for it, and so he happily returned to the studio again with Hugh at the end of the *North and South* campaign.

I liked Hugh Murphy a lot. He was very genuine – an honorable gentleman who was never scared of hard work. We worked together on numerous artists. I got him in to produce Paul Brady's *Hard Station* album; I introduced him to Van Morrison and Hugh ended up working on Van's critically acclaimed *Beautiful Vision* and co-wrote three songs on the record, 'Across The Bridge Where Angels Dwell', 'Aryan Mist' and 'Dweller On The Threshold'.

Hugh also did a demo session for me with an 18 year old girl from Basingstoke... but more on her later. Suffice to say that, in all of Hugh's work, he was a top notch producer and much, much more besides.

Sadly, Hugh Murphy passed away in 1988, after he lost his fight with cancer. I don't think Gerry really got over Hugh's passing; they had worked together and been best friends for over thirty years.

He may not always have relished touring, but Gerry Rafferty loved to travel. He is quoted as saying that a certain album had cost him £200,000 to deliver. £100,000 of that went on travel, £75,000 on equipment, which didn't leave a lot for making the record.

During the last few years of his life, Gerry would ring me out of the blue from somewhere exotic on his travels. On one occasion, he said he was thinking of doing some shows and asked if I could get him on to the Glastonbury Festival. I assured him Michael Eavis would love to see him at Glastonbury. He said he wanted to tie in a Glastonbury show with an appearance at the Celtic Connections Festival, Glasgow. Celtic Connections annually put in a request for a Gerry Rafferty appearance. Gerry liked the fact that both locations started off with GLAS. He suggested we could maybe do a few other concerts around the same time. Glastonbury to Glasgow routing is known in the agency world as a dart board tour. Wherever the dart you throw at a map lands, the agent sticks in a show. With Gerry, I didn't dwell on the distance between locations. Artists have been known to travel halfway around the world for the chance to play at Glastonbury. But I did explain to him it might be a wee bit difficult as Glastonbury is always the last full weekend of June and Celtic Connections is the last two weeks of January. "Oh they're merely details

Paul, I'm sure you can work all that out for us," he said. We had a few more conversations about it, but in the end he decided to leave it till later.

Sadly, very sadly, the man who gave the world,
'Your Father Didn't Like Me Anyway'
'Look Over The Hill and Far Away'
'Patrick'
'Please Sing a Song For Us'
'Mary Skeffington'
'Can I have My Money Back',
'To Each and Everyone'
'Get It Right Next Time'
'Whatever's Written In Your Heart'
'Stuck in The Middle With You'
'Baker Street'
'Take The Money And Run'
'Shipyard Town'
'Moonlight and Gold'
'On A Night Like This'
'Don't Give Up On Me'

had run out of road – and of years – in 2011.

The last time I spoke to Gerry Rafferty, he had just flown up to Scotland in a charter plane – and he rang to tell me that he'd gone up to surprise his mate, John Patrick Byrne. John had been the mastermind behind The New Humblebums artwork and was also the subject of a Gerry Rafferty song, 'Patrick', as well as the writer of 'Tutti Frutti' and *so* much more. Gerry had forgotten to bring his address book with him and wanted me to track Mr Byrne down. I was busy working on it when he rang back a few minutes later to say it was okay, he'd just bumped into someone at the airport who knew Patrick and he was about to head over to see him. "Don't tell him, I'm coming," he whispered. "I want to surprise him." In those few seconds, I was convinced we were experiencing the genesis of a new Gerry Rafferty song.

Sadly, not one that time allowed.

Fruupp

Jackson Browne & David Lindley

Eric Bibb

Kendrick Lamar

Little Village 1992

Ronnie Spector by Debra Greenfield

Nanci Griffith

The Communards

Van Morrison

Mary Coughlan, 1992

Mary Margaret O'Hara by Don Rooke

The Notting Hillbillies: Guy Fletcher, Mark Knopfler, Steve Phillips and Brendan Croker
February 1990

The Kinks

Nick Lowe   Kate and Anna McGarrigle

Tom Waits

CHAPTER TWENTY-NINE

WHAT HAVE YOU GOT TOULOUSE?

As a promoter you barely get to meet the artists. You meet and work with all their representatives. As an agent I always make a point of introducing my artists to the promoter, usually with a "this is our promoter for the evening." The only exception would be at a show where Harvey Goldsmith was the promoter, for no other reason than that Harvey usually drapes himself all over the artists from the moment they arrive in the building. He's attempting to "bond" with the artist, trying to make an invaluable direct connection. I'm not saying he is entirely alone: some promoters do try to develop relationships with the artists. I guess the hope is that it might help them to secure a better deal or if – next time around – the agent feels the need to use a different promoter, they might be able to lodge an appeal and cry about how much money they lost on the previous tour.

Sometimes promoters have been known to make a pitch to the manager and/or artist directly, claiming, "Look I can save you 10% of your fee if we do the deal and cut out the agent." There is a very important distinction to be made here: the more an agent gets, the more the artist receives, whereas the more the promoter gets the less the artist (and agent) makes. I always caution the artist/manager with Parable No 666: "For it is written, beware of a man bearing a larger slice of a smaller pie."

****

On the first tour I did with Crosby, Stills and Nash, I went to visit them at Wembley Arena and the tour manager said, "Come on back and meet the boys." I said, 'It's okay; I'll wait until after the show." I've always felt the period before an artist goes on stage to be a hallowed, protected space. Acts approach it in different ways. Some artists will want to send for their brown trousers. Others will hang out in the catering room with their crew. Status Quo will get out their sleeping bags and, as a band, have a wee nap on the dressing room floor.

Christy Moore and his musicians play a few tunes together. Robert Plant irons his white T-Shirt. Don McLean retreats to the peace and quiet of his dressing room and doesn't like to be disturbed. In this time of social networking, some artists, like Jean Michel Jarre, will be working the web literally right up until the second he's about to hit the stage. Joan Baez gathers everyone involved around in a hand-holding circle and wishes everyone a great show. Paul Brady – a contender keen to be a champ – pounds the dressing room floor like Anthony Joshua, hammering – or rather sparring – away with his guitar. Mike Scott enjoys a computer link-up with his kids. Lucinda Williams complains about the pre-show music her sound man is playing on the PA system. Jackson Browne will get into a vibing huddle with the members of his band, crescendoing into a joint reaching for the sky moment. John Cooper Clarke, a real living legend, nips outside the venue for a last-minute ciggy.

Famously when he was playing Sheffield, Octagon, JCC along with mate Richard Hawley, nipped out for a ciggy – the big problem was the house lights had already gone down and they were locked out and couldn't get back into the venue again to get on stage... well, eventually he did. It was very funny at the time but not if you were the promoter, Stuart Basford.

Ray Davies usually wanders around the backstage area very relaxed and talkative. Some artists take that even further, going out of their way not to have any predetermined ritual, as a way to avoid being nervous, but, thereby – in some cases I've seen at least – making themselves even more nervous by the pre-show ritual of not having a pre-show ritual. Some are like warriors pumping themselves up as they prepare to do battle. Tanita Tikaram was always very nervous. James Brown had his hair in curlers. Blues artist Buddy Guy starts off his shows at a tempo, pace and energy most artists finish at. I often wondered what he did to psyche himself

have to be careful picking the promoters you work with and the fees you charge. And fair. There will always be promoters who'll pay anything you ask and sometimes even more, because they are attempting to get into the business or are desperate to get a particular artist. It'd shock you the number of people I've met who feel that promoting concerts is a bit of a bank raid. They go to a concert, or even a festival and think – wow, that isn't hard. I could do that. "Look," they'll say to you, "There must have been 3,000 people in the venue and that's what, £50 a ticket and so that's £150,000 at the box-office. So what would the Blues by Five cost me? Even if I pay them £50,000 that still leaves me £100,000. Ker-ching! Money for old rope. I'll have a bit of that!"

Then you'll patiently tell them that the venue they are talking about only has a capacity of 1,000 and in fact the ticket price couldn't be over £18.50 and after VAT, ticket commission, venue hire, equipment hire, advertising, social media crew, stage crew, security and catering, there'd probably only be a few grand to play with. They'll come back with, "That's simple, we'll just put them in a bigger venue. We've got the money; we'll pay you in advance. There'll be a pony in it for you."

We've never worked that way. Chuck Berry always seemed to go to the highest bidder, irrespective of the promoter or the event. Perhaps that's one of the reasons his shows (behind the scenes) appeared to be such train-wrecks, with disputes over fees, taxes, backup band, equipment, set lengths and so on and on.

They say the devil always arrives with the biggest cheques. Maybe there's a bit of truth in that. Either way, the point is that we really do need the good promoters to stay in business, which is why we need to be fair. But being fair doesn't mean that you cut the fee for an act worth $250,000 to $225,000 at the drop of a hat.

How good are CSN? For me, 'Suite: Judy Blue Eyes' is a marvellous slice of modern music, classical in its own way, and the perfect piece to display their collective talents. The blend of the voices is sometimes so tight you believe you can hear a separate distinctive voice. Theirs is easily the best combination of voices since George, John and Paul. On CSN's special nights, when the stars are aligned, the room is full and the sound is with you, CSN performing 'Suite: Judy Blue Eyes' can make you believe you are in heaven.

Another stand-out, show-stopping, live song is 'Helplessly Hoping', also from their near-to-flawless first album. Yes of course there's great music on the rest of their albums – and on their second album *Déjà Vu*, there is a career high song 'Carry On'. Plus, 'Teach Your Children', the anthem for the Woodstock generation (musicians and fans). But, to my ears, they never bettered that astonishing debut. This may have been because there was no pressure on them, and no expectations. No one was looking over Stephen Stills' shoulder as he built the layers of music which formed the backing tracks, playing most of the instruments himself, and all the while creating the foundation for their wonderful voices. They weren't even a real group at that point. And yes Crosby's *If Only I Could Remember My Name*, Stephen Stills' self-titled debut and Graham Nash's *Songs For Beginners*, were all albums of real substance– but as a unit, they never bettered, *Crosby Stills & Nash*.

On one European tour, I was with the band for most of the shows. We were all worried about David Crosby. Bill Siddons and myself felt we needed to be near at hand, in case of any "emergencies." It was the first tour I encountered that had a gentleman on the road who acted as what was called an Ambience Director. This character was like the advance party: he would hit the tour stops the day before the show to ensure *ambience* was available when the tour hit the town. The three principals traveled in 3 separate tour buses. On one particular night, Stephen Stills' bus was either still in the last town or had gone on to the next. I was traveling on Graham's bus and we pulled into a service station off the autobahn, on a T&CF (toilet & comfort food) pit-stop. Crosby's bus pulled up behind us.

Don't get me wrong here. Crosby was always well behaved on stage: two roadies would lead him to his mic and he'd stand there and sing as sweet as a bird all night until the two roadies came back to lead him off the stage again at the end of the show. But it was broad daylight when he waddled off the bus, carrying a bowl (more like a basin), full of sweet red cherries bobbing up and down in water, eating them one after the other as he walked. But that wasn't the strange part. The strange part was that he didn't have a stitch of clothing on: he was butt-naked as the day he was born and carrying his bowl of cherries in a strategic, embarrassment-saving position. Luckily enough one of the roadies came after him and led him back onto his bus before an international incident occurred.

On midsummer's day 1983, shortly after the cherry-eating incident, the tour pulled into Toulouse, the French red brick city. That night, during 'Suite: Judy Blue Eyes', Stephen Stills – pleading with his one-time paramour Judy Collins to come back – does his best to persuade her with the line "*What have you got to lose?*" The first time the band sang it, it was perfect, spot on, and there were calls of recognition from some sections of the audience. The second time – with Stills singing it by himself – the audience missed it. But the third time they sang the line, "*I'm going to fly away, What have I got to lose,*" the Toulouse audience got it big time. A massive shout went up and then the band understood. The fourth time – Stills is getting desperate for Judy's attention pleading for, "*Thursdays and Saturdays, What have you got to lose,*" the audience and the band lifted the roof off in a special shared moment.

Sometimes, the real magic happens entirely by accident.

CHAPTER THIRTY

THE MYSTERY OF THE SECOND BEST SELLING BAND IN THE WORLD

At one point in the late 1960s the best-selling group in the entire world – with the possible exception of The Beatles – was a group no fan ever screamed at. There were no known photographs. No one ever sought their autographs. No one knew their favourite food, drink, actor, actress, movie nor even the clothes they liked. In fact, no fan was even aware of their existence. For good reason: the record companies didn't want anyone to know, especially the fans. The identity of this collective was the record companies biggest, and their most carefully guarded, secret. Were anyone outside the hallowed corridors of the Capitol Records circular building in LA, CBS's Blackrock skyscraper in NYC, Warner's rambling, timber-based, hillside enclave on the edge of their California movie lot, and the like, to discover the secret, it could potentially have killed the careers of some of the biggest groups in the industry and totally reshaped the landscape of the music business as we know it today.

If I dropped the names Hal Blaine, Carol Kaye, Tommy Tedesco, Al De Lory and Larry Knechtel into a conversation, one would be forgiven for mistaking them for a bunch of lawyers.

However if I mentioned (in no particular order)...

'He's A Rebel'

'Surfin' USA'

'Da Doo Ron Ron'

'Be My Baby'

'I Get Around'

'Everybody Loves Somebody'
'You've Lost That Loving Feeling'
'Help Me Rhonda'
'Mr. Tambourine Man'
'California Dreamin''
'Eve of Destruction'
'I Got You Babe'
'Good Vibrations'
'Monday Monday'
'River Deep Mountain High'
'I Am A Rock'
'Strangers in The Night'
'These Boots Were Made for Walking'
'Never My Love'
'Up Up And Away'
'San Francisco (be sure to wear some flowers in your hair)'
'The Beat Goes On'
'Wichita Lineman'
'MacArthur Park'
'Mrs Robinson'
'Young Girl'
'Classical Gas'
'Galveston'
'Holly Holy'
'Let The Sunshine In (Aquarius)'
'The Boxer'
'(They Long to Be) Close To You'
'Cracklin' Rose'
'I Think I Love You'
'Bridge Over Troubled Water'
'Rainy Days and Mondays'
'It Never Rains in Southern California'
'Yesterday Once More'
'The Night The Lights Went Out In Georgia'
'The Way We Were'

'Rhinestone Cowboy'
'Love will keep Us Together'
'I'm Not Going to Miss You'
'Half Breed'
'Dizzy'
'Indian Reservation'
'Young Girl'
'Surf City'
'This Diamond Ring'...

there would be a warm wave of instant recognition.

The recording session for each and every one of the above 50 classic singles centred around the house band, a.k.a. The First Call Gang, a.k.a. The Phil Spector Wall of Sound Orchestra, but mostly known around the LA recording studios as the legendary Wrecking Crew. The not-so-Motley Crew featured, amongst others, Carol Kaye, on bass and lead guitar, Hal Blaine on drums, Tommy Tedsco on guitar, Al de Lory on keyboards and Larry Knechtel (later a member of Bread) on keyboards. They were frequently joined by future recording stars in their own right, Leon Russell, on keyboards, and Glen Campbell on guitars. The Wrecking Crew were also on occasion part of a much larger ensemble. It's well known for instance that, in search of the Wall of Sound he was forever hearing in his head, Phil Spector loved to absolutely pack the studio to overflowing in an attempt to fulfill his dream sound.

None of these musicians were shrinking violets. It was just that they didn't want to become road warriors, trying to retain a personal life as they endeavoured to make ends meet by touring. This group of musicians by far preferred to work for a dollar in the studios. .

The centre disc and sleeve on many a record may have proclaimed the names of acts like...

Jan and Dean
Sonny & Cher
The Mamas & The Papas
The Beach Boys

CHAPTER THIRTY-ONE

HOW LUCKY TO BE IN THE PIED PIPER'S NEIGHBOURHOOD

One of the biggest advantages of being an agent – and representing the artists I am lucky enough to represent – is the trips I get to make to NYC and LA, and a few points in between, to take care of business. That might mean meeting American artists who I already represent (or their representatives); meeting American artists I don't represent but would like to; or meeting American agents who look after some of our European based artists in America.

For my LA trips, I had a routine down to a fine art, where I would drop my bags off at the hotel, usually the Hyatt Hotel (aka the Riot House) on Sunset Boulevard in West Hollywood. I'd then walk back up to where Holloway Drive (where Marilyn Monroe shared an apartment with Shelley Winters in 1951) intersects with Sunset Blvd, to one of my favourite bookstores, Book Soup.

It was a bit of a walk but my head would still be regularly rotating through 360 degrees as I took in all the signs, sights, sounds and scents of the place I'd been dreaming about since I was barely a teenager, watching *77 Sunset Strip* on TV. The intro – with Kookie combing his hair for the first of many times that evening – was filmed at 8524 Sunset Boulevard, which was on my walking route. Kookie was played by Edd Byrnes, who had a million-selling, No 4 hit single in the *Billboard* Top 100 with, 'Kookie, Kookie, Lend me Your Comb'. The fictional *77 Sunset Strip* was in fact 8524 Sunset Boulevard, the one time entrance to the famous Dino's Lodge. Dino's – as in Dean Martin – was where all the real stars of the day used to flock. The other good reason for my brisk walk in the American fresh air was that I always found it a very effective way to fend off any tedious, time-wasting, jet lag. West Coast air smells totally different to European air. I always put it down to the fact that even when it's dry in England and Ireland there are still tiny droplets of damp evident in the air, whereas in Hollywood where the sun always shines, it is essentially damp-free.

Tower Records used to be located directly opposite Book Soup. On my walk up to Holloway and Sunset, I'd always ponder which of those two stores to visit first. It mostly depended on which new albums or books I was hoping to find. Tower Records usually won. American album releases would often be months ahead of the UK.

1982. I was just in the door of Tower Records, when I noticed a display for *One From The Heart* album – a soundtrack album recorded by Tom Waits and Crystal Gayle. I was a big fan of Tom Waits. I had tried over the years to forge a connection with him, to make a pitch to become his agent. Unfortunately, for me, the people I contacted – lawyers, managers, record company staff – became ex-lawyers, ex-managers and ex-record company staff and so the trail went cold. Nonetheless I tried to make *One From The Heart*, the first album purchase of that trip. I searched in the Tom Waits section, the Crystal Gayle section, the soundtrack section, the new releases section. Nothing doing.

I approached one of the assistants and asked her, "Do you have any copies of the new Tom Waits' album?"

"Sorry we're all sold out," she announced proudly. A fan I guessed. She leaned across the counter and dropped to a conspiratorial whisper as she continued. "And you'll never guess who I sold the last copy to. Don't look now as he's right behind you, but it's Tom Waits with his wife."

I'm afraid I couldn't help myself. I did, look, and there, just one aisle over, were Tom Waits and his wife Kathleen Brennan.

Sometimes in this life you have one chance and I wasn't about to pass this one up.

I walked over, apologised for my intrusion, and introduced myself. Luckily enough they had heard of my attempts to make contact and so we retired to a local café and several cups of tea and a few hours later, I became their agent. And I have remained so for forty years now. Working with Tom and Kathleen has been one of the joys of my life.

I was soon to learn that with Tom Waits you were expected to do more than just book or promote the concerts. It was, quite literally, all hands on deck to get the show on the road. On the first tour I booked in 1985, the opening night was in Edinburgh Playhouse on Monday 18 October. I met Tom at Edinburgh Airport on the production day and took him straight to the venue. En route, we took a pit stop in a café for a quick cup of tea, to allow Tom a chance to catch his breath before heading for the stage door, which is at the end of a ridiculously long, steep and deep, external staircase.

I soon sussed out the chores Tom had earmarked for me. At one point, during the show, Tom wanted "rain" to fall from the overhead lighting truss. At another, he wanted a light placed in the inside crown of his top hat so that when he lifted his hat slightly from the top of his head a bright light would shine back down over his head. And my final trick was that when Tom walked over and opened the door of a tall fridge standing on the stage, a massive column of light would engulf him and spill directly into the audience. Of course you know that if I disclose the secrets of the above three tricks I would be thrown out of The Magic Circle. This would prove difficult as I'd never been in The Magic Circle in the first place. But better to be safe than to be sorry, and say that I really did manage to produce the required rain; and the bright light shone forth from the fridge. The third illusion, the light from within the top hat, took a lot of time and a few scalded skulls to perfect.

Tom Waits was originally marketed by Asylum Records as a singer-songwriter. And, yes, he most certainly is a singer and a songwriter. But he wasn't part of the singer-songwriter genre at all. No disrespect to those who are: that's where my musical preferences lie. But Tom Waits uses a completely different pallet of colours for his songs. He also actually lives in them – and this is nowhere more apparent than in his live performances.

For that first tour we booked 32 concerts taking in 9 countries in six weeks. We promoted the show in Edinburgh as well as eight nights in The Dominion Theatre, London. The tickets sold out in jig time – he could literally have sold out a month in London – and the reaction to his performances was nothing short of extraordinary. It was a musical and visual experience the likes of which had never been witnessed before.

Kathleen is, of course, Irish. She was born in Cork in 1955, before her family moved to Johnsburg, in Illinois, where she grew up, close to the Great Lakes, in the Chicago Metropolitan area. 'Johnsburg, Illinois' is the title of a song – on Tom's *Swordfishtrombones* (1982) album – which is a beautiful love letter to Kathleen. She began collaborating with Tom officially with a co-writing credit on 'Hang Down Your Head' on *Rain Dogs*, in 1985. Since then, she has collaborated with Tom at every stage, both as a songwriter and producer, becoming completely integral to the Waits-ian artistic process.

In 2004, Catherine and I landed in San Francisco International Airport. Tom and Kathleen drove to meet us, at a village halfway between their place and where we were staying, for dinner. Afterwards, we hopped into their car, which was parked behind the restaurant, and sat there for a couple of glorious hours while they played us Tom's forthcoming album, *Real Gone*, from beginning to end. Listening to the album in that way, on what was a gorgeous California evening, enjoying the new music they'd recently created, was the kind of once-in-a-lifetime special treat that it would have been utterly impossible for the boy from Magherafelt to even begin to imagine when he first set off for London.

****

The demand for tickets to see Tom Waits live has never waned for two main reasons. One: a Tom Waits gig really is the show to end all shows; and two: he tours so rarely. Preparing for the 2008 tour I had a long series of chats with Tom about returning to London. We had agreed to pencil in four nights at Hammersmith Odeon as the conclusion and climax of the tour. Timing-wise it just didn't work out. Tom and Kathleen, Casey Waits, one of my favourite drummers, Sullivan Waits, who made his debut during the tour playing saxophone and crew member Kellesimone Waits (it *really* was a family affair) had to return to America a few days earlier. We discussed whether to leave London till another time, or to do the one night in Hammersmith that their schedule permitted. I felt he should do the one night. Tom voiced a genuine concern that he wasn't sure how many tickets he could sell in London.

I laughed.

He laughed back at me, saying, "So you think we could sell more."

"A lot more," I suggested.

"Two nights?"

"More," I countered.

"Four nights?"

"More,"

"Ah come on," he rasped, "do you think we could do a week?"

"More, much more," I continued.

He didn't believe it. "So how long do you think we could do at Hammersmith?"

"I think you could sell out at least a month in Hammersmith," I replied.

I think he might have suggested that perhaps I should consider going on stage myself, with a comedy routine like that.

Two weeks later, I rang him for our nightly chat and advised him that the tickets for one night in Hammersmith had sold out in record time. I also told him that in the first hour the box office was open, they had an additional 150,000 requests for tickets, another box office record.

"Hmmm, that's just over the month you predicted," he said.

I didn't bother to mention that each of the 150,000 requests was for two tickets, which would have meant more like a two month run.

Promoters are passionate about working with Tom: they're ecstatic if they secure the show, moody in the extreme if they don't. A Dublin promoter fell out with me due to the fact that he didn't promote Tom's shows in Dublin on the 2008 tour. He hasn't spoken to me since. Irish audiences have always been big into Tom Waits.

On one of his early visits, he appeared on *The Late Late Show*, the biggest show on the national channel RTÉ. When the then-host, Gay Byrne, walked over to Tom at the piano, for a quick chat between songs, he asked Tom how he was doing. Tom, quick as a flash, in that beautiful craggy voice of his, said, "Oh, I'm alright, the piano might have had a few drinks before the show, though." He was, of course, referencing one of his own lyrics. The Irish nation, already massive fans, took him into their collective hearts from that point onwards. I suspect that Tom might be even bigger than Garth Brooks in Ireland.

It was very high on both Tom and Kathleen's wish-list to do Irish shows, and they relied on me to come up with something. Tom has very strict rules on where he performs. He mostly prefers proscenium arch, theatre-type venues. He rarely plays outdoor shows. He's been offered everything under the sun, the moon and the stars, but he's very protective of the relationship he enjoys with his fans and goes out of his way to honour that relationship in how his concerts are presented. Michael Eavis has been trying unsuccessfully to book Tom for Glastonbury for years.

One day, I was having one of my regular chats with Peter Aiken – the son of Gentleman Jim Aiken, who single-handedly invented the wheel that is the Irish live music business. In my early days Jim was very kind to me and a treasured mentor, always very generous about sharing his knowledge. Jim was one of those rare promoters who you knew would always give your artist the same Rolls Royce treatment if there were 100 people or 100,000 people in the venue. Sadly, Jim is no longer with us, but Peter has very successfully taken over the reins of Aiken Promotions and brought it to another level.

The previous year, I'd been to see Christy Moore play one of Peter's Live at The Marquee gigs in Cork. Christy has played a concert there every year now for a decade, successfully creating a situation where people are going to the Christy night at The Marquee, not only to see and hear Christy, but to be part of the occasion – something which usually only happens at Gospel shows. The night I was there, the tent was full, and the atmosphere was like an amped-up revivalist meeting.

I brought the idea up with Peter. "If only we could find something in Dublin like The Marquee in Cork, that might work for Tom."

"Leave it with me, Paul," Peter said, proving he had an identical, 'don't make a fuss, make a solution,' of his father.

The following day, Peter rang to let me know that he had booked the Cork Marquee for the days we needed. Not only that, but he had also secured Phoenix Park, which is also home to the President's house Áras an Úachtaráin, and the US ambassador's residence, to pitch The Marquee. Peter had his art people do mock-ups of the venue and surrounding area,

the reaction from the audience to Tom's performance was a bit like that phenomenon in reverse, spreading the awe.

By the time he reached 'Come On Up to The House', his pleading style of singing was so heartfelt and emotional, I had the feeling that every member of the audience was going to take him up on the invitation, and follow him, Kathleen and Casey back up to the Waits' house.

A lot like the Pied Piper, in fact.

Tom is that kind of artist, who inspires a very intense feeling of devotion, as if the people watching are like the narrator in one of the many memorable songs from his 1974 album, *The Heart of a Saturday Night.* "*And I'm blinded by the neon,*" he sang then, "*Don't try and change my tune/ Cause I thought I heard a saxophone/ I'm drunk on the moon.*" We all were drunk that night, on what was Tom's only outdoor appearance.

But it didn't require any booze or stimulants. He led. We followed. It was Tom's live sorcery and the magic of the music that had us entranced.

CHAPTER THIRTY-TWO

AMERICAN PIES, DENTAL FIXATIONS & STRANGE SENSATIONS

I was always a big fan of Don McLean. I'd go and see him at least once, whenever he was in Europe, if I had a night off that coincided with a gig of his. I remember a particularly moving show he gave in Paris when just about everything seemed to fall into place. Don has such an amazing, soulful voice. It is also an exceptionally powerful one: I swear to you, if his PA system packed up one night, he would still be heard delivering every lyric in pitch-perfect style.

Some of the most finely written and beautifully nuanced songs of our generation have come from his pen and he sang them all that night, including 'American Pie', 'Vincent', 'And I Love You So', 'Castles in The Air' and 'Three Flights Up'. He also does show-stealing versions of the great Percy French song 'Mountains O' Mourne' and of Roy Orbison's 'Crying' – which receives a standing ovation at each and every show, and quite rightly so.

I noticed that Don had stopped visiting Europe during the early 1990s, so I contacted his registered agents in the USA. They weren't interested in any proposal, so I forgot about it for a while. Then, I noticed that Don was on the bill at an Irish festival, where we had also booked Jackson Browne. I was in America at the time of the festival and so I asked the promoter to pass on a message to Don that I'd like to speak to him about a possible tour. He rang me almost immediately. He was very friendly, approachable and very honest. He told me he came over to Europe only rarely because he felt there was no longer a demand for him. He was very nervous that he might not sell enough tickets. I told him I didn't believe that fans were so fickle and that, quoting the old adage, absence makes the heart grow fonder. I was very confident he could do a very substantial tour. Having agreed to it, he was shocked when I proposed The Royal Albert Hall for the London concert. It was one of his favourite venues, and also one of mine. When I first moved to London in 1967 I decided I would try to get a part time job as a steward at the Royal Albert Hall, so I could enjoy the venue and the music. I set up the interview, dusted down my suit and went to the hallowed hall only to be advised by the interviewer, before the interview had even started, that my hair was too long! I still get such a thrill from just sitting in places like the Royal Albert Hall and The London Palladium: it's a rush for me, even before the artists come on stage.

The 'comeback' tour went ahead and was a big success. We sold out the Royal Albert Hall on 26 October 2007 and he was graceful enough to thank Asgard from the stage. I noticed he had made an album titled *Addicted to Black*, but it was only available on his web site. I felt this sent out the wrong signal. Don didn't have a manager, so I secured him a deal with Proper Records to release the album in Europe.

A couple of tours later – this one took in Australia, mainland Europe, England and Ireland – Michael Eavis booked Don for the Sunday afternoon Legends Spot, on the Main Stage at Glastonbury. Don drew a massive crowd, young and old, and had over 100,000 fans singing along to 'American Pie', a wonderful moment. Don truly felt he was back in the big time. He showed how grateful he was to me and to Asgard by writing out a hand-written set of lyrics of 'American Pie'. It is currently in a bank vault.

Earlier in 2011, Don McLean had played the final gig of his stint in Australia and New Zealand in the Town Hall in Christchurch. On the way to the airport the following morning, Don felt drawn to the Cathedral. He didn't have much time to spare, but he had a morning walk around the Cathedral, returned to his car and continued his journey to the airport. At 12.51, a few minutes after his flight for Wellington took off, an earthquake that registered 6.2 on the RIchter scale shook Christchurch, destroying the spire of the Cathedral and part of the town, causing untold havoc and city-wide damage. One hundred and eighty-five souls lost their lives in the earthquake.

Over the next few years, there was a noticeable difference to the songs Don was writing. They all shared a new voice, big melodies, and wonderful lyrics. He had sent me demos of six of these songs. I felt they were strong enough to secure him a good record deal. BMG came on board and I acted as Executive Producer for the album – a grand title for someone who sets up a deal and organises the recording. The creative duties were left to producer Mike Severs, and a fine job he did too. It is still one of my favourites of all the projects I've ever undertaken, with the additional benefit that EMI decided to re-release the original Don McLean albums in their back catalogue.

Looking back now, I recall some of the great lines from his songs.

"*I was a lonely teenage broncin' buck,*" he sang in 'American Pie', the title track from one of those EMI records, "*With a pink carnation and a pickup truck/ But I knew I was out of luck/ The day the music died.*"

It is, of course, impossible to predict the strange twists and turns that life will take further on up the road...

****

One morning, I received a call from the original Galway girl, Fiona Commins. Fiona was an instantly friendly, no nonsense sort of character. She explained that she represented Jean Michel Jarre and EMI had recommended me as a good person to talk to, citing the success of our Don McLean tour campaign. Jean Michel had decided to take his Oxygene Show on the road, using all the original revolutionary instruments. Jean Michel was famous for his one-off events/installations where he would "dress" iconic locations (including the Pyramids, London Docklands, the Eiffel Tower and The State University of Moscow) in music and lights. On this occasion, however, he wanted to play small venues. Fiona wondered where Jean Michel should perform in London. I immediately suggested the Royal Albert Hall. She asked me if I could organise the concert, I said of course. I asked her where else Jean Michel would like to play. She had been planning to put the tour together herself, but I explained my role as an agent, what we did, and how much we charged. I convinced her that I could make her life a lot easier and everything was agreed in that first

15 minute telephone conversation. Now I had to put the shows together!

I went to work on what became the Oxygene 2008 tour, booking 40 shows in two legs and playing just about everywhere. JMJ and Fiona visited London in advance of the tour to check how to make the show work at the Royal Albert Hall. I'd frequently catch the Eurostar on a day trip to Paris for lunches and meetings with both of them. He was very charming, friendly, French and very easy to get on with. The Oxygene Tour sold out in advance. The shows were a phenomenal success. He was grossly underplaying each city, but on a high ticket price. The reaction from the fans was ecstatic.

In 2009 we did another 18 shows, stepping up from concert halls to arenas. JMJ changed the programme to more of a "Best-of Show," and the production values were elevated to another level. The lights and lasers and effects were stunning, a bit like David Copperfield meets E.T. This was part one of a multi-part arena tour. It was, surely, a great start to a relationship.

I got a call from Fiona later in December, while Catherine and I were on holiday, saying that they loved working with me BUT – the big but – another agent had been onto them and he was prepared to book Jean Michel Jarre for less commission than Asgard charged. HOWEVER – the big however – if I was prepared to reduce my commission they would stay with me because they loved me and I'd done a great job (she said).

I repeated my TCC address: "We charge all our clients the same commission. In fairness to all our clients, some of whom have been with us for thirty years, we never reduce our commission rate." She said she was sorry, JMJ was going to be doing a lot of touring over the next few years, but unless I would reduce our commission, JMJ was going to have to move to another agency.

"It's not always a good idea to use the cheapest dentist," I said, drawing a line under the matter and wished her well.

And that was that.

Or was it?

A few months later I was talking to top French promoter, Gerard Drouot. He told me that he'd met Jean Michel Jarre in Monte Carlo over the weekend and that he'd confessed that he had made a big mistake by leaving Asgard. The new agent seemed to be having trouble putting the tour together.

I said it's water under the bridge and we got on with our business – I believe it was discussing some CSN dates Gerard was putting together for me.

I thought nothing more about it – okay, okay, maybe I did gloat for a few seconds, but no more than that, I promise.

Later in the week I received a call from the man himself, Jean Michel Jarre. Major respect to him for having the small round things required to make the humble pie call himself.

"Le dentiste le moins cher n'était pas bon, je m'en excuse. Sorry Paul, I messed up," he apologised, remembering I didn't speak French, "it's all a mess. I don't have a tour. I just have eight dates, most of them in Germany."

I chose not to remind him that these were the same German shows I had booked for him before he left Asgard for the cheaper dentist. "What happened?' I asked.

"I don't know, no shows. Will you book my tour for me?'

"Of course Jean Michel," I replied. I had no wish to see anyone grovelling. He was very appreciative and my Eurostar day trips to Paris resumed. I got the feeling that there were a few people in the JMJ office who were not entirely happy at the outcome, but that was their problem not mine. I committed to getting JMJ at least 60 shows and in fact I secured 88 shows on that leg for him, including some high-paying outdoor shows. The tour's fifth and final leg concluded in Zurich at the AG Hallenstadion on 20 November 2011. Along the way, on 31 July 2010, JMJ did a spectacular event in Praza do Obradoiro in Santiago de Compostela, where he dressed the square in lights, sounds and fireworks to the delight of the huge audience that attended.

Jean Michel Jarre was an unusual act for me to work with, in that songs are generally so central to what I like and what I do. In fact, I always thought that JMJ could have made an amazing album if he brought the astounding Lisa Ekdahl in as guest vocalist on a few of the tracks. But he really went for it on stage every night. And he was never scared of hard work. I liked that. It was also a delight to witness how much joy his music was capable of spreading. I enjoyed working with him. Most of all, he was great company.

****

In 2002 I booked Robert Plant and his band Strange Sensation to headline The Acoustic Stage at Glastonbury. Backstage, Robert was very approachable. In fact he was so approachable that he did the approaching, popping his head through the Asgard production office door and politely asking for the ironing board as requested on his contract rider. He was about to disappear across the field with it when he asked if it would be possible to attend to his ironing chores on the spot. Apparently, it was his regular pre-gig ritual to iron a Daz-white t-shirt, each night prior to going on stage. I told him he was very welcome and so he started ironing. We began to chat. He asked about Asgard and about all the great acts we worked with. He was particularly interested in Sonny Terry & Brownie McGhee, Buddy Guy, Taj Mahal, John Lee Hooker and Nick Lowe, who he noted was on the bill that night as well.

"Everyone loves Nick Lowe," he offered as he expertly tackled the complicated maneuver around the short sleeves with the iron. In a free-flowing conversation, we rabbited away for ages. It reminded me of chats I had with my mother while she ironed. She felt that talking to someone, anyone – like her son for instance – would help the time spent ironing to pass more quickly, maybe even more pleasantly. I loved these sessions because my mum would tell me things about myself that I'd never otherwise have known – like, for instance, when as a kid I had asked her if I could wear my spectacles to bed just so I could see my dreams better.

Robert Plant talked away about music. He was absolutely consumed, obsessed even, by it. I don't think I have ever met anyone who knows his music so well. Van Morrison used to have a sax player called John Altman. He's now a world famous film composer and conductor. John not only knew the musicians present at the various famous recording sessions but he also knew the tape operator, and who made the tea and whether it was Typhoo or PG Tips. Maybe John – with his encyclopedic mind – knew a bit more, but I can tell you it was close. Anyway I very much enjoyed my first meeting with Robert Plant and he and his wonderful band of musicians, Strange Sensation, brought the proceedings to a brilliant close that evening.

I didn't think any more about it until several months later when Robert rang me up out of the blue and said, "I have a strange question for you, 'Do you, or your partner, have any plans to sell your company'?"

I said hello before answering, "We've always felt," I responded, "that whatever it might be worth to others, it would always be worth more to us. So, no, we don't have any plans to sell Asgard."

"Okay, good to know, so, in that case can I come and talk to you about representing me?"

Even if I had wanted to say no, and I didn't, I could never have said no to the man whose band, Led Zeppelin, had debuted 'Stairway To Heaven', one of the classics of the modern era, at the Ulster Hall in Belfast on 5 March 1971.

I figured that Robert might be one of a rising number of artists who were becoming concerned about the fact that the agency that represented them was owned by the same company who owned the promoter, some managers *and* some of the important venues on the circuit. You could totally understand why discerning artists might ask themselves: "But who exactly is representing my best interests in this equation?"

Robert explained that he was fiercely loyal to his current agent – they were very good friends – and that the conversation he was now having with me was awkward. We chatted about his plans, what he wanted to do. I didn't want to put him under any pressure, so I kept it loose saying we'd love to work with him, but we would totally understand if it couldn't happen.

He went away to think about it. A month passed. Then we had a cup of very sweet tea in the Moroccan café at the top of Parkway, in Camden Town, and chatted as we watched the world go by. We discussed our commission rates. He asked for a better deal. I advised him it just wasn't possible. He asked me why I wouldn't reduce my commission. I told him that it just wouldn't be fair to the artists I'd worked with for decades.

"But they'd never know, I wouldn't tell them," he said.

"But I would know," I replied.

I couldn't tell if he was upset or pleased with what I had to say, but either way we couldn't finalise a deal.

Another few months passed and then we bumped into each other on Regents Park Road as he was jumping into a cab. He shouted across that we needed to chat again and he would give me a call the following week.

He kept his word. He was getting ready to move, he said, and raised the commission issue again. Nothing had changed at Asgard. I told him what we charged and once again he replied that his current agent was doing it for less. He wanted me to go and discuss the matter with his manager, the renowned Bill Curbishley.

Bill fondly mentioned Robert's legendary tightness.

"If anyone wanted Robert distracted, all they'd need to do would be to put a 6-penny bit down in front of a Routemaster," is more or less how he actually put it.

It was a very pleasant, entertaining meeting. Bill is a wonderful raconteur. I could quite literally sit for days listening to Bill Curbishley. But the bottom line was Bill and I couldn't do a deal.

I met Robert months later on a Saturday morning in Primrose Hill by accident, "I need to come and see you again," he said. He kept his word and at that next meeting, Robert Plant confirmed that he had decided to move to Asgard. He asked me for a day's grace so that he could tell the current agent. The plan was that he would go and see the current agent in the morning, tell him the news and then come around to see me in the afternoon, so that we could start to make our plans. He rang me up after his morning meeting. Robert was quite distraught. The agent he had been working with was very upset and Robert said he, in turn, was so upset he wanted to delay our meeting until the following day. Robert claimed he was still going to come to Asgard.

I feared it wouldn't happen.

The next day however it was all confirmed and I started to work on booking a tour. It was in the summer of 2003. Robert was mega-keen about the other acts who were going to be on the various bills. You had the impression he was working out in advance which acts he wanted to stay around and catch or arrive early to see. Robert was a huge fan of live music.

We got to the end of the tour successfully. Time passed. A few months later Robert called me to say that his previous agent had been on again, offering to book him out for even less commission than last time – for half the rate I charged. He wanted me to reconsider my rate. I explained I was sorry but I couldn't. He said he too was sorry, he'd enjoyed working with us but he couldn't refuse the current offer from his ex-agent. His last words on the phone to me were, "But don't worry Paul, we'll work together again."

Robert's tour manager and sound engineer was a man called Roy Williams. Roy was one of the best sound engineers in the game. He was a delight to work with, very professional, very together and he loved a laugh. He should have been the Lord Mayor of Dudley. Sadly, that won't happen either. He is no longer with us. But I will forever be grateful to Robert for enabling me to get to know Roy.

CHAPTER THIRTY-THREE

THE WORLD IS A LITTLE VILLAGE

A chap called Chesley Millikin rang me up one day out of the blue. A mutual friend, the great guitar player David Lindley, had given him my number. Turned out that Chesley used to do PR in America for an Asgard act called The Chieftains. After a few phone calls I established that he was a real character, cut from the old (high quality) cloth. He would ring up newspapers with the line, "Hold the front page. I've got a great story for you." Honestly! And he'd get his stories in, almost without fail.

He was also the kind of chap who could sell Roy Keane to Manchester United, to play midfield in today's team behind Marcus Rashford. Chesley would, of course, insist on performance bonuses.

He rang me because he wanted me to listen to his "amazing" new act, a wunderkind he'd discovered playing guitar in a bar in Texas. He duly sent me a cassette and he was spot on. Stevie Ray Vaughan, the guitarist on the tape, was on fire. I could tell straight away that he'd do a great live show. Chesley was wheeling and dealing and had the interest of a few record companies, but an important part of his plan, he explained, was to NOT wait for American success before hitting Europe. He wanted to start to build The Kid's profile in Europe at the same time.

Stevie Ray Vaughan and band, Double Trouble, signed to Asgard. Soon afterwards, they did a record deal with CBS/Sony. Stevie managed to very successfully incorporate a couple of the old Jimi Hendrix tricks – plucking the guitar with his teeth and playing it behind his neck – into his show. Within a few years he was very big on the European concert circuit. A lot of quiet introspective musicians, who strive for success, discover when they reach the dizzy heights that it wasn't what they'd had in mind. At all. Sometimes the pressure is unbearable. Artists generally start out because they love writing songs and singing and playing live. That doesn't necessarily mean that they're going to be okay doing the meet-and-greets. It doesn't mean that they're going to enjoy everyone wanting a little piece of them. It also doesn't mean that they're going to be comfortable with the media, which can be quite alien to those of a sensitive nature.

Sometimes when you reach the plateau, you realise that Dylan was spot on when he sang: "*And don't go mistaking paradise/ for that home across the road.*" When paradise isn't all you expect or need, then just like Adam and Eve, you look for something else, maybe even forbidden fruit to keep you going.

I met Stevie Ray Vaughan and I always found him to be a beautiful sweet man; a classic Southern American gentleman in fact. I remember spending a truly wonderful afternoon with him, Chesley and the band, in Willie Nelson's studio in Austin, Texas. Willie Nelson even made an appearance that day, to add to the sense that this was a special occasion. If you want to get a quick flash of SRV's brilliance check out his stunning guitar solo on David Bowie's, 'Let's Dance' (18.5 million YouTube views and counting), and 'Heroes' (154 million YouTube hits).

In a sense, SRV was like Rory Gallagher. If anything, Stevie was even more painfully shy. Sadly at the peak of his success, he found the need to turn to medication to help him through the night, only to find that the remedy proved to be the poison. It all ended very sadly.

He had been ill, but he'd cleaned up his act, had a new lady in his life, found religion and arrived over here for a seven-week European tour with Asgard. There were plenty of good reasons to feel optimistic. The opening night was a sold-out show in Paris and I went over to catch him in action. During the performance, his demons came back to haunt him in the most vicious way and he lost the plot completely while on stage. Stevie went into a series of long, disjointed monologues, leaving his band and crew, not to mention the audience, very confused. He had to be checked into hospital that night and the rest of the tour was cancelled.

He battled with drink and drug addiction for most of his career, but very sadly, in a different twist of fate, he was to meet his end in a helicopter crash in East Troy following a gig with Double Trouble on the night of 27 August 1990. He was just 35 years old.

You look at this and similar tragic stories and there's only one conclusion possible: it's just not worth it. But it's never easy because, as the saying goes: "The devil always arrives bearing the sweetest brews."

Be careful out there.

****

John Hiatt is a fine songwriter with a wonderful gravelly, lived-in voice. He always looks so comfortable when he's up on stage, like he's just out for a drive in his favourite pick-up truck, one hand on the steering wheel, with the elbow of the other arm resting on the open window. When I represented him, he played solo and travelled by himself. He was very popular in Holland and toured there a lot. Life on the road can be lonely, even if you're travelling with a band, so I'd spend some time travelling with him to keep him company. I remember one journey in particular. He was playing an early spot at a Dutch festival, and later that afternoon, we drove on to the next city. Nowhere in Holland is far away from anywhere else in Holland, so it couldn't have been a long drive. Out of the blue he announced he had something to tell me.

"I'm an alcoholic," he said quietly.

The confession took me by surprise. I genuinely respected the fact he was brave enough to talk about it. It was more that I felt blindsided. If anyone was suffering from this terrible disease it had to be a mutual friend. I confided as much to John.

"No, you see the difference is he *enjoys* a drink, I *need* to drink," he said stoically.

We talked about it on our travels and he seemed happier to have shared it with me, so that I could have the promoters check out where the local, vital for him, AA meetings took place.

We kept in touch after he returned to America. We'd chat on the phone and discuss how he was getting on, and what songs he was writing. He started to share a few of these with me. Songs like 'Have A Little Faith In Me', 'Alone in The Dark' and 'Memphis in the Meantime' all sounded brilliant. We began to discuss how to record the songs. I wondered, aloud, if Ry Cooder might get on board and play on a few songs. And then, if he got Ry, there would be no better man for the skins than Jim Keltner. Every time we talked, John would get more and more enthusiastic. He didn't have a manager, or a record company, and wondered if I had any idea who might release the record if he ever got it made.

I immediately thought of Andrew Lauder, who was running Demon Records. I spoke to Andrew. He was a big fan of *Warming Up To The Ice Age*, the album John had released on Geffen Records. Andrew would fund the recording, but only up to an agreed level. He had to make the sums work. John Hiatt was buzzed by the news – even more so a few nights later when he announced he'd got a 'yes' from Ry. Next, the legendary Jim Keltner, a real live Traveling Wilbury, was on board. We started to run into problems with LA-based bass players. The top three on John's hit list were unavailable. Meanwhile, the deal was proving difficult. But Andrew, being Andrew, stuck with it and eventually we had our ducks in a row. John booked Ocean Way Studios in Hollywood. Two weeks to go and still no bass player. I'd already suggested Nick Lowe: I thought he'd be perfect for the project and his expertise in the studio wouldn't hurt either, but there wasn't the budget to add a transatlantic airfare and a hotel stay into the mix. Three days before recording and no bass player on board, I insisted that we really had to try to get Nick. In truth I couldn't have imagined a better combination of musicians than Ry Cooder, Jim Keltner, Nick Lowe and John Hiatt. On top of which, John's collection of songs deserved the de luxe treatment. I spoke to Jake Riviera, Nick's manager, and the main man behind Demon Records. Nick was up for it, and being Nick Lowe, he refused to take any payment for his services. Twenty-four hours later, Nick was picked up at LAX by John and driven straight to the studio. Work finally commenced on *Bring The Family*, with John Chelew in the producer's chair.

The album was released by Demon Records in 1987 and was eventually picked up for the USA by A & M Records. I much preferred the Demon

Records album sleeve (well worth the investment to check out the zany cover photo). *Bring the Family* was John Hiatt's eighth album. It was his first to chart on the Billboard Hot 100 and featured 'Thank You Girl', his first single to chart in the US.

The *Bring The Family* gang regrouped in 1991 under the name Little Village, to record an album for Warner Brothers. This time, songwriting and singing duties were split between Nick Lowe, Ry Cooder and John Hiatt. The album was released as *Little Village* in 1992. It was a fine album. But the playing on the European tour that summer was on another plane entirely. The ticket sales were also incredible. I figured that, if they could have got back into the studio immediately, they'd have made a contender for Greatest Album of All Time. It didn't happen. But the tour yielded some of the finest live music I have ever witnessed. I remember in particular the show at the Ahoy in Rotterdam. With its 11,000-plus capacity, it was a far cry from the clubs John Hiatt used to play in Holland in the early days. But Ry Cooder, Nick Lowe, Jim Keltner and John Hiatt filled every cubic millimeter that night with some of the most beautiful and brilliant sounds it has been my privilege to hear. There are times when you really do feel: I wouldn't have missed that for anything.

CHAPTER THIRTY-FOUR

MARK TWAIN WITH A MARTIN D 28

If there wasn't a music business some people would still make music and write songs. The absence of recording contracts, or publishing contracts, or the unavailability of a streaming platform, really would not matter to them. They'd continue to embrace the honourable art of making music and creating songs because their existence, the essence of their lives even, depended on it.

John Prine was one such true musician.

Like a lot of the artists I've been lucky enough to work with, he found his way into the music world via an unconventional road map – in his case literally! He was a US mailman, delivering letters on a well-trodden route in Chicago. Once he'd learnt his route, he could deliver his letters and simultaneously daydream his days away. He did this for six whole years before he picked up the courage to hop on stage at an open-mic night at the Fifth Peg Folk Club in Chicago. That night he performed one song. The reaction was enough for the club owner to book him for the following three Thursday nights. Upon discovering that he was expected to play a 60-minute set, John spent the rest of the week writing enough songs to do just that. The first week 12 people turned up. The ticket price was 50 cents and John was paid half of this. One of John's most famous songs came into being because he had the street smarts to read an audience from his first few gigs. He noticed the same man sitting in the same seat in the front row for the first two shows. John figured that, if the man in the front row turned up for the third gig, he would probably be annoyed if the fledging singer-songwriter did exactly the same set again. So, in order to add some variety, he wrote a new song, 'Sam Stone', in the taxi on the way to the club on the third night.

John Prine started to play around Chicago's folk circuit. He was a natural entertainer and so it didn't take long for him to start earning a lot more from performing than he was from being a mailman. He happily hung up his US mailbag. It was around this time that he encountered another young singer-songwriter, Steve Goodman, and they became good buddies and later best friends. Kris Kristofferson happened upon the talent of Steve Goodman and booked him as the opening act on a three-night Chicago run. Goodman browbeat Kristofferson into travelling across to the other side of town after one of his shows to see his mate, John Prine – "the real deal" – performing. Kris was so taken by John's songs he had him sing them again for him in the dressing room afterwards. As a result of this meeting, John was signed to Atlantic Records.

John Prine, Loudon Wainwright III and Steve Goodman were the first artists (but not the last) to be unimaginatively marketed by their record companies as "the next Bob Dylan." Bob Dylan himself became a fan of John, citing him as one of his favourite songwriters. "Prine's stuff is pure Proustian existentialism," he said. "Midwestern mindtrips to the Nth degree. And he writes beautiful songs." Dylan played harmonica on stage when John made his debut in New York.

From his first album, John Prine set up shop the way he meant to continue. He liked the recording studio, but he never wanted to live there or have one in his house. He preferred to keep visits to the studio rare. He wanted them to be special. His priority was to always follow the song and he endeavoured to record versions of his songs that he could perform live. The stage, and not the recording studio, was to be his priority.

While he was in the studio he worked under the rule that the song was the boss. "I don't know where a song comes from," he claimed, "but when I get a pretty one, I don't want anyone messing it up."

His trademark was creating a story within a song. His lyrics were always intelligent, funny but never highbrow and, just like Mark Twain, there was never a wasted word. He confessed that he came from the Chuck Berry school of song-writing where every single syllable of your lyric had to have a note. He thought the bridge was a crucial part of a song and he loved writing them. On his co-writes, he could always be relied upon to come up with the perfect bridge.

When John finished writing a song he was particularly proud of, he had a habit of keeping it under wraps for a few weeks. He said he just loved the feeling of walking around, knowing that no one else in the world had heard the song in question yet. One such song was 'Jesus The Missing Years', from the Grammy award winning album, *The Missing Years* (1991). He kept that one under wraps for a fortnight. I just can't imagine what it must have felt like to be walking around knowing you were the only person in the world to have heard what was to become a classic. I have always thought that 'Jesus The Missing Years' was a film begging to be made.

An important piece of advice John offered songwriters was to make sure they liked the songs they wrote. He suggested that if the song became a big hit, then you'd most likely be asked about it every day for the remainder of your life. You'd be expected to perform this song every time you appeared on stage. So, it helped if you genuinely liked your own songs. He performed 'Sam Stone', 'Hello In There' and 'Paradise' (three songs he wrote when he was 21 or 22) just about every time he appeared on stage. John liked them all – and he really enjoyed singing them.

His mentor, the legendary Cowboy Jack Clement, taught him to be "friends with the microphone." The microphone is an artist's vital link with their audience, so Cowboy Jack encouraged John to get to know it, to understand how it worked and to master how best to use it.

I know I've said this about a few people, but I found the always dapper John Prine to be a true gentleman. He was a great storyteller on and off stage and had many wonderful different spins on life. For instance, he believed that eras with bad pop music also produced bad looking cars and he felt a lot of modern vehicles would have been so much better if our current pop music scene was hitting the high notes. It's not surprising then that John *was* a big fan of the 1950s automobiles.

On the sleeve notes for his great friend Iris DeMent's debut album, *Infamous Angel* (1992), John wrote: "And if pork chops could talk, they'd probably learn how to sing one of her songs." If we don't know exactly what he means, it doesn't really matter because it sure sounds good, and if it sounds that good then he couldn't be talking about music that would be anything less than amazing, which turned out to be the case. John was always very generous in his praise of other artists. One of the big secrets of the music world is that truly great artists are *always* big fans of other artists.

Although never tarnished by the chains of notoriety or fame, John Prine achieved a level of critical praise that was coveted by his peers. He had, from the very beginning of his career, learned the secret of a long run: always keep some reserve in your tank and maintain a direct connection with your fans. He achieved the latter when, in 1984, he set up his own record label, Oh Boy Records, with his manager Al Bunetta. Oh Boy Records was a true independent record label – indeed, it might even have been the first to use the crowd funding system to produce albums.

It was not by accident that John Prine's final album, *The Tree of Forgiveness* (2018) – his first in 13 years – was not only one of the best of his career, it was also acknowledged as such and had the sales and chart position to prove it, reaching No. 5 in the hallowed Billboard Top 200 albums. This was his highest ever USA chart position. 'Lonesome Friends of Science', one of the many beautifully crafted songs on the album, could have nestled cosily on his very first album, *John Prine* (1971).

John also wrote songs that were ideal for other singers to interpret and make their own. Most people will recall how Joe Cocker managed to reinvent 'With A Little Help From My Friends', to the degree that when you hear the title you think first of Joe's version, and The Beatles original afterwards. With John Prine', I'm thinking of Nanci Griffith's version of 'The Speed of The Sound of Loneliness' – which truly brought home the brilliance of this song to me. Then there was Bonnie Raitt's version of 'Angel From Montgomery', a career-defining moment for her. And as if that wasn't enough, didn't Carly Simon only go and gift us an equally vital version.

In and out of song, John Prine had a turn of phrase which would always bring a smile to your face. I'm thinking of lines like *"I can hear the train tracks/ Through the laundry on the line."* ('Knockin' On Your Screen Door' from *The Tree of Forgiveness,* 2018)

Those two pictorial lines take you straight there: you're right beside him as he narrates the story. Once again you have been effortlessly transported into the ultra-visual Prineworld.

That same visual sense is at work in 'The Other Side of Town', from *Fair & Square* (2005)

"A clown puts his make-up on upside down/ So he wears a smile even when he wears a frown."

Then there's the beautiful early song, 'Souvenirs', from his second album *Diamonds in the Rough* (1972).

"I hate graveyards and old pawn shops," he sings, *"For they always bring me tears."*

I spoke to him about that one and it turned out he actually *liked* pawn shops – he really loved to see other people's junk, he said – but he confessed that in his songwriting, sometimes the sound of the word was more important than the meaning. For the lyric of 'Souvenirs', he preferred the sound of the word "hate" over the words "like" or "love". On top of which he felt "hate" sat much better with "graveyards."

Some of his songs – like 'That's the Way the World Goes Round'. (from *Bruised Orange*, 1978) – are so friendly that the first time you hear them you think you've known them all your life. Similarly, with 'In Spite of Ourselves', a pitch-perfect duet with Iris DeMent from the album of the same name (1999).

What it all comes down to is that John Prine was a master storyteller. Some of his introductions to his songs while on stage, or the stories he told off stage, suggested he had a few great books in him as well as all those beautiful songs.

We did several tours with John, starting with a concert at The National Stadium, Dublin on the 24 October, 1981. John's show was part of the incredible series of legendary concerts we were doing in the National Stadium around that time, featuring artists like Eric Clapton, Dire Straits, Carole King, Ry Cooder, JJ Cale, Loudon Wainwright III, Rickie Lee Jones, Sonny Terry & Brownie McGee, Gerry Rafferty, B.B. King, Van Morrison and Kate and Anna McGarrigle. The National Stadium was the best place in the world to be when John Prine – or any of these illustrious artists – were onstage. For as long as I can remember, John was very popular in Ireland, where the audiences embraced all of the original Americana artists way before the rest of Europe did.

The last time I met John was when I bumped into him and his wife Fiona in the lobby of the Westbury Hotel in Dublin a few years ago. I hadn't seen him for ages. He did like a chat though and pretty soon we were catching up over a cup of tea and debating the quality of the scones. Talking about the important things…

Talking to him again, I remembered how beautiful his concerts always were. It's infectious to witness an artist who so obviously enjoys being on stage. John's gigs were a beautifully balanced mix of songs and storytelling. He was very generous with the length of his sets – and yet the time seemed to fly.

After the shows, we'd have to fetch John a fish and chip supper from one of the local chippies. Following one very successful concert in the Royal Festival Hall, London, and while everyone else was dining in the posh area with white napkins and legit cutlery, I found John in his dressing room, happily sitting on the floor with his fish and chips spread out on the newspaper wrapping in front of him, tucking in finger-style. I believe he even travelled with his own salt and vinegar. He definitely travelled with a tube of mustard. Oh, the comforts of life on the road.

John Prine died amid the Covid madness of 2020, but that'll be my lasting image of him, turning on a sold-out venue to the magic of his wonderful, and totally uncorrupted, music – and then celebrating afterwards by tucking into his fish and chip supper.

CHAPTER THIRTY-FIVE

THE MULTI-MILLION SELLING PAUL SKEFFINGTON

As an agent you're always on the lookout for new artists. Part of the joy of being an agent is to be part of the team involved in bringing an unknown artist onto the stage and into the recording studio. To experience the absolute buzz of spotting their potential, can be rewarding enough. Of course, there is a major thrill in representing artists you have been a big fan of, artists who already have a successful career. I'm thinking of artists like Ray Davies and his band The Kinks, Tom Waits, Loudon Wainwright III, Jackson Browne, Van Morrison, Christy Moore, John Lee Hooker, Ronnie Spector, Robert Plant, Nick Lowe, Paul Buchanan & The Blue Nile, Mike Scott & The Waterboys, Gilbert O'Sullivan, Graham Nash, Sonny Terry and Brownie McGhee, The Clancy Brothers and Tommy Maken, and, of course, The Chieftains...

But what about the future legends?

I'm a big fan of songwriters and, in the mid-1980's, I'd started to think, if only I could find a young Paul Simon or a young Gerry Rafferty, I could launch a career like few others before. In fact, my dream artist would probably have written Paul Simon class songs; sung like Paul Buchanan; played guitar and fiddle like David Lindley, bass like Paul McCartney, drums like Jim Keltner, piano like Tom Waits, and organ like Steve Winwood; and looked like Elvis Presley circa late 1950s and early 1960, or around the time he was stationed in Germany and stopping off on UK soil for the one and only time in his life.

I was very serious about my quest and spent a lot of time listening to tapes and going to gigs. I was totally convinced there was someone out there – the perfect artist – waiting for me to discover them. I had my Master Plan in place. Paul Skeffington – the nickname I'd given my artist – would always be photographed holding a guitar to emphasise he was a serious songwriter and not a celebrity. I'd start him – or her – off doing solo shows to hone the material. I would endeavour to persuade Mark Ribot and David Lindley to play guitar on the album. Peter Van Hooke had to be a dead cert for the drummer's seat. I remembered Peter Gabriel – or was it Phil Collins? – once made an album without any cymbals on it. I liked that idea a lot, so my artist's statement would be the obvious absence of backing vocals. I figured this would focus the listener's attention more on the voice and therefore on the songs. My plan was to sign the artist to Warner Brothers, who had my favourite stable of artists by far: I wanted my artist to sit comfortably in that illustrious company. I planned that by the time the album was released (following, of course, a top ten single,) Paul Skeffington would have put together a great band. He – or she – would then head off on the road and we'd make agent's hay booking ever-bigger and more sophisticated venues.

Three years later, my grand project was still stuck in neutral. I even took a few adverts in the *Belfast Telegraph* to no avail.

Then one night, in the death throes of 1987, I was at the Mean Fiddler in Harlesden, in North West London. I had booked the great Irish troubadour, Paul Brady, to play a few nights in the Fiddler. I arrived early and the main room, where Paul was performing, was packed to the rafters, mostly with my fellow countrymen and women, all of them keen on acquiring a drink or three. I decided to slip into the smaller Acoustic Room for a quiet cup of tea before Paul's set. There was an open-mic night on, where several new, pre-booked, artists would show up with their own mates and fans in tow. The idea was that the sum total of all these thirsty attendees would add up to the capacity of the Acoustic Room (approx. 120) and the bar would do well. When I walked in, there were about 20 people evenly spread over five tables. I ordered my cup of tea.

A few moments later, the lights went down and Paul Skeffington walked on stage.

"You're kidding!" I hear you say.

Well no, I'm not really kidding.

'Define "not really"?'

Just let me tell the story! Paul Skeffington, the songwriter I'd been searching for, for three years, most definitely walked out on the stage... but that wasn't the artist's name. In fact he was a woman – and she did this very special thing that night that I've never forgotten in the intervening 35 years. Basically all the acts had a few friends and supporters in the sparse audience. Which meant that when "their act" was on stage, their supporters would pay attention, while the rest of the audience would chatter away.

This young woman came on stage with a Washburn guitar slung over her shoulder. The date was Friday 18th of December 1987. She was just 18 years old. In fact, I discovered later, this was her very first time on stage. Clearly she didn't have any friends or supporters in the audience because *everyone* talked through most of her short set. At one point the chatter from the table closest to the stage became so loud they were in danger of drowning out her performance altogether. Mid-song, she stopped singing and, while continuing to play her guitar, walked over to the side of the stage closest to the noisy table and glared down at the talkers until, one by one, they grew very self-conscious, and shut up. When she had silenced them, she walked back over to the microphone, positioned centre stage, and continued singing as if it had been the most natural thing in the world to do. Now if I had just done something like that my heart would be beating its way out of my ribcage, but the singer immediately dropped back into the spirit of her song as though she just swatted away a troublesome fly.

The name of the very striking young singer was Tanita Tikaram. That night, she performed 'Sighing Innocents', 'Poor Cow', 'Good Tradition' and the 'Cathedral Song'. And I was hooked. I had to dash back into the Main Room to see Paul Brady give one of his typical blistering-hot sets and left a message for Tanita to say I'd like to see her later. By the time Brady was finished, Tanita had left a message for me saying she'd had to leave to catch a train back to Basingstoke. She might have entered the annals as one who got away.

Thankfully not. Tanita called me the next day and came to see me in Asgard's Camden Town offices. She was immediately impressed with my morning's shopping – Christmas presents still in their Liberty bags.

She brought a musician – a bass player – with her. I couldn't work out if he was a boyfriend, a band member, or a security prop. We chatted away. I told her I thought her songs were easily good enough to secure her a record deal. I told her I'd like to be her agent and explained to her exactly what an agent did. I said if she came with me, the first thing we would need to do would be to find her a manager. The bass player asked if she signed with me how much would I pay her? Tanita had the good sense to look embarrassed, but equally she couldn't hide the look of hope in her eyes. I explained that this wasn't what agents did. I advised them both that the job of an agent was to find her gigs, ensure that she was paid for those gigs and take a 10% commission on the shows. She rang up the next day and said she wanted to sign with Asgard and no, her companion wasn't either her boyfriend or her bass player. For whatever reason, I never saw him again.

I started to book her on a lot of shows, mostly as a support act. She opened for a number of artists I had out on tour at the time, like Paul Brady, John Martyn and Warren Zevon. I booked her on a London TV magazine show and tipped off a few friends in record companies to watch. They were impressed. I set up a photo session for her and, as part of my Master Plan, every time she was photographed she had her distinctive Washburn, nylon-string guitar, with her in the shot. There were numerous single-named, female, pop artists at the time. I wanted Tanita Tikaram to be considered as a serious musician, a singer who sang her own songs.

In truth, we didn't have to veer too far off the original Paul Skeffington Master Plan. Tanita looked as beautiful as a young Elvis Presley. In fact the resemblance was uncanny – and she would play up to it by uttering "Daddy" every time she saw a photo of Elvis Presley. Tanita had a deep – you could say masculine – voice, with hints of Leonard Cohen. It was the perfect voice to deliver her coded lyrics. She had a unique turn of phrase, but also the necessary ambiguity to ensure that her lyrics were generally open to personal interpretation. She was an excellent guitarist too, with that magic thing of creating enough interplay and drama not to need a band. Some artists, when they perform solo, essentially strum along. But others – like Paul Simon, John Prine, Joni Mitchell and James Taylor – create a different kind of musical tapestry. Paul Brady's version of his exquisite 'Crazy Dreams' is a very good example. Tanita had the potential to play in that league. But I would have to demonstrate as much, if I wanted to attract record company interest.

I had met Hugh Murphy through his work with Gerry Rafferty on his breakthrough 'Baker Street' and *City to City* campaign. I had also booked Hugh to produce Paul Brady's classic, crossover from traditional to contemporary music LP, *Hard Station*; and I made the link between Hugh and Van Morrison, who brought him in to work on *Beautiful Vision* and ended up giving Hugh three co-writer credits on that album.

I still hadn't found a manager for Tanita and so to get things rolling, I started to talk to record companies myself. The ultimate game-plan was still to land with Warner Brothers, but I figured Roger Ames and Colin Bell at London Records might be interested. I decided that Tanita and I would nip up to Hugh's home studio and record a few of her songs. Hugh would engineer, and I'd produce the "voice and guitar" session. We headed up on a quiet Sunday afternoon – it was the final day in January, 1988. Hugh had the desk primed for a good guitar sound, we made Tanita feel comfortable in the studio and the tape started rolling. Hugh and I were assuming we'd need a long session to get a decent few demos. We recorded 'Cathedral Song' and it sounded amazing: first take and she'd nailed it. Three songs later Hugh gave me a knowing squint. "She's really got something," he muttered. "This is special." Nineteen songs later, Hugh's jaw was on the floor. So was mine. Had we really just heard this young artist sing all of those 19 songs, without needing a second take on any of them? Some were big songs, some were cheeky songs and others were simply gorgeous – but they all passed the Old Grey Whistle Test in that they had unique, catchy, powerful melodies, which you could whistle immediately. I still have that original tape. And I can assure you, it still sounds utterly brilliant.

On the strength of the Hugh Murphy session, and with no commitment on either side, I persuaded London Records to put Tanita in a recording studio. This time, I got Peter Van Hooke in to produce. I knew if there was a great record to be made, Peter was the one who could deliver it. He and

I had worked together on Herbie Armstrong's beautiful, *Back Against The Wall* album for Peter's hi fi friendly label, MMC Records. Knowing what kind of an artifact we wanted, Peter pulled in his cohort Rod Argent. Rod had first been spotted as a member of the seminal band The Zombies and wrote their biggest single, the classic, million-selling, 'She's Not There' (Decca 1964). The reason I wanted these sessions to be "produced" was that I wanted to see how far some of Tanita's songs could be pushed. A great song won't turn into a great record if the producer makes a mess of it. A great record becoming a great *hit* record is a different matter again. So we needed to explore how to make the most of Tanita's songs.

Peter Van Hooke and Rod Argent produced the 'Cathedral Song' by placing Tanita's wonderfully distinctive, husky voice in the centre of their stereo picture, and creating a stunning, lush, majestic, soulful sound around her. We all knew immediately that we could make a great album.

I set up a meeting for Tanita with another potential manager, Lorna Gradden, who was manager of The Communards – another London Records artist we were enjoying great success with. She was very together, on the case and was doing brilliant work for The Communards. I figured she'd be the ideal manager for Tanita. I played 'Cathedral Song' for Lorna and she loved it. I fixed a meeting between Lorna and Tanita, but for whatever reason, Tanita didn't feel comfortable. She explained that she thought she needed to get to know someone really well before she made that important call. I have to say that I was taken aback by what she said next. "I would really like you to be my manager, Paul," she offered. She argued that I was already doing most of it anyway and that she felt comfortable working with me.

I found her a solicitor, Russell Roberts (independent from Asgard's legal representation), and we did a deal. Asgard Management took on the job of managing the career of Tanita Tikaram. I paid her a retainer so she could give up her tele-sales job and offered her the spare room in my flat, so she had somewhere to stay when she was in London. I felt it was important to visit her parents, knowing that if I was one of them, I'd be really worried about her spending her time with this older Irishman up in the big smoke. Her dad was a Fiji Indian and her mum was from Malaysia. He had been in the Armed Forces and so, like Jackson Browne, Tanita was an army child, born in Germany. They made us tea and sandwiches and I explained to them exactly what I did, what I charged for my services and how we would go about managing their only daughter's career. They were excited by how confident I was in Tanita and her songs. I gave them my number and told them if they ever had any worries or concerns to please give me a call. Tanita, although she could see the need for the meeting, was very keen to get proceedings over with as soon as possible. I was quite hungry by now, so I went to nab one of the sandwiches. One of my biggest faults is that I'm a very fussy eater. I hate myself for it, but there's nothing I can do about it. It's the way I've been all my life. Anyway, these were all cheese sandwiches and I hate cheese. I really do. I mean, not as much as I hate tomatoes, but that's another story.

So when Tanita's mum saw I wasn't taking any of her sandwiches, she lifted the plate and personally offered me one. I didn't want to offend her on my first meeting, so I took the sandwich and held it in my hand. For.... a... long.... time.... I could feel Tanita's mum and dad occasionally glancing at the sandwich and then at me and then back to the sandwich again. I think I must have been hoping for a convenient flowerpot or a hungry pet dog. Neither came to my rescue and so I decided I really had to bite the bullet. I chomped into the sandwich – and I can still remember that single bite, of all the bites I have taken in my long life, far too vividly. It tasted just like... cheese. I started to feel nauseous. Maybe I was overthinking it, but for a moment I was sure I was going to get sick. To kill the taste, I took a generous swig of tea, and beads of sweat started to prickle on my forehead. Gradually, the feeling subsided. Tanita, meanwhile, was very happy at how the meeting had gone and was very keen to get me out of the house quickly, in case her mum and dad started to ask embarrassing questions about the seedier side of the music business. Yes, she was very happy to see me go, but nowhere near as happy as I was to run away from the prospect of having to attempt to eat another cheese sandwich. You wouldn't believe how quickly I scooted out the door and down the road.

London Records loved the recording of 'Cathedral Song' as well as the voice and guitar songs from the Hugh Murphy sessions. They were ready to do a deal. With their interest as a back-stop, I still wanted – if I could – to stick to my Paul Skeffington Master Plan. I asked a good mate of mine,

Fraser Kennedy, to ring up a mutual contact at Warner Bros and spin the – truthful – line: "Have you heard this brilliant artist Asgard are looking after? She's called Tanita Tikaram. She writes her own songs, looks more like Elvis Presley than Lisa Marie does, has an amazing voice and London Records want to sign her." I'm paraphrasing there, but whatever he said, within minutes Paul Conroy was on the phone.

"Have you signed a deal yet?" was his opening gambit.

"No, but we're well progressed with London, and CBS are keen and Virgin want to…"

"Can you come around now and play me some music?"

Ten minutes later, we were sitting in his office in Broadwick Street grooving to the sounds of 'Cathedral Song'.

Like John Peel with The Undertones, he played it again. And again.

The production sounded like a million dollars. It was a great track. Paul saw the potential and said he wanted to sign Tanita Tikaram to a long-term recording contract with Warner Bros.

I went to see Colin Bell and Roger Ames and explained the situation, and they were totally fine about it. Given her style, they understood the logic of wanting Tanita to be seen as a Warner Bros artist and in the same company as legendary Warner stars like Neil Young, Joni Mitchell, Jackson Browne, Paul Simon, Cary Simon and Van Morrison. I really don't think Roger and Colin were tremendously upset. I suspect that, rather than seeing Tanita as a future star themselves, they were happy to back my intuition. Either way, they gave us the demo version of 'Cathedral Song' to take with us as a gift. In fact it was exactly this demo version which appeared on her debut album.

Once the news was around town that Warner Bros were closing in on a deal with a new songwriter everyone wanted to make a pitch. One label even did the clichéd, "We'll send you a blank cheque," approach. Yes it happens – and we actually received such a cheque. Tanita Tikaram was 100% happy to let me get on with doing the deals on her behalf. Of course she was always kept in the picture, but was never preoccupied with it. She always signed off on the deals saying, "If you're happy with it, PC, then so am I." Her approach made negotiating on her behalf a lot easier.

I did the Warner Bros deal with Paul Conroy and Rob Dickens. I wasn't after a major advance. I thought the last thing an eighteen-year-old fresh out of school needed was a bunch of money. I was prepared to sacrifice a hefty advance in favour of a high royalty rate. I was convinced that Tanita was going to sell a lot of records and so I wanted her (and, needless to say, by extension, myself) to be fairly compensated for those sales. So, with a bit of investigation, I discovered the superstar's royalty rate – being paid at the time to artists like Paul McCartney and Elton John. I wasn't greedy. I didn't ask them to match that to start with. I suggested a reasonable royalty rate for a new artist, but then I asked for the rate to be escalated, to be triggered on reaching specified sales platforms such as 50,000, 100,000, 250,000, 500,000 and on every addition 250,000 until, at 3,500,000, album sales Tanita would be to be on a superstar royalty. Rob Dickens laughed at me as he said, "Paul, if Tanita's album ever sells a million copies, I'll be happy to pay you what you're asking for." I was okay with him laughing. He agreed to the escalations. So I guess we were all very happy when Tanita's debut album, *Ancient Heart*, sold 4.8 million copies. Rob later confessed to me he had originally thought if we had managed to sell 20,000 copies of Tanita's first album, we'd have been off to a flying start with her career.

Getting the right publishing deal was also of crucial importance. I knew Warner Chappell as a first class operation and they had just appointed a new MD, Robin Godfrey-Cass. I had met Robin first when he was a radio plugger for Heath Levy publishers, who administered Future Legends Music, Fruupp's publishing company, back in the mid-1970s. I liked Robin. I knew I could talk to him honestly and so I explained that I was in no hurry for Tanita to sign a publishing deal.

There was no need. Publishers had become just like banks, in that they collected your money for you, sat on it for as long as they could, and took an unfair share of it for the privilege. Gone were the days of publishers earning their share by going out there and aggressively securing covers for the artists. I explained that I was convinced Tanita's record was going to be very big and all she really needed to do was register her songs with Copyright Control and take the lioness' share – and consider a more lucrative deal down the line. Robin very patiently heard me out and when he was convinced I was finished, offered, "But you must have some kind of deal in the back of your mind you'd agree to today?" He knew me just as well as I thought I knew him.

I outlined what I thought would work for Tanita as follows.

I wanted Tanita to have her own publishing company.

Warner Chappell would act as the collection house for Tanita's company.

On all of Tanita's original compositions she recorded she would receive an 85% publishing royalty.

However, in order to encourage Warner Chappell to go out and find covers for Tanita songs, we would reduce Tanita's percentage to 60% on all the income generated by those songs recorded by other artists.

Tanita would have the final say on how, and if, her songs and music were used on TV and in films.

No offers would be entertained for any of Tanita's songs to be used for advertising.

Warner Chappell would contribute an agreed un-recoupable sum of money annually for two years for additional marketing and promotion of her records and tours.

I also wanted a rather large advance for Tanita – an unheard of sum for a new artist. I had three reasons: one, at that stage 85% was as high a royalty rate as we were ever going to get in London for a new artist, so there was no need to trade part of the advance against a higher royalty rate; two: Robin succeeded Rob Dickens as the managing director of Warner Chappell. Rob appointed Robin and I believed that Rob was still actively involved in Warner Chappell. My logic being, if things ever got a wee bit sticky for us, we needed the record company to keep the pedal to the metal – in which case the Warner "family" exposure might, just might, be handy as an insurance policy. And my third reason was that I wanted to secure a nest-egg for Tanita, to compensate for her giving up her academic studies and any career that might have flowed from that.

I'd saved my most difficult deal point for last. I knew it was the point Robin would have the most difficulty selling to "his board."

I wanted Tanita to retain the copyright to her songs, so that, at the end of the deal, after four years, she could, if she wanted, take the full rights to her songs with her, to wherever or whatever she was going to do next.

Robin smiled a lot, exhaled air through his teeth a bit, moaned plenty, groaned even more, cried a little. He'd obviously been to the Michael Eavis class on The Art of Negotiating. But, here's the big thing: he didn't say no. He said he'd get back to me. I asked him to play 'Cathedral Song' again just before he spoke to his board.

He rang up the next day and said he couldn't get the board to approve either the advance or the copyright issue. They were offering half the advance and a return of copyrights after 15 years. He seemed genuinely down when I advised him we'd have to let the deal with Warner Chappell go.

He tried again a few times throughout the day and I repeated my original case: that there really was no need for Tanita to sign a publishing deal at that point. We were happy with the idea of reaping the publishing dividends directly.

He rang back towards the end of the day.

"So, do you have a name ready for Tanita's publishing company yet? We're ready to do the deal."

It so happened I had always felt, with Tanita's unique way with words, that Brogue Music would be the perfect name for her publishing company. When I suggested this to Tanita she agreed immediately.

Brogue Music, Tanita Tikaram, Warner Bros, Warner Chappell's and Asgard Management (all thanks to Paul Skeffington) were open and ready for business. But we had yet to make the difficult first album.

Shortly after the record contract was agreed and signed, I received a phone call from Malcolm Dunbar the head of A&R at Warner Bros. Malcolm said how excited he was about the fact they'd signed Tanita. He said he was really looking forward to sitting down with me and discussing potential producers for the album. Alarm bells went off immediately. I thought, "Gee" – well I didn't really think "gee", but I'm worried that if Tanita's mum ever reads this she might retrospectively be concerned. But the words 'record company interference' came up on my inner screen. I told Malcolm that Tanita and I were very happy with Peter and Rod and we wanted them to be the producers. Malcolm suggested they were fine, but just for the demos – and we should get some names in. "I've got a few people in mind who would be perfect," he said. I liked Malcolm. He sometimes went a wee bit too far in describing the recording process, telling me on one occasion that delivering an album, "was just like giving birth." I wasn't quite sure that was the best way of describing it at all.

I had a wee chat with Paul Conroy and Rob Dickens to ensure we were going to avoid the postnatal approach by sticking with Peter and Rod. They intended to continue with the template they'd developed during the recording of 'Cathedral Song'. They would record Tanita's voice and Washburn guitar to a click track.

The click track was vital to the next stage, which was completing the stereo picture by adding other instruments in sympathetic and arresting arrangements around Tanita's voice. As per the original master plan, there would be no backing vocals. The idea was to not have 'an album sound' that each song would be forced into. Rather, every track would be different and feature a distinctive signature. Like an oboe, a folk-flavoured fiddle, a mandolin, a keyboard pad, a flugelhorn, a trumpet or various guitars. Tanita's voice would be the common link throughout.

The very first time I heard 'Cathedral Song' I suggested to Tanita she should call her first album *Ancient Heart* after the line in the song. Those two words totally summed up Tanita: her voice, her words and her music.

We were very lucky in the musicians we secured to play on the album. David Lindley, best known for his work with Jackson Browne's band, was staying in my basement at the time. He was in London filming a role for a film about *Blackbeard* and he happily made an appearance at Rod's Red House studio.

Marc Ribot from Tom Waits' band was passing through town and popped in to contribute. In addition, we inveigled the marvelous Helen O'Hara from Dexys Midnight Runners; Mark Isham from Van's band; Brendan Croker and Mark Creswell from The 5 O'Clock Shadows and, from the Paul Brady Band, Paul Brady himself. On top of that, Peter Van Hooke did all the drum parts and the maestro, Rod Argent, handled keyboard parts, and all those beautiful string arrangements. Rod and Peter dipped into their wee black books and gathered the cream of the session-musician scene to complete their dream audio pictures.

The tracks were coming together very well. There was a folk feel on 'Good Tradition', swinging like never before with Helen O'Hara on violin, Paul Brady on mandolin, and Van Hooke creating a racket on the drums, remoulding the song beautifully. Thanks to Mark Isham, 'For All These

Years' became a soundscape haunted by the ghost of Miles Davis. I'd always felt 'Preyed Upon' was a brilliant piece of soulful, confessional lyric writing, with a stunning makes-you-want-to-cry melody, and so it proved. If anybody wanted to know about Tanita, it's all laid out in that song, especially heard alongside 'Little Sister Leaving Town' and 'Harm In Your Hands' from the second album, *The Sweet Keeper*.

'Twist In My Sobriety' was the only track Peter and Rod were having a problem getting a shape on. Tanita had already recorded a flawless vocal, but nothing seemed right to fill out the rest of the soundscape. Late one night, as Mr. Van Hooke was dropping me home, I invited him indoors. We really needed to crack what to do with 'Twist In My Sobriety' and its cryptic lyric about entering, and traversing, the dangerous foreign lands of post-teenage years – and I had an idea. I played Peter a track from one of Tanita's favourite albums, *Famous Blue Raincoat*, by Jennifer Warnes. The track was a Leonard Cohen song called, 'Ain't No Cure for Love'. The second I played it to Peter, he shouted in excitement, "I get it, I get it, it's fours on the floor, that'll work."

Pretty soon we had the final song on *Ancient Heart* finished and were ready to go.

'Good Tradition', the first single, was released mid-June 1988. We didn't want to put one of the album tracks on the flipside, for fear it might stigmatise a first class song as a B-side. Peter and Rod were off working on another project, so Tanita and I nipped into the studio and jointly produced a solo version of 'Valentine Heart'.

Months before, I'd sent Ken Woollard, the legendary creator and curator of the renowned Cambridge Folk Festival, a cassette of a few of the voice and guitar versions of the songs we'd recorded up at Hugh Murphy's studio. Ken rang back within the hour of receiving the cassette. He loved it and booked her on the spot for that year's festival and offered her a very generous fee on the strength of the music. Now, as Tanita was walking onto the Cambridge Folk Festival Main Stage on 31 July 1989, Bruno Brookes had just concluded the weekly run down of the singles charts on BBC Radio – and Tanita's first single had entered the Top 40, at No. 36, totally justifying Ken Woollard belief in Tanita and the fee he'd offered. Three weeks later 'Good Tradition' reached the Top 10 in the UK. Of the nineteen singles Tanita has so far released, that's her highest ever chart position. On 13 September, the album *Ancient Heart* was released. I've seen very few artists work as hard as Tanita Tikaram did over the following fifteen months.

I've always tried to ensure that artists don't see the record label as the enemy. They're only trying to sell your music. I told Tanita we should never use the word "no" with Warner Brothers. If they suggested something we felt was not appropriate for her music, we would respond with something like, "That doesn't really work, for us, but how about if we…" – and make suggestions as to what it would be possible to do. You say "no" to your label too often and they move on to the next artist on their priority list. Of course it's easier to work as hard as Tanita worked when you see, on a weekly basis, the fruits of your labours. Her album was going Gold and Platinum absolutely everywhere. She was No 1 in Norway, Sweden, Poland, Switzerland, Austria, Germany and Ireland. Ireland, in fact, was the first country to award Tanita a Gold Disc for sales of *Ancient Heart* – which reached the top ten in most territories. It peaked at No. 3 in the UK charts, where it enjoyed a 59-week run. The second single 'Twist In My Sobriety' sold over a million copies and topped the charts in several countries including Germany. *Ancient Heart has* now sold a staggering 5 million copies.

It cost under £40,000 to record.

Not everything went exactly according to plan. 'World Outside Your Window' is one of my favourite Tanita songs. The minute you hear the melody your mind automatically flips the words, *the world outside your window*, back at you. Peter and Rod's production of the track is magnificent, as is Mark Creswell's beautiful high life guitar, giving the song an inspiring feel-good vibe. I saw it as the perfect song for Helen Sharman – the first British astronaut as well as the first woman to visit the Mir Space Station – to take into space with her and play to the entire universe outside her window. I imagined looking out through Helen's window, into the galaxy, with Tanita's wonderful voice and 'World Outside Your Window' helping to immortalise the magic moment. I always thought it was going to be Tanita's biggest single, but by the time it came out – the fourth single to be released from 'Ancient Heart' – everyone on planet earth had already bought the album. Either way, it didn't click in the way I had hoped.

By the time we came to make the "difficult second album," *The Sweet Keeper*, things had changed.

Tanita has since confirmed that she is comfortable speaking about her sexuality, so I'm not talking out of turn. Looking back, I think she found those early years on the road very challenging. Being stuck with a mostly male band and an exclusively male crew and not having someone to go home to, she must have been thinking, "is all this hard work worth it?" She must have been wondering, "Is my lifestyle in direct conflict with my search for love?" These were the kind of late night conversations we were having when I recommended to her that she take some serious time out, in order to directly address the personal issues we were discussing.

Tanita relocated to San Francisco for several months, from where she wrote me numerous, powerful but always totally hilarious, not to mention long, letters. They were so good and entertaining that I started to have discussions with Faber about signing her as an author. Faber were very keen, but in the end Tanita decided that she was more comfortable as a songwriter.

I believe she felt she needed to assert herself more in her approach to life.

Maybe she felt she was either sharing the spotlight too much with Peter and Rod; or maybe she just wanted more of it. She suggested that she should produce her own records. I advised her that not everyone who can write great songs, and perform them well, can produce those songs with the same degree of expertise. I made the case that Peter Van Hooke and Rod Argent knew what they were doing in the studio; separately and together, they had made more than one multi-platinum selling record. Once an album was completed I knew what then needed to be done: how to take the project through the record company, set the touring up, find a way to take the music live, to the fans, and give it the best possible chance of selling by the truckload. But I had to accept some very important essential facts. I was her manager (and agent). She was my client.

I felt it was important to remember that this was not my album. This wasn't Peter and Rod's music. This would be Tanita's record and she really had the right to do it whatever way she wanted to. She also had a right to decide who she wanted to work with. I might think that she is wrong. I might believe that I know a better way. But that was beside the point. Peter, Rod and I had a big say on *Ancient Heart*. Now, Tanita felt it was time for a change – and so it was. Tanita was far more hands-on in the making of *The Sweet Keeper*. By the time it came time to record the difficult third album, *Everybody's Angel*, Tanita was the co-producer.

There were also other serious behind the scenes issues. The first album was on Warner Bros, my dream label for this project. But between albums, Warner Bros decided they were now so big, and so successful, that they would divide the company into two labels. Warner Brothers and East West were to be two separate divisions with separate teams under the one roof, but both under Rob Dickens. We were told that Tanita was going to be on East West. It didn't matter that Tanita had signed to Warner Bros, or that Warner Brothers (worldwide) had been my label of choice for this artist.

As a set-up, East West was not in the same class as Warner Bros. Yes, they were nice people, and all that, but we no longer had Moira Bellas and Barbara Charone in the PR department working on Tanita's records. Moira and Barbara could break an act every day and before lunchtime. Tanita and I loved, and got on famously with them. They were vital to the success of *Ancient Heart*. Neither was Paul Conroy to be on Tanita's side of the company and believe me Paul Conroy is the kind of record company executive you *really* want to have on your side. East West's one major plus was that they had hired Fraser Kennedy to be on their team, but there's only so much one man can do.

It is never entirely clear why something works, but the end result of all these changes was that *The Sweet Keeper* didn't sell anywhere near as many copies as *Ancient Heart*. We weren't far off the 2 million mark – and it is still selling – but because of the stratospheric sales of *Ancient Heart* it was considered a failure.

Give me some more failures like that, *please*!

From an artistic perspective, no album containing a track as flawlessly brilliant as 'Harm in Your Hands', could be considered a failure. It is one of Tanita's finest pieces of songwriting.

Tanita's third album, *Everybody's Angel* sold fewer copies again. But what bothered me greatly – and still does – is that it was considered a failure, when it sold a million copies. The first single was a wonderful Tanita original song called 'Only The Ones We Love'. It celebrates the importance of family. Jennifer Warnes, Tanita's favourite singer, had turned up at her first LA gig and came backstage to meet Tanita. Her goodbye to Tanita, as she departed the madness that was happening backstage, after the show, was, "if you ever need me to sing on anything with you, please just call." We took her at her word and she added beautiful background vocals to the song in Groove Masters recording studios, in LA.

****

Just before the release of 'Only The Ones We Love' as a single, Tanita and I were travelling by train up to Manchester for a day's promotion. I made a call to Alan McGee, Head of Promotions at East West Records, to check the vital first week chart position and to see how we had fared on the BBC playlist. The news was not good. When I told Tanita that we hadn't made the BBC Radio playlist and the single had charted at No. 69 in its first week, she was devastated. She broke down and started sobbing. Failing to make the playlist – combined with a disappointing chart position – was a very reliable code that the single was not going to do the business. If it had charted in the Top 40, there was definitely something left to play for. It might have been all the encouragement the BBC playlist gate-keepers needed to add 'Only The Ones We Love' the following week. On the flip-side, if we had made the playlist, the guaranteed airplay would have pushed the record into the Top 40 the following week and the game would at least be on. But to receive the double negative news was the knockout punch. Tanita knew my shorthand. When I prefaced the news with the word, "You" – as in, "You are in the Top 40" – it was always going to be good news. But when I said, "We" – as in "We didn't make the playlist" – she knew it was going to be bad news.

I'll tell you, I have rarely felt as out of sorts as I did on that train journey. I didn't feel upset that the single wasn't going to make it. Sure, it was a brilliant single and deserved to succeed but... that's the way this business works. However, I felt devastated because she seemed so distraught. There are no acceptable words of comfort you can offer. Nor were there any words she wanted to hear from me. In that moment, I understood where she was at. I had a feeling, from the way she was glaring at me, that she was thinking, "You're my manager, this is your fault. I wrote the perfect song. You should have made it a hit." In a way, it was the same treatment she had very effectively given to the five people at the Acoustic Room in the Mean Fiddler, the first night I saw her. She did the same thing (and just as effectively) to me. There would be another day, and another album, when the world wouldn't seem quite so bad and eventually that claustrophobic feeling that she was fretting over – "this is all I have, this is my life" – would be gone. Yes, it would eventually go, but it would never ever be forgotten. I think, in hindsight, if I had the slightest inkling, on the night I first saw her, that she was going to be capable of making me feel so heart-sick, I would have happily walked away or, at the very least, made sure I found her a manager and stuck to my instinct of being her agent and only that.

****

When we were struggling to make the desired impact with the third album, I tried in vain to persuade East West that, even though it wasn't doing the numbers expected, predicted, or accounted for in their projections, they still should be supporting the album in general and the artist in particular. But no, they wouldn't budge. They had decided the album's life was over and stopped promoting it. By making that decision when they did, they also made their decision a self-fulfilling prophecy. Their argument was that the album had bombed and they would not throw good money after bad. My point was that the record company should still have continued promoting the album. More importantly they needed to be seen to be still promoting the album, and to be supporting Tanita as an artist. Her future was at stake. So too was their investment. But they didn't get it. Or maybe it was just that they didn't want to get it. They had made their money. Tanita, as an artist, had broken even for the label on the release of her very first single, 'Good Tradition'. I'm serious. The record company were fully recouped on one single! The good *old* Warner Bros had stuck with Ry Cooder for an incredible seven albums before they broke even on his account. By the time of her third album Tanita's account was ridiculously in credit. I wasn't asking the record company to do something Asgard as managers and promoters were not prepared to do. Tanita's concert at the London Palladium on 21 May 1995 still stands as the biggest loss we ever suffered, on a single show, in our history as promoters. But from the record company's side, they'd all enjoyed their big bonuses and were already onto their next, new, big, hot, young thing. That's fine.

Maybe that's the way it works. But you know what: they should sometimes maybe pause and view their overall profits and losses before deserting the artists they profess to love. They might even find that they would prolong their bonus income if they just stuck with their artists through the more difficult times.

They should have remembered the Monday morning on the original campaign when Jeff Beard, the Head of Sales rang me up and asked, "Guess how many copies of *Ancient Heart* Tanita has sold this morning?"

I figured it must be good because he'd never made such a call before. So I went high.

"7,000?"

"Try again," he chuckled.

"10,000?"

"Much higher, Paul," he continued, clearly enjoying himself.

"20,000?" I offered in sheer disbelief.

"No!"

He kept replying to the negative. I gave up when I reached a staggering 50,000.

"89,500," he eventually declared, putting me out of my misery.

Actually misery is not the right word. The other funny thing about that morning is that the magical sales figure wasn't enough to get the album to No.1 in the UK charts that week. In today's marketplace, you can get to No.1 in the album charts by selling 5,000 albums in the first week. In the entire life of an album today you're very lucky if you sell 50,000. So Tanita Tikaram sold more in that single Monday morning than would be needed to keep her at the top of the charts today for at least 19 weeks. But of course you can't really say that – because that was then and this is now and pretty soon it won't be anything at all. It's kind of like you are never meant to compare apples with pears. I quite like both apples and pears, so maybe a better comparison would be between lemons and pears. I'll leave it to your imagination which era would be the lemon.

CHAPTER THIRTY-SIX

TALKIN' 'BOUT POSTERS... WHAT'S WRITTEN ON THE WALL...

Asgard started promoting gigs for two core reasons. One, I was very keen to work with Van Morrison; and two, because it was often difficult to get promoters to buy into the level we felt our artists were at. So, we would promote the artists ourselves and then, after a tour or two, the other promoters would want to join in. And that was all fine. If things go well, you can make more money being a promoter than an agent. However, as with Tanita Tikaram at the London Palladium, you can also lose a lot of money – a fate which will never befall you as an agent.

I also stopped promoting for two reasons. One, as a promoter, I felt I owed it to the artist to be at every show I promoted, but the more successful we were, the more impossible that became; and two, the whole game became far too corporate. Whether it was good for selling tickets or not, the idea of branding became a kind of a fetish, with the artists' management demanding that all promoters, the world over, use the artist's standardised, self-produced artwork.

Which meant that the pleasure I took in creating artwork for posters and adverts was finished. I had always loved that aspect of the business – travelling around Europe and seeing, on the hoardings in cities, the posters the various countries would come up with. Leon Ramakers (Holland), Thomas Johansson (Sweden) and Assaad Debs (France) always did brilliantly distinctive and very classy posters. Under the new dispensation, that was all kaput. Indeed promoters worldwide would not only have to use the same artwork, they'd also be charged for the privilege of doing so.

I remember being forced to use a dank, depressing black and white piece of artwork – and the same insipid visuals – for two successive Jackson Browne tours. You couldn't even read the artwork when it was reduced for small press ads. And so every promoter would ring up and say, "Paul we know you like Jackson, but this artwork is dark, dank and depressing and is unreadable to the extent that it is useless."

What could I say? "Yes I know, and I agree with you, but I've already had the conversation with management, and they insist you use it… and pay for it!" And they'd say, "Even though we used it and paid for it for the last tour?"

All I could say in reply was, "Sorry." Because I really was.

There was an infamous instance when a manager refused to allow a French promoter to use "en concert" instead of the artist's original artwork version of "in concert". In a Spinal Tap moment, I tried explaining – to no avail – that "en concert" was in fact French for "in concert."

"It doesn't matter," I was told, "it has to be as it is in our artwork."

You couldn't make this stuff up.

I had been brought up to believe that when you enter someone's house you should honour and respect their ways. Should it not be the same when you enter someone else's country? Should we not be respectful enough to honour their traditions – in this case their style of artwork? So I stopped promoting.

Tanita Tikaram's debut was the second biggest selling album ever in Norway, behind Leonard Cohen. *Ancient Heart* had been No. 1 there for 12 weeks. So she was mega. My favourite Norwegian promoter – a tall, handsome gentleman by the name of Rune Lem – came up with the idea of putting Tanita Tikaram and Tracy Chapman together for a special outdoor show at the beautiful Isle of Calf one-day festival. It takes place in a stunning location on the outskirts of Oslo and in previous years I'd already booked Santana, Van Morrison and Jackson Browne in as headline acts. Now, in Norway, Tracy Chapman was not quite as mega as Tanita. So, in our opinion, Tanita deserved the top billing and Rune did the posters and adverts accordingly. The only problem was that Tracy's people felt she should be top. Rune explained his dilemma to me.

As it happens, there was a wee bit of history here. Very early in Tanita's career she had been booked to support John Martyn at the Saddler's Wells Theatre in London. At the last minute the promoter, John Lennard, was persuaded by Tracy Chapman's agent to add her to the bill. At the soundcheck on the afternoon of the show, when Tracy – or her people – discovered that she was going on before the unknown Tanita Tikaram (who didn't even have a record contract at that point) they threw a wobbler. Tracy had to – *just had to* – go on immediately before John Martyn. John Lennard asked me if they could swap Tanita and Tracy's spots. He said he didn't care either way and he was only asking me because he'd been requested to. I said, "Sorry, but we need to keep the billing the way it was agreed." I was also John Martyn's agent and John Lennard was his manager, so he really didn't have a problem. Tracy's people kept making a fuss, but eventually they headed back to their hotel to get ready for show time.

Tracy and party arrived back at the venue way after the time she had been told she was due on stage. They apologised profusely, the traffic was really bad, they were very sorry that Tanita had to go on early...

That was when the promoter admitted that he had intentionally told them the wrong stage time, thereby ensuring that they would be back in plenty of time for their correct stage time. They were further advised that Tracy was due to go on in five minutes and Tanita would be on after Tracy as per the original plan.

To say they weren't best pleased is like saying Lewis Hamilton enjoys losing.

That was then and this was now – and Rune was having problems over the billing on the poster.

"So", I said, "these posters of yours." I was examining the one he'd already sent me, now unfolded across my desk, "Well, no disrespect Rune, but they look very cheap".

"I know, but it's the printers up here."

"I wasn't complaining. I was just thinking, that if you need to print up, say, six posters, with a different layout, switching names, for instance, if you need to send them to someone, you know, in America or wherever, well... it wouldn't really cost you much, now would it?"

"Say no more PC," he said, and off he went, to complete his chore.

CHAPTER THIRTY-SEVEN

STRANGE FRUIT: THE TRUTH ABOUT LIFE ON THE ROAD

Lonnie Donegan was the banjo player in The Big Chris Barber Band. Born in Glasgow to an Irish mother and a Scottish father, Lonnie had a soupcon of swagger, a smidgeon of agony and a hell of a lot of style – but left to his own devices he probably would have been just as happy to have remained as a working musician in what was a very popular big band. However, in 1954, towards the end of one of the Barber's band's recording sessions, Lonnie recorded the vocals on an up-beat tune by American Blues artist, Lead Belly (aka Huddie Ledbetter), called 'Rock Island Line'. It was, it turned out, the birth of what became known as skiffle music.

Skiffle was a very successful fusion of unlikely bedfellows: black rhythm and blues and UK folk music. Predictably, you might say, Barber's record label, Decca Records, weren't in the least bit interested in Lonnie's tune and it remained an obscure album track until radio producers and DJs picked up on the song all by themselves. Well, golly gee. "By popular demand," Decca were forced to release the track as a single and it became a smash hit, peaking at No 8 in the UK Charts in January 1956. Extraordinarily, the single also made No 8 in America. It was the first of Lonnie Donegan's seventeen UK Top 10 hits, three of which occupied the coveted No 1 spot. Lonnie was the first artist whose debut single sold a million copies in the UK alone. 'Rock Island Line' went on to sell three million copies worldwide. Lonnie was paid a measly sum of £3.50 – the session-fee for the recording session as stipulated by the Musicians Union – for his performance on the hit. But, on the flip side, he had been launched as a successful artist.

Taj Mahal was influenced by Lonnie's sound. A young American called Phil Spector admitted Lonnie had inspired him to take up guitar. The Quarrymen – John Lennon's first band – were another Lonnie Donegan-influenced, skiffle style band. Even The Traveling Wilburys tipped a cap towards their skiffle roots.

Lonnie was one of the first great road warriors. He was a real live-wire; he'd do up to four shows a day and sold over a quarter of a million tickets on a three month tour. Media wise, Lonnie was like a combination of Bruce Springsteen and Oasis on stage, only twice as hip and far more cool. Lonnie was the big thing around the time The Beatles were becoming the next big thing. Now, over 30 years later, he wanted to get back to the limelight and I was more than willing to help out.

Lonnie made an album with Rory Gallagher, Chris Barber and Van Morrison. Donal Gallagher, Rory's manager, was helping Lonnie out and wanted me to become his agent. We took him on in 1999, and started to put shows in for him. I got him the Cambridge Folk Festival and The Acoustic Stage at Glastonbury and several concerts – plus Van was using Lonnie as special guest on some of his shows. And, being Van, he was very generous in relation to payments. Van was always unstinting with his musicians and his opening acts. Lonnie was such a glutton for gigging that he always had many irons in different fires and sometimes even two different irons in the same fire. He'd ask you to do stuff, you know, like putting some gigs together for him, which we would do, only to find someone else would be holding the same gigs for him. So I told him we couldn't work that way and we parted on good terms.

A year or so later, he wrote me a nice letter saying he'd sorted out all his other stuff and he'd like to talk about us working together again, and this time on an exclusive basis. He wanted to know if I'd mind having a meeting with him to discuss his touring. I was a great admirer of his talent, his energy and I liked him very much as a human being, apart from which he's an entertaining storyteller, so I readily agreed and we put in a lunch for the following Monday. About 11 o'clock that morning his wife, Sharon, rang up to say that Lonnie was a wee bit under the weather and would I mind if we postpone the lunch. Of course not, I said.

Later in the afternoon I received another call, this time from Lonnie.

"Sorry about lunch, mate," he said.

"No problem Lonnie," I said. "We'll do it another time. You sound terrible though, are you okay?"

"Actually, I'm in hospital, I came out of surgery about an hour ago."

"What! Listen Lonnie forget about all of this stuff, we can discuss it when you're feeling better. Now, away off with you, and rest," I said, finding it incredible that he'd be thinking about business so quickly after coming round after an operation.

The following day, I read in the newspapers that he'd had a quadruple bypass heart operation – his fourth I think – and he was still so desperate for work he was on the phone to his agent within an hour of coming round.

So much for him being, 'A wee bit under the weather.'

You see, Lonnie was part of the old school of show business, where you always had to be working. Equally you always had to be seen to be working. It was a bit like Ray Davies ringing me up after he had been shot in the leg to tell me he was okay and would be back.

The last time I'd seen Lonnie, before his "procedure", was when he opened for Van Morrison in The Oxford Apollo the year before. He was brilliant: he worked the audience like a trouper and had them all begging for an encore which never materialised, because the house lights came up before Lonnie even had a chance to get off the stage. It was a treat, though, to watch someone so in love with being on stage and so comfortable up there. In October and November 2002 some of his road crew reported to me that he was like two different men during what was to be his final tour. His last gig was in Nottingham, the city where, supposedly, he started his live career over half of a century earlier. Off-stage, he'd look tired, ill, weak, defeated and each and every one of his 71 years. But the minute he hit the boards, he was 10 foot tall and like a teenager giving the show of his life... *again*, just like he'd done every single night of his career.

Lonnie had written a few frequently covered songs like 'I'll Never Fall In Love Again', as well as picking up the publishing on classics like 'Nights In White Satin' by The Moody Blues and 'A Whiter Shade of Pale' by Procol Harum. So you'd have to figure he wasn't fixing up meetings with an agent while on his sick bed just to pay for the weekly provisions. That's the thing about artists like Lonnie. Health permitting, they never have an off-night.

It *really* is in their blood. They are true gigging musicians and I guess that means there also has to be a bit of a gypsy in them. You'd have to think that artists like Ray Charles, BB King and Bob Dylan have made enough dollars over their careers not to have to continue to live on the road. And the simple answer is: yes, they have made enough money – and yet they still do it. Or in the case of Ray and B.B. they did till they finally shuffled off stage for the last time.

These musicians carry on playing live, not because they want to, but also because they *have* to. Lonnie didn't start off doing this so he could still be on the road at 71 years of age, putting up with hotels, airports, stage doors, musicians, crew, cars, buses, trains and bad weather; not to mention four heart by-pass operations. He just ended up that way. When you're on tour, as Lonnie probably discovered early on in his career, something takes you over: it colonises your life. When you wake up, you can feel you are connected to something, like a magnet whose strength grows as the day progresses. Your days disappear in a haze of travel, hotels, sound checks, food, fans and autograph hunters – often the professional kind, who are not about the music of the person whose signature they are after, or even the show itself. They are merely chasing celebrities because they know the bigger the celebrity status of the owner of the squiggle, the more money they will get for it when they sell it, which is what they will invariably do. But through all of this, the magnet is growing stronger and stronger until it gets to the point where you no longer have the will to resist. And then you step out on the stage and it all falls into place.

The magnet is the magic of being out there in front of an audience.

The second you step out onto that stage, the rest of your day starts to make sense. In an indefinable way, you realise exactly why you want to do this. If the feeling was something you could put into words, it wouldn't have as much power over you. But it does.

The great artists mostly look and behave comfortably on stage. It is often where they feel most at home. They genuinely look like they were born to be up there. They are not scared of being on stage; they enjoy it immensely. Because of this, they are more likely to give a life-enriching performance, and not a recital.

The main difference between two seemingly talented tightrope walkers of equal ability is where one crosses the wire checking his fingernails while the other walks across respecting the distance between himself and the ground. The latter high wire artist has learnt from experience that showing off should not be part of the act.

Similarly, a real artist will never feel the need to display his or her superiority vocally or as a musician. But at the same time, the consummate performer will be aware that talent doesn't grow on trees and that a performance is expected.

Lonnie was happy doing what he did right up to that final night in The Royal Concert Hall in Nottingham, on Wednesday 30th October 2002 – and even then he was giving all he had to give, happy to be at home with his audience.

Ironically the title Lonnie had chosen for his final tour was, "This Could Be The Last Time."

****

Sadly not all artists are so well equipped for life on the road. Clifford Thomas Ward (or Clifford T. Ward) released a truly beautiful single 'Gaye' in 1973. It was an exquisitely written song with a melody which won a spot in the affections of Irish and English audiences alike from the very first listen. The single deservedly rose up the charts peaking at No 8 in the UK that summer and went on to sell a million copies. I bought the album a few weeks later. I loved it. It was called *Home Thoughts*. The album quickly became a great friend and I checked in vain trying to discover if Clifford T. Ward had any appearances coming up. The album was on the renowned Tony Stratton-Smith's Charisma label.

The Famous Charisma Records, to give it its full title, was also the home of Genesis (with and without Peter Gabriel), Lindisfarne, Rare Bird and Van De Graaf Generator, amongst others. I knew the Head of Press at Charisma, a loveable character by the name of Waxie Maxie. He was a real live, loud and proud Teddy Boy and he'd a fun weekly column in one of the music papers. Waxie Maxie (somehow it never seems right to call him just Waxie) told me that Clifford was a very talented artist – I could hear the "but" coming up – *but* he was painfully shy. Apparently

Clifford's chronic shyness made photo sessions, TV, shows, radio shows, and interviews virtually impossible. It also turned out that he'd only ever done one concert and there were no more planned.

Ireland, as it had a habit of doing, had taken Clifford T. Ward to its big collective heart. He *had* managed to do some TV and promo in Ireland and so the single had picked up great airplay and the album was doing really well. This success generated a buzz, which in turn was creating an audience who, the same as myself really, wanted to see him live. But there was nothing doing, apparently, and so I put it to the back of my mind.

A few years later Waxie Maxie put me in touch with Clifford. Waxie Maxie had mentioned my interest and as a result Clifford invited me up to his house, not too far from Kidderminster, for a meeting. It was a beautiful spring day and as my cab dropped me at the top of their drive, Clifford and Pat, his wife, were contentedly working away in the garden. The imagery of the title track, 'Home Thoughts From Abroad', immediately whacked me right between the eyes. A man (Clifford) has to work abroad – in the song, it was in Italy – and while he's doing so, he deals with the homesickness he feels, by putting his emotional thoughts of his home and his wife into the lyrics of this stunning, heartfelt song. Neil Diamond dealt with this same subject matter, also very effectively, in his classic 'I Am, I Said'.

There is this one live clip on YouTube where Clifford is performing this song, 'Home Thoughts From Abroad', and I swear to you he's not just singing the song, he is living it. It's very clear from his eyes how much he's hurting again. It's a TV talent show, The Castlebar Song Contest in 1982, and Clifford is the "entertainment" between the last act performing and the results being announced. You can't help feeling for him. You get the impression from his demeanour that onstage is the last place he wanted to be. Yet when he starts to sing he's immediately back in the sentiment of the song, feeling that debilitating pain of homesickness all over again.

Clifford and I discussed some concerts. He desperately wanted to do some live shows, but it was clear that this would be an uphill struggle for him. With that in mind, the idea of doing low key launch concerts in Ireland as a backdoor way to shows in England really appealed to him. I made a few suggestions and left Clifford and Pat to the tranquility of their garden. Clifford rang me a few days later and said how much he'd enjoyed our chat and he wished to go ahead by starting off the plan with some concerts in Ireland – but not to include any shows in the UK for the time being. He wanted to see if he was comfortable with the Irish shows first.

Clifford T. Ward sold out his show in the National Stadium, Dublin the minute it went on sale. Normally such a quick sell-out would mean you'd start to add additional shows. I felt that merely suggesting it would only make Clifford even more nervous. I had already explained to Clifford the magic combination of the intimacy of the venue and the uniqueness of the Dublin audience."It's just like having a few friends around to your house to sing some tunes for them," I said, a style Kate and Anna McGarrigle had very successfully perfected. Personally, I wasn't convinced Clifford was the type of person who would have a "few" friends around to his and Pat's beautiful house for a "come-all-ye", but it was the best I could come up with.

Clifford was very excited about the Dublin concert selling out so quickly. Of course, if you were of a nervous disposition, the next level on, from being very excited about selling out a concert would be getting *too* excited about it. Sadly, very sadly, this proved to be the case. Five weeks before the Irish shows, Clifford rang up and said, "Look Paul, I'm very sorry but I just can't do these concerts in Ireland." The key words for me were "Sorry" and "can't" because I knew beneath it all he really *was* extremely sorry and he really *couldn't* do the shows. He painfully explained that he and Pat had discussed it over and over again – but the bottom line was he was finding it impossible to contemplate. I believe Clifford wanted to do these shows as much as, if not more than, I – and the audience – wanted him to do them. He seemed very relieved that I didn't attempt to persuade him to change his mind. I figured that he'd put himself through that particular set of wringers already, plus I knew my conscience would never forgive me if I tried to force him to do something that was clearly anathema to him..

I had a sense also that the Irish audiences would never have forgiven me either, that they understood and perhaps even sympathised. If you ever catch the YouTube clip, you'll see why you would never want to put someone, anyone, in a position of such transparent liquid trauma: it's literally oozing from each and every pore in his body. Clifford and I agreed we would keep in touch and we would address the live situation at another time. We did keep in touch; I really enjoyed our chats and his honesty. Sadly he never felt comfortable enough to make the leap. I suspect that if Clifford T. Ward had been an "overnight sensation", his nervousness wouldn't have been an issue. Singing live to an audience would just have been another natural chore he'd have had to do in the new life he'd found himself in. Clifford had been in a few professional groups pre-'Gaye'. He'd even made an album, *Singer-Songwriter*, (1972) for John Peel's Dandelion Record label. But because he had time to see and observe how the business works from the inside, he'd have worked out what stressed him so badly, and realised what the anxiety was capable of doing to his nervous system. Many industry luminaries have said that, if only Clifford hadn't been so nervous, or shy, he'd have been a mega singer-songwriter. Even though, in the several years I worked with him, I never actually succeeded in doing a single concert with him, I was always very proud to represent him. To me he was one of the perfect Asgard singer-songwriters.

Sadly Clifford T. Ward passed away a week before Christmas, 2001.

****

Carly Simon was another one of my favourite singer songwriters. I loved her albums *Anticipation* (1971) and *No Secrets* (1972). More recently, I really enjoyed her very revealing book, *Touched by The Sun* (2019), about her friendship with Jackie Kennedy. She is a hugely talented and genuinely fascinating character.

Although she did occasionally suffer from bouts of stage fright, Carly wasn't nearly as anxious about performing as Clfford T. Ward. She did a few phenomenally successful American tours and it often occurred to me that we were missing out on something special, not seeing her in Europe. However, there was a major obstacle: she suffered from a severe fear of flying. I was told that Carly is what airlines refer to as "a runner". They'd even go as far as marking her up on their manifest accordingly.

Runners might book a seat and even board the flight – but at the last possible moment, they're likely to dart out of the aircraft, just before the door is shut, and scarper down the steps. This particular anxiety made it difficult to imagine her touring Europe. I eventually met Carly through a mutual friend, a very fine singer songwriter called David Saw. As it happens, David is also "a runner," but I set up some shows around London for him and it all worked out. David was good mates – and played guitar – with Carly's son, Ben Taylor. Thus, it happened that word came back from Carly, via Ben and David, that she was very interested in finally doing a European concert tour. I spoke to her representative, who put me in touch directly with Carly and it was true: she was very keen to do some shows. She knew from David that Catherine and I had occasionally visited Martha's Vineyard. As we were planning to be there that summer, we decided to meet up. I remember the summer of 2007 well, mainly due to the fact that a Fruupp song I co-wrote had been sampled and covered by Talib Kweli with Norah Jones on vocals and while we were on Martha's Vineyard the album containing the song entered the US album charts at No 2. Needless to say, I was rather pleased!

The night before I met up with Carly Simon, along with Ben Taylor, her daughter Sally Taylor, and David Saw, she gave an impromptu performance in a cool venue on the island. It really was a beautiful, spiritual, family type of occasion. The following day I met Carly at her home, and we discussed everything under the sun to do with the tour, including, but not limited to, the musicians – David and Ben were to be in the band – equipment, crew, venues, cities, countries, routing, taxes, commissions and what have you. The idea was that Carly and her troupe would arrive by QE2. The tour buses would pick them up in Southampton and the tour would be routed so it was doable by bus and ferry and then she would return to the USA on the QE2. By that point, tour buses had become very cool, decked out with 5 Star hotel-class comfort and finishes. It sounded like a plan.

Catherine and I left the Island and returned to London in good spirits: it had been an enjoyable and worthwhile trip. Carly and I kept in touch and I painstakingly put together a tour which would take in 24 concerts, during the spring of the following year. Then just before I was given the green light... I was given the red light. David Saw said everything was great, apart from the transatlantic travel bit – which, of course, was fundamental. The two boat trips were making the timescale too long and flights weren't a possibility, so the tour was put on hold.

Carly eventually came to London on the QE2, to do some album promo.

Alas she stayed for less than a week but managed to include a live Radio 2 showcase, which was genuinely incredible. Carly sang her heart out and looked like she was thoroughly enjoying herself. I thought the brief trip might re-invigorate Carly's interest in a concert tour. But sadly (several years later) it hasn't... or not so far at any rate. I hope a tour will eventually happen. I'm a patient man.

****

I was a major fan of Jennifer Warnes's brilliant work with Leonard Cohen. I eventually met Jennifer at a Tanita Tikaram concert in LA. Subsequently, Jennifer did some beautiful harmony vocals on a couple of Tanita's albums, including on 'Only The Ones We Love' and 'I Might Be Crying' – on which Jennifer put an incredible multi-voiced, multi-tracked Polynesian chant. An element of serendipity entered the picture. The manager of one of the acts I was already working with also became Jennifer's manager and signed her to Asgard for agency representation. At the time, we'd been discussing how great it would be to get Jennifer to finally do a tour of Europe in her own right. Again we sketched in a routing for Jennifer with a few special events, festivals included. Sadly we never managed to get anything off the ground. The new manager became the ex-manager but Jennifer and I continued to have our chats directly. She covered Mike Scott's majestic 'The Whole of the Moon' for one of her albums, but still no tour.

When I noticed she was doing some American dates I got in touch with Jennifer again. She was very excited about being back out on the road and hoped that the North American dates would be a stepping stone towards some European shows. Whatever was going on behind the scenes, the US tour hadn't come together easily. Then she signed a new record deal and so the dates we'd been discussing had to be shelved. Any live work would have to tie in with a future album release. The next album took a long time – as in years – to finish. Still there was no sign of a tour. As the process of nothing happening extended indefinitely, it struck me that, if you're not careful – and you're not like The Waterboys, or Nick Lowe, or Lonnie Donegan, or Dylan on his never ending tour – then you're in danger of falling into a slumber, wherein not touring grows to become more attractive than touring. This is the agent's worst nightmare. In different ways, Clifford T. Ward, Carly Simon and Jennifer Warnes had all made it real for me. But not for a minute did I love their music less as a result.

CHAPTER THIRTY-EIGHT

THOSE GRAND OLDE BOYS, FROM ROY ORBISON TO NOTTING HILLBILLIES

In case you hadn't noticed, I am a major fan of singer-songwriters. Not just the ones I've been lucky enough to work with, but also master craftsmen and women like Carole King, Paul Simon, Leonard Cohen, Nick Drake, Joni Mitchell, Neil Diamond, Joan Armatrading, Lesley Duncan and Bob Dylan. I've always been in awe of those people who can create a perfectly formed song from, seemingly, out of nowhere. I was even a sucker for Inigo Jollipant from the thoroughly enjoyable *The Good Companions*. It wasn't meant to be enjoyable because JB Priestley's most popular tome was a school course book for that long lost year. I won't ruin it for you by telling you whether or not the singer-songwriter (Inigo) wins the heart of the girl (Susie) or not. But ever since my first gig, that night in Rasharkin, when I was caught in a trance by the lyric to 'She Thinks I Still Care', it has been about that unique combination of the music, the melody and the lyric for me. The economy with which the writer could convey the twists and turns of a broken relationship in a short song, struck a chord with me. It might have been because if you knew the singer and/ or writer was going through the same pain as you, it made your pain easier to bear. Either way, when – as in the Elvis hit 'His Latest Flame' – your fate was sealed and you knew she was in the arms of another, well, you could always turn to Roy Orbison with his majestic 'It's Over' or even his gorgeous, show-stopping 'Crying'.

Roy was another of those singers I'd been chasing for ages. In my book he'd always been a singer-songwriter in the finest sense of the word, and up there with the best of them. After a few years of trying, a friend of mine, another USA manager, casually dropped into one of our regular catch-up conversations that he'd heard that Roy's wife Barbara was now his manager and she was bringing a whole fresh energy to Roy's career. I tracked Barbara down. We spoke on the phone. A no-unnecessary frills type, she was immediately friendly. She was interested to hear what I'd recommend. I was clear: I'd avoid the lucrative chicken and chips in the basket circuit in favour of aggressively promoting Roy as a current artist. He had started to be considered cool again by a lot of the younger acts, some of whom were enjoying success with covers of Roy's classic songs. My plan was to bring him back to London around the time of the release of his (1987) album, *In Dreams: The Greatest Hits* and play somewhere totally unexpected. The idea was to invite everyone down to the show, create a major post-show buzz and then bring Roy back again the following year for a full scale European tour around the time of his next album – which Jeff Lynne had already agreed to produce.

Barbara liked the idea. She went off to check me out with some of the managers of the artists I work with. We spoke again a few nights later when she reported that she had discussed Asgard with Roy and they had decided to work with us. You can't imagine the buzz you feel when someone of Roy's stature agrees to take you on as their agent.

The venue I picked for the showcase was the Mean Fiddler. Together, we made such a fuss over the show that absolutely everyone in London was talking about it by show-time. The guest list was rammed: just about everyone that mattered was there. No matter how much an artist is hyped, there really is no hiding place for them from the minute they walk on-stage, especially when the venue is so small that most of the audience could see their own reflection in Mr Orbison's trademark sunglasses.

Hiding places didn't come into it. When Roy's band – all smartly decked out as if it was the opening night of a long run at the Copacabana in New York rather than the Mean Fiddler in Harlesden – started up they were tight, but not in a "we've got the chops" show off kind a way. You could tell immediately that it was going to be good. But when Roy Orbison himself stepped up to the microphone and opened his mouth and started to sing, the audience shivered in pure delight. This was a mas hairs-on-the-back-of-the-neck-standing-up moment. Roy might have been from a different era, but he and his band were *soooo* good that nothing else mattered. They played all the hits you'd have seen him perform on Top of The Pops: his first UK No. 1, 'Only The Lonely'; the mighty 'Crying'; the heart-breaking, 'It's Over' also a UK No. 1; 'Pretty Woman' his other UK No.1, with the catchy guitar motif, more effective than a chorus and completed with his unique the gargle sssssnarl. Then there was the painfully sad, epic, mini opera, 'Running Scared' and more... much more. If the audience had their way, Roy Orbison would still have been on stage singing, not for his supper but for his breakfast the following morning. To hear all those songs back-to-back from the man who created them, was an extraordinary experience. I met Roy after the show and discovered that he was a gentle, quiet man, and entirely unassuming despite the fact that he wrote very complex songs musically and lyrically. The Mean Fiddler show was a major success. It achieved all our objectives. Roy Orbison was back in the limelight.

The following year was a very busy year for Roy. 1988 started off with a television special recorded at The Coconut Grove, a night club in LA – the award winning, *Roy Orbison and Friends: A Black and White Night*. The band that night consisted of Elvis Presley's TCB band: Glen D Hardin (piano); James Burton (lead guitar); Jerry Scheff (bass); and Ronnie Tutt (drums), with special guests Bruce Springsteen, Tom Waits, Jennifer Warnes, k.d. lang, J. D. Souther, Steven Soles, Jackson Browne, Bonnie Raitt and Elvis Costello. What a band, what a night, what a singer-songwriter and worth the price of the DVD, even just to catch Tom Waits's organ solo. Meanwhile, with Jeff Lynne producing, Roy continued work on his new album. Jeff was also producing George Harrison's new album and Roy agreed to sing on one of the songs for the B-side of George's first single from the album. George and Jeff put together a bunch of mates to record the track: George Harrison, Jeff Lynne, Roy Orbison, Bob Dylan, Tom Petty and Jim Keltner. The song was called 'Handle With Care' and – rather than being relegated to anyone's B-side – it became the first track for a new album the six musicians went on to record under the band name of The Traveling Wilburys.

I met up with Roy and Barbara again at a beautiful apartment they had, in Dorset Square, for when they were in London. They were in town on

Wilbury promotion business, but Roy was still hoping his album would be completed by the end of the year and then we could start to plan the tour to tie in with record company release dates.

I can't remember if I cried when I heard the news on December 6, 1988, that Roy had died. He had been so full of hope when we met. 'You Got It', a song Roy, Jeff Lynne and Tom Petty wrote for Roy's final album, *Mystery Girl*, was released a month after Roy's death and reached No. 3 in the UK and No 9 in The USA. *Mystery Girl*, which was Roy's twenty-second album, raced to top the charts in USA and the UK to join *The Travelling Wilburys Vol* I, which was also a huge hit. Bono and The Edge pulled off a masterstroke by writing 'She's a Mystery To Me' (from whence the album title came) – the perfect Roy Orbison song for Roy Orbison to sing.

Roy Orbison's glorious gig at the Mean Fiddler would turn out to be his final London appearance and the one and only show I got to do with him and Barbara. It was also one of the greatest gigs I was ever involved in – and for that I am very grateful.

****

It's the story of my life, I know, but I'd been chasing Gordon Lightfoot for decades to come to the UK and Ireland for concerts. I was a big fan of his songwriting. I'd had one of his albums, *Sit Down Young Stranger* at the time when I didn't have a lot of albums and so I knew it inside out. I have always thought it funny that when you buy a new album, no matter how much you might enjoy it the first few times you play it, you will, eventually, without even being conscious of it, start to play other albums at its expense – until, eventually, you stop playing it altogether. *Sit Down Young Stranger* was not one of those. I suspect I bought it because of the haunting, 'If You Could Read My Mind', or because Ry Cooder and John Sebastian played on the album. But I grew to love it because, in racing terms, it was a stayer.

The years rolled around. I noticed that Gordon hadn't been to Europe for ages. I spoke to Gordon's PA, Anne Leibold, conspicuously failing to remark that she had the perfect name for someone in showbusiness. As it turned out, Anne couldn't have belied her name more completely: she was always very polite, pleasant, gracious and extremely together. And so I kept in touch with her. If I noticed that Gordon was doing another long run in the Massey Hall in Toronto I'd get in touch. Gordon Lightfoot is to the Massey Hall – he has done a record 160 concerts there in 60 years – what Eric Clapton is to the Royal Albert Hall. Except that Eric's tally is even higher at 214 concerts.

Eventually, on one of my regular calls, Anne surprised me by announcing, "Yeah Gordon said that the next time you called to tell you he's ready to come over." So in the early summer of 2016, he did just that.

The expectations were high. Gordon Lightfoot features on most people's favourite singer songwriter lists, including Bob Dylan's. He's written songs everyone knows, though they may not know that they are Gordon Lightfoot songs. Realistically it was too late in his career to win over any new fans but there were more than enough to fill the venues, including a wonderful evening in the Royal Albert Hall, on Tuesday 24th May 2016.. It was a successful tour and another ambition to be crossed off my bucket list. Sometimes, you gotta just keep picking up the phone to make it happen.

The Notting Hillbillies

I was in the Asgard office in Dryden Chambers when John Illsley and David Knopfler walked in. They were touting their new band Dire Straits, who had started to cause a stir in London, thanks mainly to Charlie Gillet's show on Radio London. Dire Straits consisted of John (bass guitar), David (rhythm guitar) David's brother Mark Knopfler (lead guitar and vocals) and Pick Withers (drums). They sounded like their main influences were Bob Dylan, Ry Cooder and JJ Cale, but with a very refreshing cinematic spin in their lyrics. I imagine they came to see us because (a) we listened to Radio London; and (b) my partner, Paul Fenn, represented Ry Cooder and JJ Cale.

We thought Dire Straits were great. I had reservations about their name, particularly in light of the then current punk movement, worrying that people might assume they were a punk band. We secured a few gigs for them around the London club scene, including one at Dingwalls Dance Hall in Camden Town. Man about town, Ed Bicknell, was dragged down to see them by his mate at Phonogram. He fell in love with Mark's red Stratocaster, and decided on the spot that he wanted not just to be the band's agent but also their manager. Ed eventually hooked up with the very together, super-efficient, extremely cool, and always dapper Paul Cummins, to form Damage Management. Dire Straits and Damage Management went on to fame and fortune, breaking records all around the world in terms of albums sales and box office receipts. It's always heartening to see the good guys win – and there are always more than enough other great acts out there to keep us occupied 'round the clock. We continued to promote Dire Straits shows in Ireland, including our second ever massive outdoor gig, Dublin Festival No.2, at Punchestown Racecourse, on Sun 17 June 1983, with The Undertones (playing their final gig with Feargal), Nick Lowe, The Chieftains, Hotfoot and Paul Brady on the bill. Paul Cummins became a major fan of Paul Brady that day, and signed him to Damage Management.

A lot of people turned up outside Punchestown that day, trying to get in free. They seemed to be well organised to me. In Italy, the music-should-be-free-movement protested regularly outside gigs, usually leading to riots. I'd never been aware of it in Ireland before, but it was for real – indeed there were riots the following year outside the Bob Dylan gig in Slane. As the tension built that afternoon, I was convinced it was all going to kick off. And if people got hurt, I started to worry, it would likely be seen as my fault. After all, I was solely responsible for bringing the audience there. We doubled the security on the gates fearing violence was going to explode at any moment. Then the air started to go out of the balloon. Some of the people who had been chomping at the bit to get free access to the site seemed to sense the danger, because, in a matter of five vital minutes, about half of them literally disappeared, melting away into the afternoon. But I was scarred by the experience. It was scary knowing that it could all have gone horribly wrong and ended up a disaster with lots of innocent people being hurt or worse. I decided it just wasn't worth it, no matter how much money you could potentially make. There never was a Dublin Festival No 3. In fact I never promoted a gig outdoors again.

In truth, there had been a wee bit of trouble backstage at Dublin Festival No.2 as well. One of the musicians in the main act complained to their Manager that there were no suitable dedicated toilets available for him. So the Manager in turn complained to his co-manager, who complained to the band's tour manager, who in turn complained to the band's production manager, who complained to the band's stage manager, who complained to the promoter – yours truly – who complained to the promoter's rep, who complained to the site manager, who complained to the venue's representative, who complained to the venue's caretaker, who complained that the whole fecking lot of us were making a mountain out of a molehill. He took the artist to the private club-house underneath one of the stands and, not only showed the artist through to their luxurious 5-star toilet (allegedly a former stall for horses suffering from stage fright), but also guarded the door from the outside while said business was being conducted. Apart from anything else, the whole exercise did serve to display the way the smelly stuff moved through the music business.

****

I'd still occasionally bump into Mark Knopfler at Brendan Croker and The 5 O'Clock Shadows' gigs and on a few special nights he joined Brendan, and a third mate, one Steve Phillips, on stage for an incredible performance at the Acoustic Room in the Mean Fiddler. Mark clearly enjoyed the contrast between the small intimate gigs and the 60,000-plus audiences Dire Straits were playing to worldwide on their lengthy tours.

So much so that during a break between *Brothers In Arms* and *On Every Street* albums, Mark formed a band with his mates Brendan Croker (guitar and vocals), Steve Phillips (guitar and vocals), Guy Fletcher (keys from Dire Straits), Marcus Cliffe (bass from Five O'Clock Shadows) and Ed Bicknell (drums – yet another drummer manager). The new group was called The Notting Hillbillies. They released a skiffle-influenced album called, *Missing... Presumed Having a Good Time*, which climbed to No 2 in the UK albums charts in 1990. As Ed was busy (very busy) in the drummer's seat, he and Mark appointed me as agent for the band and I booked a UK tour for them. They did 40 sold out shows (including 5 nights in London) in just 43 days in April and May 1990, and then went back to their day jobs.

****

Paul Cummins was managing Paul Brady. I was his agent and I wanted to do something different. We had worked on highly successful London runs for Tom Waits, Christy Moore, Van Morrison, Jackson Browne and Elvis Costello & The Attractions. Why not have a go with Paul? A successful run of shows can be the equivalent of a hit single or a chart album, for a great live performer, in that, if successful, it can gain similar high profile exposure and shine a bright light on the artist's complete body of work.

Late in 2000, I approached Peter Aiken of Aiken Promotions with the idea of a Dublin run, in Vicar Street. Although he wasn't Paul Brady's regular promoter, Peter was very enthusiastic about the project. It certainly helped that he was already a major Brady fan.

At the outset, Peter felt I was being too ambitious with my proposed Paul Brady Month at Vicar Street. He countered with a commitment for a week with an option (on his side, natch) to add an additional week, with further weeks added, subject to demand. The thing about a run is that you really do have to make a statement. You have to go out with all media and marketing guns blazing. You have a chance, with your initial campaign to capture the public's imagination and for ticket sales to catch fire. If you go out cap in hand, and are half-hearted with your launch, the audience tends to react accordingly and you never get to your option shows.

Peter Aiken totally bought into the logic and we went on sale with Paul Brady's Month (Oct 2001) at Vicar Street. When you factored in the necessary rest nights, we were left with 23 show nights. Ambitious? Perhaps. But when you take into consideration Paul Brady's reputation as a live performer, and the potential contained in his wee battered telephone book, I remained quietly confident. As Paul got to work, the ingredients came together: Brady's live reputation; a stellar cast of guest artists; and Brady returning to his folk/trad roots for a few of the nights. So, the event became much bigger than the sum of the parts. For all of that October, music fans in Ireland and some from as far away as London, Nashville and even San Francisco were talking about the Paul Brady Month in Vicar Street. Peter and Bren Berry from Aiken Proms stepped in, above and beyond the call of duty. Paul Brady's office, namely Liz Devlin and John Munnis, kept it all running smoothly. There were no wobbles, no shapes were thrown and it was all about getting the artist on stage each night.

Aer Lingus even threw in a few tickets to get some of the special guests in from the USA and London. It was intense, as Brady and his band worked really hard, each and every afternoon putting that particular evening's show together with the special guests. Most of the audience didn't have a clue as to who would be sharing the stage on any particular night, but I'm pretty sure that no one went home disappointed.

Over the years I've been very lucky with my adventures in wonderland. I've witnessed some incredible performances – but Tuesday 23 October 2001 was right up there with the best of them, when Paul was joined onstage by Van Morrison and the original lead singer with the Royal Showband, Brendan Bowyer. It was one of those magical concerts where every single song took the show a step further on up that rare ladder of perfection. Both Paul and Van were so turned on by the magic they were tapping into, that neither of them wanted it to stop, nor the night to end. I remember seeing them stealing an occasional look at each other as if in disbelief that they were on stage, at the same time, sharing these utterly unique moments with *the* legend from the Irish Showband world, Mr Brendan Bowyer. On that night, they were part of something so special that it was never, ever going to happen again. In fact, we all were. The following year I took a variation on the Paul Brady Month at Vicar Street idea to Julian Vignoles at RTE, suggesting it would make a great TV series. Julian bought into it immediately and produced a wonderful TV series called The Paul Brady Songbook. Reflecting on it afterwards, I thought, one more time with feeling: really, who needs hit singles?

Not me, that's for sure...

****

At Asgard over the years we've been lucky enough to work with some of the world's greatest blues artists. I'm talking about people like John Lee Hooker, Buddy Guy, Taj Mahal, Dr John, Robert Cray and Sonny Terry and Brownie McGhee.

We represented Sonny and Brownie towards the end of their career together. My first meeting with them was very bizarre. Although I'd been through all the tour details in advance with their American representative in NYC, the artists insisted on meeting me at their hotel the minute they arrived in London. I sat down with them. Sonny was probably the best blues harp player who ever lived and was a big, gentle, warm, smiling man; in contrast, I always felt that Brownie was somewhat underrated as a blues artist. Maybe he too felt that to be the case, because he was always guarded, withdrawn even. Anyway, I sat down with them and, as requested, went through the tour details with them: the cities, the venues, the fees and the state of the deposits. All artists are keen to ensure that 50% of their fees have been deposited with their agent before stepping on stage for their first concert.

Brownie asked me a few questions as we went along, and then, just when I thought we'd covered everything, Sonny asked me the same questions all over again and had me repeat the fees. By the time I sat down with them, it turned out, they hadn't actually spoken to each other for about 17 years. Although they would never allow any meetings to take place unless they were both in attendance, they insisted that you address them both separately and directly. It didn't matter that they both had to hear the information twice: it was only important that (a) you addressed each of them as individuals and (b) you never spoke to one of them without the other being present.

I still find it quite incredible that two artists could never communicate with each other for 17 years, yet still gel so brilliantly on stage every night. The shows we did with them were at the end of a long career, but I was dumbstruck by the power they generated nightly on stage.

When you hear Sonny howling through his harmonica you don't just think you can hear the long black train coming down the line. No, you sense that the train is coming for you. Like it is coming – in the end – for us all.

CHAPTER THIRTY-NINE

IT'S FUNNY WHO YOU CAN BUMP INTO ON THE ROAD

I met Dave Stewart once at Heathrow Airport in London. We were on our way to a festival in Belgium, where he was playing with his band Eurythmics, formed out of the ashes of The Tourists. He and his entourage, and the party I was with – I can't remember if it was Van, Buzzcocks or The Undertones – were all suffering from delayed flight syndrome. When we found a space to decamp into, I happened to be sitting next to him and we had breakfast together. He was very chatty. He had a copy of *Music Week* with him and was very excited that Eurhythmics' new single had just charted. Dave was clearly a scholar of the mechanics of the music business: he knew all about how the charts worked. But the conversation wasn't all about him – he was very interested in my acts and we exchanged yarns until our flight was called.

Post-festival some members of Eurythmics were being driven back from the festival site to the hotel in the same van as me and my band. Annie Lennox plonked herself down next to me. Again, we had a good old natter as the vehicle bounced over the rough terrain close to the festival site. She was particularly interested in Van and Jackson: these were artists that other musicians respected and maybe even loved. The thought occurred to me that I might like to represent Eurythmics, but the moment passed and I was too busy to think about it afterwards.

Many years later, I became agent for Shakespear's Sister, who featured Dave Stewart's then wife, Siobhan Fahey, late of Bananarama – who, of course, had been a huge crossover pop success. Shakespear's Sister were on London Records and they had an excellent manager, Steve Blackwell, who was always on the case. The music business is a bit like a train station, with all sorts of lines criss-crossing in the most unpredictable ways. Steve was also manager of an American artist, Nan Vernon. Dave Stewart, it transpired, was her producer and so our paths intertwined again. Nan had made an encouraging start to her career. We did some double bills with the Belfast singer-songwriter Andy White that were well received and all seemed to be going well for Nan. For some reason, however, the album she was working on got shelved and – pretty much overnight – Nan just disappeared. I assumed she must have returned to the USA.

The big wheel kept on turning. Dave Stewart and Fun Boy Three singer Terry Hall formed a group called Vegas. They had two very promising singles and made a great album that was sadly ignored. Steve was manager and Asgard were agents and Vegas toured a bit – but they never really caught the public imagination. Perhaps they were missing Annie's very distinctive, soaring vocals.

I always find myself putting Eurythmics, Queen and Abba in the same section on my CD shelves. To me, they are all trapped in an, "I prefer their singles" syndrome. I mean I'll be happily going about my day and – if I accidently tune into a radio station playing good music – I'll be ecstatic to hear 'Sweet Dreams' by Eurythmics, 'The Day Before You Came' by Abba, or Queen's 'Somebody To Love'. Later on in the day I might dig out one of their albums and put it on – but by the third or fourth track I always need to play something else. One track on the radio is magic; several tracks on the CD player and I find myself automatically reaching for *Moondance* or *Traveling Wilburys Vol I*. I do believe it might just be a character flaw on my part and I plan to build it into a character for one of my Christy Kennedy mysteries. I just need to work out exactly what it says about a potential character first.

CHAPTER FORTY

HE WRITES SONGS THE WHOLE WORLD SINGS

Who is the best-songwriter-never-to-make-an-album? I'm thinking about one of the all-time great songwriters, Mr. Bob McDill. He's had over 30 (and still counting) No. 1 hit singles on Billboard's US Country Charts. He's been covered by everyone from Alan Jackson, Waylon Jennings, Perry Como, Grateful Dead and Jerry Lee Lewis to Bobby Bare, who recorded an entire album of McDill songs under the inventive title of, *Me and McDill*. And a very fine album it was too. Still is. But here's the rub: Bob McDill songs are at their best when showcased by Don Williams, who always included at least 2 or 3 Bob McDill songs on each of his excellent albums. In fact, *The Essential Don Williams His Greatest Hits* has no less than eight classic Bob McDill songs or co-writes. Every time I hear his version of 'Amanda' (another Bob McDill song with intricate lyrics and the sweetest of tunes) I wonder what kind of song the master craftsman might have come up with if he'd turned his spotlight on the object of my teenage, unrequited affections, Margaret Hutchinson. I can almost hear it now, a story-song telling how her Hollywood looks resulted in tailgating around the Diamond; her strolling hand in hand, with a mysterious out-of-towner, along the banks of the Moyola; not to mention the Wall's Corner Boys' synchronised head-turning. It might have been the ideal song for Ulster's finest country-music artist, Brendan Quinn, to cover. If only it had been written, that is.

On a rare Nashville trip, I tried to track down Bob McDill. I ended up speaking on the phone to someone from JMI, the publishing company

Bob was signed to. The gentleman on the other end of the line turned out to be none other than the legendary Cowboy Jack Clement and we'd a great, lengthy chat.Cowboy Jack worked as a producer and engineer on sessions with the likes of Roy Orbison, Carl Perkins and Johnny Cash, for Sam Phillips at Sun Records. It was he who 'discovered' and recorded Jerry Lee Lewis when Sam Philips was outta town. As far back as the 1960s, Jack Clement signed two songwriters, Dickie Lee and Steve Duffy, to his publishing company. They delivered a song to him which Jack took a big shine to: it was, he believed, a classic. In 1962, he single-handedly persuaded country music superstar George Jones to record the heart-breaker. The resulting single spent 23 weeks in the Billboard Hot Country charts, six of those weeks at No.1. It became a cornerstone of George Jones' career and the most requested tune in his repertoire. The song was in fact 'She Thinks I Still Care' – the song I'd heard The Driftwoods perform back in Rasharkin at my first dance. The Driftwoods, it turned out, were in very good company because Elvis Presley, Cher, Jerry Lee Lewis, Anne Murray, Glen Campbell, John Fogerty and James Taylor, amongst numerous other artists, also recorded it. Anne Murray's version – renamed 'He Thinks I Still Care' – also reached No. 1. in the Billboard Hot Country chart. It was a good one.

Successful as Jack Clement could be at convincing artists to do what he wanted, he confessed that he'd never been able to persuade Bob McDill to make a serious attempt at a recording career of his own. The writer was more than happy spending his time writing songs and lecturing English classes at a local University. Just as I was giving up hope, Cowboy Jack Clement mentioned in passing that Bob had recorded several of his songs with his musician friends, and collected them onto a demos album – mainly to be sent out to producers who were looking for songs for artists they were working with to record.

"Any chance of buying one of those?" I asked, with all the subtlety of an X-Factor contestant.

He laughed (as you do).

I got the picture (as you do).

We chatted some more and as I eventually prepared to leave, he threw me a scrap by saying he'd have a wander around the office next time he had a moment, to see if he could find a copy of the McDill demo album. "But that was ages ago," he added, "and we didn't press up very many copies."

I got back to London, and forgot all about it until – a month or so later – a mint copy of Bob McDill's extremely rare album turned up in the mail as a gift from Cowboy Jack Clement. The album was called *Short Stories*. It had 'escaped' rather than being released in 1972, self-produced, front-room sounding, and contained 10 beautiful songs written or co-written by Bob McDill. The 'some of his friends', who played on the album, turned out to be regulars on Don Williams' albums and tours. The album was in a lovely sleeve, made from very stiff American cardboard, which protected the album and the art – which is probably why I still have it today.

In addition to Don Williams, Bob had songs recorded by Bobby Bare, Crystal Gayle, Waylon Jennings, Ray Charles, The Grateful Dead, Joe Cocker, Anne Murray, Emmylou Harris, Dan Seals, Alan Jackson, Kathy Mattea, Mel McDaniels, Sammy Kershaw and Pam Tillis, among many more. He had 31 – that's thirty-one – No.1 country hits. He was voted Songwriter of the Year on three occasions, received the ASCAP Golden Note Award and the Academy of Country Music's Poet's Award. He wrote two books. Nobel Prize for Literature winner V. S. Naipaul has written about him. And yet very few people in music know who he is. He came up with some of those great song-titles that make country music such a pleasure-ground for so many. 'Somebody's Always Sayin' Goodbye', 'If Hollywood Don't Need You (Honey I Still Do)', 'I May Be Used (But Baby I Ain't Used Up)', 'You Turn Me On (Like A Radio)', 'I Never Made Love (Till I Made It With You)', 'Lord Have Mercy On A Country Boy', 'I'm Living Up To Her Low Expectations' and 'All The Good Ones Are Gone' are just a few examples: works of art all, in just a few words. But I keep thinking of that George Jones recording that The Driftwoods covered.

"Just because I asked a friend about her
Just because I spoke her name somewhere
Just because I saw her then went all to pieces
She thinks I still care..."

The thing is, Bob, that we do. We still care. A lot.

CHAPTER FORTY-ONE

MY TOP 20 FAVOURITE LIVE ACTS

This story isn't all about live music. But it hinges on it. What is it that happens when an artist, or a band, steps out on stage in front of an audience? How has this ritual captured the imagination of so many people, all across the world, that it has become a kind of sacred action in itself? I might have done something different with my life. Instead, I have devoted the past 50-odd years to making that connection between artists and their potential audience. I have worked with great people. Been in strange and sometimes uncomfortable and even scary situations. But it obsessed me at the outset and it still does. Something mysterious happens in that interaction between the singers, the musicians, the artists – and the people that are listening. But it is hard to pin down what that mysterious something is, because it is different – or feels different anyway – depending on the artist. Van Morrison and Buzzcocks are worlds apart. As are Maria Callas and Joni Mitchell. In order to try to understand all of this, just a little bit better, I decided to type up a first draft of a list of my personal favourite Top 20 live acts, in order of preference. Big mistake. I was okay with it to start... but then as I began to read down the list, I'd remember some of the amazing shows by other acts – mostly but not always already on the list – and I'd have to revise my sequence accordingly. So, in the end, I thought: there has to be a compromise here and – like any good agent or promoter – I decided to go and look for it.

A Taste of Musical Greatness

Ah, the memories come flooding back. I was home for Christmas from London, one year. So too were Taste. They'd always treat us to a few shows around the North of Ireland and so – along with a couple of mates – I scooted up to Portrush to witness Rory (Gallagher), Wilsie (John Wilson) and Charlie (McCracken) playing at Kelly's up at the Port. It was their third gig of the night – in fact, as they took to the stage at 2am., it was technically tomorrow already. A Taste gig was a powerfully physical experience – but it was just after 4am when they finished their set. The three heroic musicians and their audience were equally drained. Was it bedtime yet? Not for me and my mates. We still felt high from the sheer electric energy and the superb, intricate musicianship of the band. As they headed off to get a few hours' kip somewhere, en-route to another three-show night, my mates and I slipped down to the East Strand and, perfectly exhausted, we walked the beach (I do believe we were about two foot above the sand) until the morning broke and we could head to Morelli's in Portstewart for a hearty Ulster Fry.

If I Were The Carpenters…

The London Palladium is one of the most beautiful venues in the world in which to experience music. The Carpenters were doing two shows there, on the final night of their world tour, on 27 November 1976. I had a ticket for the second show and so went to grab a pre-show bite at the wee café a few yards from the Palladium's stage door on Great Marlborough Street. Right between The Palladium stage door and the café was a newsstand which opened out in a major display-a-rama. This newsagent was very popular with music business types in the area, because he went out of his way to collect an early delivery of the weekly music papers. A bunch of us would form a disorderly queue waiting for these oracles to arrive. You'd have record company staff checking to see if they needed to enlarge or reduce the initial pressings of the various artists' new albums; publicists waiting to discover if they were going to be okay with that week's invoice. You'd also have agents checking the reviews and using the advance scoop to work out the fees they would be seeking for their acts over the next seven days. Then there would be managers keen to steal a first peek at their artist's reviews and to have their excuses worked out.

The Carpenters show that night in the Palladium was destined for nothing but five star reviews. I couldn't believe what a powerhouse Karen Carpenter was as a drummer. She was also one of the most amazing singers I've ever witnessed live. She was so utterly poignant and soulful – that really is the right word – on stage, I was convinced she was going to drag my heart up through my throat. Surely The Carpenters should be my No.1. It was a thought that crossed my mind.

Tom Waits: A Statement of InTent

I have probably said enough elsewhere in this book about Tom Waits that there is no need to repeat myself here. No debate, nor discussion, needed: Tom is among the greatest live performers of all time. And I've seen him in powerful close–up as well as from the back of the venue. Over the years, as you might imagine, I developed a list of favourite places to see artists that I am lucky enough to work with. I think of Belfast and Glasgow in the one breath – they can have both the cruellest and kindest audiences. Then there's Dublin, Paris, Oslo, Amsterdam, Liverpool, The Stables Wavendon, Manchester, Birmingham, Edinburgh and Berlin – amongst others, I guess. I've seen the incomparable Tom Waits in a few of these places – and every time, he has been brilliant. But for me, personally, that Phoenix Park gig we engineered with Peter Ailen, in the Cork Marquee tent, was an extraordinary musical and personal highlight. I don't think it'd be possible to see the likes of it again. Until the next time Tom plays, that is...

A Mona Lisa Ekdahl Smile

Lisa Ekdahl is a Swedish singer who was being managed by my friend, Fraser Kennedy. In 1999, she came to London, to do a week at Ronnie Scott's and FK invited me down. It was a brilliant night and the venue was packed with adoring fans. Lisa duly signed with Asgard – and she and her producer, guitarist, musical-director and partner Mathias Blomdahl have been an absolute joy to work with ever since. She was already very popular in Sweden, Norway, Denmark, France, Holland, Belgium and Turkey when we took her on, and was achieving either Platinum or Gold album sales in all those territories. I went to see Lisa and her band at The

Circus in Stockholm, at a gig promoted by Thomas Johansson and Jan Gille of EMA Telstar (the company may have changed its name but they will always be EMA Telstar for me). As it happens, Thomas was one of the very first European promoters I worked with. He booked Fruupp for a show in Stockholm in 1976, en route to a trek around Finland that lasted weeks. I think we should have had, "Have Band, Will Travel (Need Wages)" printed on our business cards. Since then, Thomas and his team have always taken care of business for me and the artists I represent: he remains the go-to promoter for all the big concerts in Sweden. It was great, that night, to see Lisa in their care, in front of her home crowd. The sound Lisa's band create is so gentle, breezy and melodic; and it's always wonderfully topped off by Lisa's soulful vocals. The reaction that night in Stockholm was completely off the charts. Of all the acts mentioned in *Adventures in Wonderland*, Lisa is the least well known in the UK or the US – well, maybe with the exception of the not-so-legendary Blues by Five.

But as a writer and performer, Lisa has few equals. To familiarise yourself with her work, *Give Me That Slow Knowing Smile* is the perfect starting point. Trust me. You'll have your own knowing smile at the end of it.

The Night Loudon Wainwright III Wanted To String Me Up
Loudon Wainwright III was selling out UK shows long before I met him. I booked him once via his then agent, March Artists, for my Irish University circuit and accompanied him on that tour. I'm very glad I did. He became my first proper client. As it turns out, he's both an exceptionally nice man and a powerful performer. Yes, he is funny, but he's also a hell of a singer. As a lyricist he is up there with the very best. On top of which he can, and often does, set his carefully crafted words to melodies in a way that'd draw tears from The Man Who Couldn't Cry – as he did with 'Five Years Old' and 'Motel Blues'.

While on the tour Loudon travels by himself – no band, no road crew, no hangers on – the end result being that he returns home after his tours with a lot more money in his pocket than most bands do. Loudon is such good company on the road that I would take off with him, just for the hell of it, whenever the opportunity presented itself. He was very popular on the folk festival circuit. At first I thought (in those pre-Amazon, MTV and

Netflix days) that the language barrier might impede his connection with audiences in Europe. This was never the case.

Loudon never worried about the billing. He'd go on whenever the festival wanted him to, and he'd do a set for as long as they needed. He would always steal the show. Audiences see someone like Loudon and they immediately clock that, not only is he great, funny, and a singer with very few peers, but they've never seen his like before. He's that original. I'd tend to go backstage to see him after he'd played. When we'd chewed the fat for a bit, he'd always go out for a wee dander around the festival site and he'd always, but always, return in the company of a beautiful woman. I don't think I'd ever met a man with so many friends, albeit mostly new friends. John Lee Hooker was the only musician who could compete with Loudon in the lodestone stakes.

I executive produced a few of Loudon's albums (*'I'm Alright* 1985; *More Love Songs* 1986; and *Therapy*, 1989) and the whole process was an absolute joy from start to finish.

In the early days at gigs, Loudon talked me through the art of replacing a broken string on his guitar. "Don't worry," he'd declare, 'it rarely happens, but if it happens, I'll hand the guitar to you, and you just do this and this, pick up the relevant string, they're all laid out for you from highest to lowest..." – he looked at my blank response – "okay from thinnest to thickest. I'll keep the audience occupied. You unwind your new string, do this and this, tighten up the string, not too tight, give it back to me and I'll fine tune it as I finish my chat with the audience and then head off into a song. Okay?"

"Sounds good to me," I bluffed.

"But don't worry it'll never happen," he offered.

But it did happen, in a rammed – as in, packed and boisterous – Theatre Royal, Glasgow.

I don't know what I was worried about. Poor Loudon was marooned out in the middle of the stage with 1,600 people, who he had just succeeded in building-up to a mighty peak, watching. But we got through it, more or less intact. The thing about Loudon Wainwright is that he doesn't play to a crowd of people. Like Christy Moore, he plays to a collection of individuals. Equally, when these artists talk, everyone in the audience feels like they are being communicated with on a personal level. So, it was never going to be a problem, that night in Glasgow. If I had realised this at the time I might have found it a bit easier to re-string his guitar. Anyhow, job done, I handed the guitar back to Loudon – and twenty minutes later he walked off stage seven foot tall and to a genuine standing ovation. Three encores later not a man, woman, nor child, had left the theatre. They were all clapping, stamping and shouting for more.

"What'll I do?" he asked me in a wee bit of a panic, as he walked off stage, "I've done everything?"

"What about 'Tubular Bells'?" I suggested, citing Mike Oldfield's 50-minute, new-age, instrumental opus.

Luckily for me Loudon has a great sense of humour and he went back on stage, laughing louder than I was and, to the sheer delight of the audience, performed 'Surfing Queen', a song about an extremely ungallant chap who used his ex-girlfriend's cadaver as a surfboard.

I've always thought that learning to re-string a guitar in theatrical darkness was the best trick I learned since I'd worked out how to remove the wrapper from a sweet, single-handedly, while said hand was still in my pocket – and hidden from the prying eyes of Wee Doyle, our maths teacher.

Upon This Rockpile I Will Build My Church... Maybe

Then there was the night Loudon Wainwright III and I drove – well, he drove, because I don't – up to Loughborough University to witness Rockpile in action. The very dapper Nick Lowe, in any of his magnificently multifarious outfits, was – and is – always a sight to behold. Dave Edmunds is no slouch himself on the boards. Put the two of them together with Terry Williams (drums) and Billy Bremner (guitar and vocals) and you've got a powerhouse to rule the world – and rule the world they would have done... if only there hadn't been a dissenter in the ranks. On that extraordinary night in Loughborough University, the future seemed to be a long way off and they were nothing short of perfection.

Mary Margaret O'Hara: Who Needs Easy Listening?

If an album review is favourably comparing the work under scrutiny to *Astral Weeks*, then I'm the sucker who will be at the head of the queue to buy a copy – even if it is with my cynical, "Oh yeah? Really?" hat on. One such album was *Miss America* (1988) by Mary Margaret O'Hara. In this particular instance, my doubt was washed away by the end of the first song, 'To Cry About'. The only similarity between *Miss America* and *Astral Weeks* is that both albums are unlike anything I had ever heard before – or since. The exquisiteness of the melodies would have been much more than enough, to make *Miss America* a classic album. But the sheer brilliance of her performance as a vocalist was something else altogether. By the time Mary Margaret reached the last song, 'You Will be Loved Again', I was convinced my life would never ever be the same. On that first play, I'd been completely floored by 'Year in Song', 'Body's In Trouble', 'Anew Day', 'When You Know Why You're Happy' and 'Help Me Lift You Up'. If anything, *Miss America* has got better and better over the intervening 34 years. Again, and perhaps this is something else it shares with *Astral Weeks*, the translucent *Miss America* is not an album you'd want to put on at a dinner party. I mean that in a good way. Who needs easy listening?

Within a couple of weeks of buying the album, I'd tracked MMO'H down in Canada and persuaded her that she should come over for a tour. She was excited at the idea. We put together a schedule to include shows at The Dominion in London (16/11/85) and The Olympia in Dublin, with about a dozen other shows along the way. The Dominion sold out. The feeling in advance was that it would be a very special night. It was – to the power of ten. It was extraordinary. Her live performance was out of this world. Mary Margaret says she feels like she keeps trying to jump out of her own skin, when she's performing. I think I know what she means. On the night, she willingly followed where the muse took her. Mary Margaret sang as though she was genuinely possessed by the music.

We hired a fine Donegal man by the name of Billy Robinson, one of the best sound engineers I've ever worked with, to do the tour. The result was that every single member of the 2,000-plus audience was able to totally join her in the experience. The reaction combined joy, shock, exhaustion, and being physically and spiritually moved. People were visibly in tears as they left the theatre.

The only slight downer of the entire tour was that the record company complained that they'd never get her on *Top of the Pops*. The really sad thing was they didn't realise how big a compliment they were paying her.

Mary Margaret didn't tour very often, mainly due to the fact that performing took so much out of her. I'd kept in touch with her and got excited when she told me that she had started work on the second album. The next time I phoned, she told me that she decided to pull the plug on the recording and put it on indefinite hold. I asked her why. She explained that everything she was writing she had written before; and everything she sang, she had sung before. She had no wish to do that. To this day, she only ever released one proper studio album; yes there was an EP and a soundtrack album, but *Miss America* is her only properly independent, full-length work. When you shoot for the stars, and you hit the bullseye first time, perhaps it's just too hard to do the same thing only differently. And when your own record company complains, after a life-changing performance, that they'll never be able to get you on *Top of the Pops*, who could blame you?

Thanks to the word-of-mouth grapevine and attention from artists like Morrissey and Cowboy Junkies, *Miss America* is now a certified classic cult album.

MMO'H continues to sing. The last time I saw her live was as a cast member of a production of Tom Waits' *The Black Rider* musical in the Barbican, London (2004). She was in fine voice.

I'm still convinced that someday, 'Anew Day' or 'You Will be Loved Again' (from *Miss America*) will be a big hit for someone. In the meantime, I am waiting, in the hope – slim as it might be – that she will release another album of original songs. If she does it could indeed be one for the ages.

Bob Dylan: Another Convert On The Never Ending Tour

After I moved to London in 1967 I went to see Bob Dylan every time he played London. The greatest memories probably come from the six-night run he did at Earls Court Arena (120,000 total capacity over the 6 shows) in June 1978. He then returned to the UK in July to play The Picnic, a one-off outdoor event at Blackbushe Aerodrome, Camberley (on the Surrey borders). It was the final stop on his European leg. For the Blackbushe show, he was joined onstage by special guests including Eric Clapton and Joan Armatrading. And what's the capacity of Blackbushe? Well, just pick any high number you can think of. I would guess that anywhere between 250,000 and 400,000 people were there to see Dylan.

I attended that show with my good friend Peter Clarke, owner of the revolutionary Supermick Lights. Supermick were revolutionary on two accounts. One, nothing, absolutely nothing, was a problem for them; and two, they never charged an arm and a leg, even when they could have got away with it. We drove up in his Land Rover and when we hit the nose-to-tail traffic, at least a few miles from the site, he said, "Wait 'til you see this." He put his hand under his seat, pulled out an orange lamp, connected it to the cigarette lighter, switched it on, checked that it was flashing properly, reached out through his open window and plonked it on the roof of the Land Rover. He then proceeded to drive on the hard shoulder, over the hedgerow, through small streams – everywhere really, apart from straight over the vehicles ahead of us, which were soon behind us. Almost immediately, we were on site, backstage and ready for some fun.

However good that gig was, my favourite ever Bob Dylan show was just a couple of years ago when I took Peter Van Hooke to see Dylan at the London Palladium, during his three-night run there in April 2017 – yet another stop on his Never Ending Tour. It was probably the smallest venue I'd seen him play, apart from the time he played Vicar Street, in Dublin. It was most certainly the prettiest place I witnessed Dylan perform, and he was in amazing, mesmerising form. I know this is impressionistic stuff, but it seemed to me that, on the night, the sound was perfect, the lights were perfect, the band was perfect – and I'd never heard the maestro sing so beautifully. The material was mixed, drawing on some of his own classics and a proper sprinkling of the standards he'd recently been recording, including a few from Frank Sinatra, plus other evergreen material like 'All Or Nothing at All', 'Autumn Leaves', 'That Old Black Magic', 'Stormy Weather' and then – to end the night – a version of 'Ballad of a Thin Man', which blew the cobwebs out of everyone's brains. Peter, unbelievably, had never seen Dylan before. He couldn't believe how wonderful the show had been. As a committed Dylan fan, neither could I.

Hats Off To The Blue Nile

The Blue Nile were one of those groups I kept hearing about, or reading about. People I knew swore by them and their legendary first album *A Walk Across The Rooftops*, was a must for all hi-fi enthusiasts – like Peter Van Hooke and another mate of the both of ours, Mark Isham. In the summer of 1990, we were together in Bearsville Studios, up in Woodstock, recording Tanita Tikaram's third album, *Everybody's Angel*. The Blue Nile were booked into the studio next to ours rehearsing for a forthcoming American tour. Peter and Mark were highly enthused about the close proximity of their musical heroes and immediately scuttled off to make contact. They returned forty minutes later with Paul Buchanan in tow to introduce him to Tanita and myself and the rest of our gang – Rod Argent, (keys and co-producer), David Hayes (bass), Richie Buckley (saxes), Mark Creswell (guitars), Helen O'Hara (violin) and, of course, Tanita herself. The Blue Nile and the TT party got on like they were one big happy family. The Blue Nile seemed to be impressed by Rod and Pete's approach to recording. In the Tanita sessions, we'd record a backing track in the morning, Tanita would then add a master vocal as Helen, Mark and Richie, retired to another room to work out a brass and violin arrangement, very much in the mode of the famous Irish showbands' joyous, signature sound as made internationally famous on Van Morrison's wonderful, *His Band & The Street Choir*. You don't believe me? Listen to it! And this was Tanita's unashamed homage to Van Morrison's album.

We'd break for lunch, come back in the afternoon and add Helen, Mark Isham and Richie's finely sculpted arrangements, and maybe polish off the track with Mark Creswell overdubbing a guitar solo or two. Then we'd be ready to start the next track by teatime, before heading off into the historic Woodstock (still very musician-friendly and with wonderful arts and crafts items on tap and a barber who had a photo on the wall proclaiming he'd cut the hair of one Van Morrison). We'd all return every night to see Richie Buckley watching Spinal Tap for the third time that evening and laughing even louder. He knew it backwards, remembered what the next line was going to be and still laughed as heartily as if it was the first time he'd seen it.

The Blue Nile, on the other hand, would start off at the crack of dawn with their synthesiser boffin, Paul (PJ) Moore, labouring over a problem concerning how to trigger something or other from his keyboard. They booked six weeks in the residential studio to prepare for the tour and PJ always needed more time.

However, when they eventually started up and played together as a band – and Paul Buchanan joined in on vocals – they created an utterly majestic sound. You could hear why everyone from Peter and Mark, to Peter Gabriel (without Genesis), Sting, Annie Lennox and Rickie Lee Jones were totally in love with their sound.

The Blue Nile said goodbye – they were off on their American tour – but in Paul Buchanan I felt I'd made a friend for life. Several months later they were in London to play the Dominion Theatre and Peter Van Hooke and I went along to see them as fans. I just wasn't, in any shape or form, prepared for how brilliant they were. Think of the best gig you've been to and double that. And multiply by five. That was the impact they had on me that night. Not since Frank Sinatra had I heard such a gifted singer. But there was a different dimension to it too:

Something that we struggle to define but which the word 'spiritual' goes closest to capturing.

A few years later, they were rehearsing in Dublin. I went along to meet them, we got chatting and they signed with Asgard . We've been their agents ever since.

It wasn't unusual for The Blue Nile to take several years to finish an album. Paul and PJ, along with fellow bandmate Robert Bell, have released just four albums: *A Walk Across The Rooftops* (1984) *Hats* (1989), *Peace at Last* (1996) and *High* (2004). But what a quartet of masterpieces they are. All four albums have enjoyed reviews to die for. The other startling fact is that although the four albums were released in different eras of the music business, they have all sold within a few hundred copies of each other. They all went Gold in the UK (100,000), yet their totals are as close as the four Beatles' houses were in the *Help* film.

The Blue Nile are not in the business to become rich and famous. They are in this business because they want, they *need*, to make music. My only worry about The Blue Nile is they are just so brilliant and get reviewed as such, that they just might scare some people away. If you want to get to know their music, I reckon *Peace At Last* is as good a starting point as any, beginning as it does with the joy and beauty of the marvellous opening song, 'Happiness'.

The Waterboys: Blue Is The Colour

It was around 1989 when I started to work with The Waterboys as agent and promoter. There was a break along the way, and we started working with them again in 2003. They are one of the most in-demand bands on the festival circuit. Every festival wants to book them. The Waterboys – currently Mike Scott, Brother Paul Brown, Ralph Salmins, Aongus Ralston, Zeenie Summers, Jess Kavanagh and, he who fiddles, Steve Wickham – are a fun troupe on the road. They're like a modern day Inigo Jollifant and The Good Companions: they travel together and play together on and off stage. It's never too late or too early in the day for a session. They love nothing more than house lights down, stage lights up, hitting the boards and enjoying a couple of hours of music, fun and joy with their favourite people... their fans.

I know very few people who work as hard as Mike Scott. He always has an album, or at least a song, on the go. I get on really well with him. He's a bit like Van in that everything is always perfectly clear. There's never any smoke and mirrors. My kind of person. I enjoy working with him. He's the quickest responder to emails in the music business (Ry Cooder is a very close second). A few years ago I had a breakfast meeting with Mike Scott in the West End. He's based his Waterboys' operation and studio in Dublin for a good few years now. He had been in London for a few days to interview a few prospective managers. We were discussing how the new manager meetings had gone and he shook his head in the negative. He explained he hadn't met anyone suitable and continued. "You know us," he said to me, "we know you. You've been one of our main advisors for a good few years now – would you ever consider being our manager?"

Mike had been sending me demos of amazing new material he'd been working on. I thought about it: (a) he'd a lot of material; (b) it was all top quality; (c) I loved the band, and (d) I loved working with Mike. So, before my scrambled eggs had time to cool I said, "Yes!" At that point, the priorities were: making the album; finding an American manager; and securing a new record deal.

Mike has a pool of people, who he canvases for opinions on different topics. Early on in the new album cycle, he sent me a work in progress recording of a new song, 'Out of All This Blue'. Thematically it was potentially an important song, around which the core of this new album might be formed. We chatted about it and he did a bit more work on the recording. A little bit later, out of all this blue you might say, a new version of the song popped up in my inbox. It seemed like a winner to me – and the icing on the cake was a stunning, soulful George Harrison-influenced guitar solo.

We had a powerful song for the album. Or did we?

There was a problem. Mike had recorded the song on his home equipment and so he had to bounce down the tracks to free up some room for additional recording. He decided to re-write the lyrics of one of the verses. This meant of course he would have to re-record the entire track. Which in turn meant the perfect version I had was unusable. Mike recorded another version, but it didn't have the same elusive magic, and so Mike decided he would leave the song to a future album. In the meantime, we agreed to use the song title as the name of the new album. He had so much material that he wanted it to be a double album.

I suggested taking a leaf out of Tom Waits' book and releasing it as two separate albums on the same day. Mike preferred the feel of a double album. Mike always finances his own albums, so that both he and the record company know what they are getting. I really liked the new team that Alistair Norbury – formerly manager of Bryan Ferry – had put together at BMG and so I approached them and we did a deal. I suggested Danny Goldberg as US manager. Mike met him and they got on well. But in the end – with a record deal already done – Danny didn't see how he fitted into the picture. We decided to press ahead anyway.

By the time the album – titled, as agreed, *Out of All This Blue* – was released, the powers that be had decided that BBC Radio 2 should become the new BBC Radio 1. The effect of this was that the majority of previous Radio 2-friendly acts – the artists who had made Radio 2 so successful – were no longer likely to make the station's playlists. Which, in turn, meant that one of the key platforms for The Waterboys' music was effectively closed off. *Out of All This Blue* was released in 2017 and reached No. 8 in the UK charts and No. 2 in Ireland – on both counts, The Waterboys' highest chart position for 25 years. The record sold well and they packed venues throughout their tour. They were an extraordinary phenomenon live and still are.

But I had then – and still have now – a sense that maybe, just maybe, the original recording Mike sent me of 'Out Of All This Blue' was one of those great rock 'n' roll 'ones that got away'. It could have been a huge hit. However, as always, it was the artist's prerogative to decide whether to release it or not. Mike wasn't happy with it and didn't want it released. So be it.

I had enjoyed managing The Waterboys for what was a relatively brief period. When we finished the *Out of All This Blue* album and touring cycle, I called Mike. I told him that, for his next move, he really needed to find a dedicated 24/7 manager, not someone like me, who was also working on at least 20 other tours at any given moment. I advised him that now would be a good time to contact Danny Goldberg again and to bring him in at the start of the new project. Danny took up the reins as manager of The Waterboys – and I'm back doing what I love doing best... being their agent.

Ry Cooder and The Chicken Skin Band

The first time I walked into the National Stadium on South Circular Road in Dublin, I immediately thought: "Oh my, oh my, how could artists be invited to play this dive?" The fact that its primary purpose was as a boxing arena heightened the sense of dread. When, several years later, I booked Ry Cooder to appear there I was still nervous about potentially calamitous first impressions..

I decided to play it safe and headed down to the venue early on showday to distract my man from the National Stadium's less than palatial surroundings. I wandered backstage mid-afternoon as Ry was restringing his guitar. As you know I've had some previous on this subject. It offered a handy conversation point, to distract him from the blood that was still clearly visible in the dressing rooms. In the end I had to face up to it. I explained to him that a boxing tournament had taken place the previous night and that this – rather than a fight between an artist and a promoter over the crowd or the money – was the source of the blood-stains that seemed to litter the place. He was easy to chat with. He wanted to know all about Ireland, Irish music, Irish history; oh, and had he really sold out such a large venue – the capacity was 2080, which was the equivalent of 20,800 in London or New York – in advance? He'd never had a hit single or a hit album, wasn't on telly worth talking about, or on radio. But it was true: he had sold out the venue. I explained to him that Dublin was a great music town. If an artist was *really* good, the Irish audience wanted to check him or her out. But he needed details. I explained that the Irish audience would have been aware of his work with Taj Mahal in The Rising Sons. That the Sound Cellar and The Tape Shop, run by the effervescent Liz Gernon, had loyal customers, who were hungry for good music, particularly live. That Dublin had been fly-postered. That we would advertise in *Hot Press* magazine and *The Evening Herald*. That for special concerts, people would organise buses from Cork, Galway and Belfast.

Like most of the artists I've worked with, he wanted to know what Van Morrison was really like. He must have believed me because when, a few years later, I extended an invitation, from Van to him, to play on Van's *Into The Music* album, and Ry showed up at the Record Plant in Sausalito (SFO) to play slide guitar on 'Full Force Gale', which became the second single from the album. Anyway, we were rabbiting away – me and Ry – ten to the dozen when sound-check time arrived. The sound in the Stadium was really good when the audience was in the venue creating a natural amphitheatre around the stage. You got enough of a feel for that when it was empty for Ry to grunt his approval. Soundcheck over, it was time for catering and then, before I knew it, show time had arrived. Whew! I'd successfully managed to divert the artist's attention away from the state of the venue.

When the audience was in and seated, you could have cut clean through the air of anticipation with a knife. Ry Cooder didn't disappoint. He was totally sublime that first night in the National Stadium. The more love the audience showed him, the more he openly displayed his love in return.

Ry made at least three visits to Dublin. The demand was such that we had to do double nights, and they sold out easily. But at the gig in 1977 with his Chicken Skin Review – an incredible big band with Flaco Jimenez (Dylan, The Rolling Stones) on the accordion – they played a blinding version of 'The Dark End of The Street' and the audience just erupted, giving him a totally spontaneous, genuine mid-set standing ovation. The audience just wouldn't stop clapping. The more they clapped, the more they were caught up in the drama, knowing they had just witnessed a very special moment – which, of course, spurred them on to even greater applause. Eventually, the clapping subsided, but the audience remained on their feet. It was quite extraordinary.

"Yeah, that was good tonight, wasn't it?" Ry admitted proudly to the audience afterwards.

Ry wasn't bragging or blowing his own trumpet. He was merely confirming what the audience had felt and expressed en masse. And the fact that he had chosen to acknowledge it, was very moving and infectious. It was *ALL* about the magic of the music being produced on the stage. I've never forgotten that wonderful moment.

Christy Moore Is The Real Deal

Christy Moore was brilliant when I first met him... and he's got better every year since. Every concert he does is a truly precious, joyous experience: a very organic, living thing. His approach is similar to the jazz greats in that he never does a repeat performance. In fact, when he starts the gig, he doesn't know where it's going to go. And so, he'll occasionally ask the audience to forgive him if he doesn't chat for a few songs, until he sees where he is heading with the concert. Audiences are cool with that. Christy has given them every reason to trust him, and they do. His fans have taken him to their hearts forever, because he is the real deal. You'd be surprised how seldom you can say that with absolute conviction...

Leonard Cohen and The Secrets of the Universe

Rather than see one of Catherine and my favourite artists perform in an arena, we caught a train up to Manchester to see and hear Leonard Cohen perform at the more intimate Opera House. I'm always happy to attend concerts wherever artists choose to perform, but I do have preferences. The Manchester Opera House. The Palace Theatre in the same city,. The Palladium and The Royal Albert Hall in London; the Olympia in either

Paris or Dublin; Carre Theatre in Amsterdam; Queen Elizabeth Hall in Antwerp; Circus in Stockholm; Liverpool Philharmonic Hall; Concert House in Oslo and either Barrowland or The Royal Concert Hall in Glasgow – Christy Moore can make both those venues in Glasgow feel like he's performing to you personally in his front living room. There's more of course, but these days I also prefer train over plane travel, and so I find myself selecting Glasgow, Amsterdam, Paris, Brussels or Antwerp for my tour visits.

Leonard Cohen was on his enforced comeback tour, due entirely to the fact that, while he was taking a sabbatical in a monastery, his funds had been misappropriated by one of his former associates. Sadly this practice is not as rare as we would like it to be in the music business. So, Mr Cohen took to the road again, much to the delight of his many legions of fans. Sometimes in life, good things happen as a result of bad deeds. Leonard was one of those artists, who I didn't represent, but who I would always be delighted to see live. I had met Mr Cohen once. He was an early supporter of Tanita Tikaram. Tanita was also a *massive*, as they say in Donegal, Leonard Cohen fan, helped greatly by the fact that one of her favourite vocalists, Jennifer Warnes, was a semi-permanent member of his touring and recording band. In my experience artists work with three different types of musicians: (1) permanent band members; (2) semi-permanent band members – an arrangement that is usually dependent on their availability due to other commitments or projects; and (3) band members who become ex-band members. On her first tour of North America and Canada, Tanita was scheduled to play Montreal. Leonard's people had been in touch with Tanita's people (as in me, her manager) and it had been loosely arranged for them to meet up at the hotel. When the extremely debonair Mr Cohen arrived at the hotel, however, Ms. Tikaram was nowhere to be found. I met Leonard in the lobby to explain in essence that Tanita was not in the building. He was charming, understanding, very funny and had a voice one could imagine Joseph of Nazareth might have used to encourage his first born. Mr Cohen wrote a wee note to Tanita, which he placed in an envelope as he continued talking to me. He smiled again, handed the note over, shook my hand and walked out into the sunny Montreal air looking a million dollars. Secretly I think Tanita was petrified of meeting her hero and chickened out. It can happen. I've already described how excited I was to meet Van Morrison. I'd immersed myself in his music, particularly *Astral Weeks*, for about 15 years before I promoted my first tour with him. You might recall that I was in my office one day when the receptionist buzzed through and said, "There's a man out here who says he's Van Morrison." I walked through to the reception and this genuine musical genius, master of words, walked up to me, stuck out his hand and said, "Hi, I'm Van Morrison." And I could not get a word out of my mouth. I was totally dumbstruck. Van, it turned out, was the forgiving type and I recovered enough to start what turned out to be a very productive relationship.Leonard Cohen wasn't the only artist Tanita "didn't meet." She'd been invited out to dinner by Madonna via "her" people (who were actually also Tanita's people, in that they shared publicists, Donna Russo and Liz Rosenberg, in the Warner's NYC press office). The problem was the Madonna invite was for the same evening I was going to see Tom Waits in a theatre piece in NYC and thence to meet up with Tom and Kathleen afterwards. Tanita took a raincheck on the Madonna dinner for the opportunity to see and meet Tom Waits. Madonna was totally cool about it, reportedly saying that if she'd been given the choice of herself or Tom Waits, she too would have voted for Mr Waits. Tanita got these invitations because there was some element of mystery about her. I remember Tanita and I went to the Music Machine (now called Koko) in Camden Town to see and hear Prince doing one of his famous after-show shows. The image of Prince chasing Tanita all around the venue in the early hours of the morning keeps recurring in my subconscious at the strangest moments.

Manchester Opera House was buzzing for Leonard. This performance was, by far, the best I'd ever seen or heard him do. His voice was honestly beautiful. He, unselfishly, performed absolutely every single song the audience wanted to hear, and more. His band, understated but brilliant, was sublime. You could – and I did – hear the proverbial pin drop. They were all dapper like their leader, and decked out in Fedoras, which were about to enjoy their highest profile since the Sinatra days. They whispered rather than played. And you sensed that you were being let quietly into the secrets of the universe. That was the way the great Leonard Cohen made you feel.

Frank Sinatra: A Genius With A Mic

My mother's influences started to filter through to me properly, after I'd totally digested the 1960s pop groups. I knew this when I suddenly found myself really enjoying the work of Frank Sinatra: his choice of songs, his arrangements and, more than anything else, that golden voice. There had been a moment when I resented his 1966 No.1 hit, 'Strangers In The Night', because it was blocking some of my personal favourites – The Beatles, The Kinks, The Small Faces, The Spencer Davies Group, Them – off the top of the British charts. But then I got sense.

The first time I witnessed Sinatra live was in the Royal Festival Hall on the Southbank, during his 6 night run in 1980. It was an unbelievable evening of music. He would always credit the songwriter and the arranger (quite a few of his finest works were arranged by Nelson Riddle). Or he'd say, "Here's a song I originally recorded with the Count Basie Orchestra." Can you imagine what those recording sessions must have been like – Frank Sinatra singing live with the Count Basie Orchestra? I remember his version of George Harrison's 'Something'. Mr Sinatra clearly had reimagined the Beatles guitar-player's soulful lyric (about his then-wife Pattie Boyd) into an episode in the crooner's own life. So convincing was he that you really felt for him personally, as he recounted the pain of a lost love, who was "like no other." It was method-singing of a kind that few other artists are capable of: he made you believe that he was in danger of having a breakdown during his performance. Sinatra sang like a talker, in that when you talk, you never – well rarely – say the same thing, in exactly the same way. The phrasing, the emphasis, the breathing will be different every time. So when Frank Sinatra is onstage and singing to you, it is like a personal confession.

Listening to the Chairman of the Board, I always got a panicky feeling that he was never going to be able to fit all of the lyrics into whatever remained of the bars available. Yet, with a verbal dexterity that was magical and the ability to manage even the greatest tongue twisters, he always did it. It never sounded rushed – and it never sounded anything but totally believable. That was Frank Sinatra. A genius with a mic in his hand, he died on May 14, 1998.

Genesis with Peter Gabriel

The first gig I ever promoted in the UK was on Friday, 1 Sept 1972 and featured Genesis (with Peter Gabriel) with special guests Fruupp, at Wimbledon Town Hall, in London. Genesis (with Peter Gabriel) were paid £400. One or two roadies hammered nails into the pristine stage to keep Phil Collins' drum kit from moving about all over the place. The council billed me for the repair work, but I was okay with that. Genesis packed the venue and there was enough left over to put a few extra tins of baked beans on our shopping list that week. I happily paid for the stage repair.

I'd always known the venue as Wimbledon Town Hall but my contract with the council stipulated that we refer to it in announcements and advertisements as Merton Civic Hall. Loads of people were reportedly asking the local On-Duty bobby for directions.

"Where the hell is Merton Civic Hall?"

"Ah, you mean the Genesis gig – it's over there in Wimbledon Town Hall," he repeated with the patience of a Saint.

Genesis were incredible. A unique band, they were way ahead of their time, with their multi-faceted live show, splendidly enriched by all that beautiful, melodic, symphonic sound and with Peter Gabriel's marvellous voice taking the whole thing to new heights. He could sing anything, including the telephone directory (ask your parents) and still give you the shivers.

Even then, Peter was considered a wee bit out there, left-field. As a cult band – before they had any recording success – Genesis were packing out all the venues on their circuit. They built their fan-base the old way. Their shows were phenomenal, creating a different level of obsession and devotion among fans. They also benefited immensely from the stellar PR work of Glen Colson. The net result was that, when they did release a record, it was treasured in a very special way. There were ins and outs in personnel and they became more adventurous musically; and when they performed 'The Return of the Giant Hogweed' or 'The Musical Box' (both from their third album *Nursery Cryme*, 1971) the audience would positively glow with pure joy. The following album *Foxtrot* (1972) contained a 23-minute piece called 'Supper's Ready': they were ready for world domination. I know that it is an absurd thought, but I sometimes try to imagine the work that original band would have come up with, if only they'd stayed together. What I will say is this: I've already admitted that I can't dance, but I'd most certainly give it another go if the original line-up ever got back together again.

Not that I'd expect my results on the dance floor to be any better...

****

So here, then, is one agent's all-time Favourite Top 20 Live Performers. I happen to have worked with a lot of them. Mostly, that's because I already loved them and then set about making something magic happen. Others I just loved. I toyed with putting them in alphabetical order here. The fact that this favours A's didn't sit right with me. Then I came up with reversed alphabetical, if only so the W's didn't seem to be pushed to the bottom, the way they normally are. I even tried mirror-imaged, reverse alphabetical. It's okay, don't worry. That, I realised, was a step too far.

So, finally, I threw the names up in the air, and this is how they landed. Honest it is...

TOP 20 FAVOURITE LIVE ACTS
1= The Waterboys
1= Tom Waits
1= Loudon Wainwright III
1= The Undertones
1= Taste
1= Frank Sinatra
1= The Roches
1= John Prine
1= Mary Margaret O'Hara
1= Van Morrison
1= Christy Moore
1= Nick Lowe
1= The Kinks / Ray Davies
1= Hothouse Flowers

1= Nanci Griffith & The Blue Moon Orchestra
1= Genesis (with Peter Gabriel)
1= Lisa Ekdahl
1= Bob Dylan
1= Dire Straits/ Mark Knopfler
1= Neil Diamond
1= Crosby Stills & Nash
1= Ry Cooder and The Chicken Skin Band
1= Leonard Cohen
1= The Carpenters
1= Paul Carrack
1= The Blue Nile

CHAPTER FORTY-TWO

KNIGHTS, I'VE KNOWN A FEW, BUT THEN AGAIN, TOO FEW TO MENTION

In the olden days, not the good old days, 'cause they're good and gone, and some of them weren't really all that good at all, the best way to do business, as a teenage manager of the Blues by Five, was to do it face to face. Doing it by phone was okay, if you'd enough coins not to embarrass yourself. By letter was also okay but very slow. Face to face, it was certainly harder for someone to say no when you were eyeballing them.

On the Northern Ireland scene at the time, most of the great clubs were in Belfast. The Belfast scene was very hard to break into, particularly if you were an act from out in the sticks. At the time, that meant anywhere outside of Belfast. Vinci, Terence, Miles and Ian were from Maghera, Paddy was from Castledawson and yours truly from Magherafelt: we were the sticks incarnate. And so, initially at least, bookings in Belfast were out of the question for Blues by Five. But in Derry/Londonderry there was a famous venue called the Embassy Ballroom, which was known to book groups as support acts to the showbands that graced the stage there several nights a week. The Embassy was even occasionally known to run exclusive beat-group nights. The team there seemed to have no hang-ups about booking an act from the country. So, armed with 10 x 8 promo photos, some colourful car-window stickers, and a few newspaper cuttings, I set out to hitch my way up to the fair city to doorstep the owner and manager, local businessman Mr Robert Ferris.

It was daytime when I arrived; it was the middle of a working week – and yet there was music coming from inside the ballroom. I banged hard. Then

I banged harder. It took a while before anyone answered.

"I've come to see Mr Robert Ferris," I offered, as what looked like a human being peered at me from behind a marginally opened door.

"He's busy at the moment," I was told.

"Can I wait for him?" I wondered. I'd come a long way and I wasn't going to be brushed off that easily.

I was advised they didn't know how long he'd be.

"I don't mind," I replied, remembering the advice I'd received from Eammon Regan, the extremely helpful manager of The Breakaways Showband: 'Always make sure you get your foot in the door'. Well, didn't I only go and manage to get my whole darned body in.

I was led through the dark lobby, into the red-shaded ballroom and introduced to Mr Ferris himself. He was friendly and asked me to take a seat. He'd be with me as soon as he could.

It turned out that Mr Ferris was actually busy routine-ing two stunning Go-go dancers in micro-mini-skirts and brown leather boots. 'Go-go dancing' was very popular at the time, thanks to BBC's *Top of The Pops*. On that particular day, in the strange confines of the Embassy Ballroom, what impressed me was not so much the two beautiful young dancers and their slightly provocative routine, but the fact that they were dancing to 'Waterloo Sunset', one of the most stunningly beautiful singles ever released. I was already a big fan of The Kinks and was intrigued by the acoustic guitar Ray played on occasion on TV shows, which appeared, to me, to have the neck and machine heads of an electric guitar stuck onto the body of an acoustic.

I must have heard the wonderful 'Waterloo Sunset' a dozen times in a row, before Mr Ferris was satisfied with the girls' routine and came over to me. He'd heard of the Blues by Five and yes, diaries drawn, he booked them on the spot, gave me a couple nights as a support act and also confirmed an appearance on one of their group nights. We'd been warned that we needed to be careful when we played the Embassy, because the local lads used to discourage out-of-town groups from venturing so far northwest, by cutting their speaker-cabinet leads with razor blades. Allegedly. But that was for another day. I hitched a lift home feeling 10 foot tall and with the words and music of 'Waterloo Sunset' permanently etched into my brain.

Sometime in 1993, a friend of mine, Fraser Kennedy, went along to meet Raymond Douglas Davies as a prospective manager. Fraser and Ray couldn't agree a deal, but, in the course of the conversation, Ray mentioned that he was also looking for a new agent for The Kinks. Fraser kindly recommended me and passed my number on to Ray.

Ray contacted me himself. We met at my house in Primrose Hill in London. I'm an ardent book collector and Ray was fascinated by the stack of new titles on my dining table. By the end of the meeting, he said he was up for moving to Asgard, but – before signing off on the deal – he wanted me to meet his "baby brother, Dave." I met Dave, a very funny man, the deal was concluded and I started work on my first tour with The Kinks. Thirty years on, I still represent Ray as his agent.

The very first time I saw The Kinks perform live was back in the heyday of punk in the late 1970s, at the legendary Bilzen Jazz and Pop Festival in Belgium. I was there with The Undertones and Elvis Costello & The Attractions. It was the year that the UK punk/new wave acts had started to get properly involved on the European Festival circuit and the entire UK contingent – including The Clash – piled into the muddy press-pit to catch the original punk, the Godlike genius that is Ray Davies. We witnessed an extraordinary, magisterial set of brilliant songs, delivered by The Kinks with the grace and power of a band who knew exactly what they were doing. As the hippies used to say, outside the rain was falling but inside the sun was shining. Ray Davies always wanted every member of the audience to have the best night of their lives. All I can say is that there wasn't one disappointed person on Bilzen's gloriously waterlogged site.

In 1994 when I signed the band, Ray had a new manager. But Ray is a hands-on type of artist, so my dealings are always directly with him.

After we put our first Kinks' tour on sale, the out-of-the-box ticket sales were incredibly strong. Yet within a few minutes of me sending Ray the report sheet, he was on the phone talking me through the sales. He went from top to bottom, commenting on the ones he felt needed attention. He mentioned a few regional journalists and DJs he knew that he'd get his office to set up interviews with. Ray has subsequently proven time and again to be a true professional in how he goes about his business. I don't believe that it's a coincidence that some of the most professional artists

I have worked with have all come from the 1960s scene. Artists like Ray, Van Morrison, Graham Nash, Lonnie Donegan, Ronnie Spector, Gilbert O'Sullivan, Peter Asher, Robert Plant, Marianne Faithful and Jean Michel Jarre all know that you don't sell tickets by accident. They know how the music business works.

As teenagers, on April 22nd 1960, Graham Nash and Allan Clark attended the Free Trade Hall in Manchester to see The Everly Brothers perform. Post-performance, they waited patiently outside the brothers' hotel, hoping to catch a few words with Don and Phil and to get their autographs. I bet you anything Graham Nash still has those autographs. The Everly Brothers also knew the ropes. They were very friendly to the two young Mancunian musicians – and years later The Everly Brothers actually covered several L. Ransford songs. L. Ransford was the pen name Graham Nash, Allan Clarke and Tony Hicks used for their songwriting adventures with their group, The Hollies. The circle was completed. The point being that it never does any harm in this business to be nice.

In early 1996, The Kinks took what we all thought was going to be a break. Over 25 years later, there's part of me that still thinks: maybe it is just a break. They played what may turn out to be their final gig as top of the bill at the legendary Norwegian Wood Festival in Oslo on 15 June 1996. I was there, not because I knew it was going to be their last gig. I was there because I loved seeing The Kinks live and Asgard also had Emmylou Harris, Ocean Colour Scene and Grant Lee Buffalo on the bill. The last song The Kinks performed that night was a rousing version of 'You Really Got Me'.

Ray goes solo, but not so low, you couldn't hear him
While The Kinks were figuring out what to do next, I suggested to Ray that he should try some solo shows. He was up for it. We booked a few, they went well; we booked a few more, they went even better. Ray, being Ray, started to develop his shows and came up with his Storyteller format, where he would play songs, read from his book X-Ray and tell revealing stories about life with The Kinks. This was way, way before VH1 started their Storyteller series, which I always took as being an homage to Ray.

He would tour with only an acoustic guitarist. The guitarist lived in Australia, which as you can imagine was a bit of a problem in relation to scheduling European shows. When Ray got more active under his own name, he asked me to find him a new guitarist. I immediately suggested Bill Shanley, a brilliant Irish guitarist. I'd first met Bill when I started to represent Mary Black. I suggested Bill to both Paul Brady and Gilbert O'Sullivan when they were looking for new guitarists and he fitted in perfectly with both bands. Bill is a very reliable man and a versatile guitarist, so I was confident he would work well with Ray. He became Ray's regular guitarist for the acoustic gigs and a member of Ray's soon to be formed new band. Ray's shows became very successful and we did highly acclaimed runs in London and one-nighters around the UK, Ireland, Europe, Australia, Japan and the USA. He was selling every venue out and enjoying the best reviews of his career.

On January 4 2004, Ray Davies was shot in the leg when he tried to protect his girlfriend from thieves in New Orleans. He rang me a few hours later from his hospital bed in New Orleans to tell me that he was fine and asking me to let his fans know he was okay and he would see them shortly. "Tell them I'll be back soon," he said.

Ray shares my enthusiasm for special projects. He was putting together the guest list for his *See My Friends* duets album, we talked through the songs and artists several times at our meeting place in Highgate. Ray prefers the face-to-face approach of my earlier Irish ballroom/showband days. I suggested he invite Jackson Browne to sing 'Waterloo Sunset' because I had heard Jackson do a stunningly beautiful version of the song on a tour bus once. Like the documentary on-bus recordings on Jackson's *Running On Empty* album, it was a performance so soulful and heartfelt it silenced everyone who was lucky enough to be on board the bus at the time. For me, the Ray Davies and Jackson Browne duet on *See My Friends* is a thing of rare beauty. In 2015, Ray and his band were again playing the Norwegian Wood festival in Oslo. Jackson Browne was appearing too, and Jackson joined Ray for a special for-one-night-only live version of 'Waterloo Sunset'.

Something beautiful started to happen around this time. With all his hard work, critically acclaimed solo records, and non-stop concert and festival work, Ray Davies became a phenomenally successful touring attraction in his own right, the equal of The Kinks in their pomp in terms of pulling power. He appeared on all the main European festivals and the Pyramid Stage at Glastonbury. He topped the bill twice at Hyde Park, once as part of the AEG British Summer Time series in 2013 and once at BBC Radio Two's completely sold out Proms in the Park show – estimated audience 90,000 – in 2017, where he was backed by The Jayhawks featuring, on lead guitar, Bill Shanley, and accompanied by The BBC Concert Orchestra and the Crouch End Festival Chorus. It was an amazing evening with the audience sometimes singing the songs back at the stage louder than the band, choir and orchestra combined. It was a fitting and emotional celebration of Ray's music and of his standing as a one of the most influential songwriters of the modern era..

Sir Ray Davies is one of those guys I was talking about at the beginning of *Adventures in Wonderland*. He found his badge to wear very early on and he has worn it with honour and dignity ever since. There are very few 100 carat, historically important songwriters out there. Ray has the gift and he knows it comes with certain obligations.

Ray Davies is great company. He has a mischievous sense of humour and is a great storyteller and a hilarious raconteur. He is also a very caring human.

He is the Guvnor. And, in this Wonderland that I have been part of for almost fifty years, I am truly lucky to have been able to work with him.

Did I ever, back home in Magherafelt, working with Blues By Five, have any inkling that I would one day be able to say something as marvellous and as mind-blowing as that?

Not a chance. But sometimes we can, indeed, exceed even our wildest dreams.

And finally, the last song...
The record shows I took the blows – and did it mum's way
After all of that I'm still thinking about Fruupp. They broke up without succeeding. But, by not succeeding – by not 'making it' – were they in fact a failure? It depends on the prism you're using.

In the early days, when the five of us – six and then seven as the road crew increased – were scooting around the UK and Ireland, and eventually Europe, it was exciting. Ninety per cent of the time it was great craic altogether. Sure, we didn't have multi-platinum discs (nor gold nor silver, nor even zinc ones for that matter). We never had a record in the charts. We never enjoyed sold-out concert tours of the UK and Ireland. But – and it's a big but – we did have our moments when it all gelled, in places like Aylesbury, Derby, Chelmsford, Southend, London, Belfast and Dublin. We were an on-the-breadline band, barely earning a living and chained to a never-ending series of one-night stands, to pay the weekly bills. We made four albums, achieving varying degrees of artistic success. In 2019, the good people at Esoteric Records released the four Fruupp albums, re-mastered in a box set under the title *Wise as Wisdom* (The Dawn Albums 1973-1975); and in 2020 they released *Maid in Ireland*, a re-mastered best of compilation, which sold very well by the standards of today's market, and scored the kind of reviews we would have been ecstatic about, back in the 1970s.

Did we all have our individual unfulfilled dreams? Of course we did. Fortunately, we were never preoccupied with them. There just wasn't time. But in the "never really made it" stakes we weren't alone. For every Genesis (with Peter Gabriel), there were hundreds of Fruupps; for every Yes there were hundreds of Enids; for every Taste, there were hundreds of Spirit of John Morgans; for every Pink Floyd there were hundreds of Quicksands; for every Peter Green's Fleetwood Mac there were hundreds of Vinegar Joes; and for every band who "made it" there were literally thousands of bands who didn't.

Most of those bands were still out gigging three and four nights a week. They were supported by loyal fans. In one way, they made a more real connection, in that the fans knew them as mates and could chat to them. At some point in their career they humped their own equipment; the blokes among them most certainly had enjoyed the company of what were then quaintly called 'groupies'; maybe the women too. They all lived the life. A lot of these on-the-breadline bands also made albums. They had their moments, on and off stage. They had their crazy on the road stories – like, maybe, losing the rear wheel of their transit van on the way back from the Madhatter Club in Maidstone.

Like Fruupp, the members of the other on-the-breadline bands had embarked on a great adventure. They were trying to write big songs, when getting to record one was a monumental milestone in itself. The trials and tribulations were many. They'd be trying not to get chucked out of their girlfriend's – or even their boyfriend's – flat before the first royalties cheque arrived. To ensure a prospective record company didn't discover one of the main members of the band was about to leave them in the lurch, before a deal could be finalised, and the advance paid. To earn enough money just to keep themselves fed. Having enough for pints would be a bonus.

In my case, without Fruupp, I wouldn't have hooked up with Paul Fenn at Asgard. By extension, if I had not met up with Paul, I would not have become the manager of (listed chronologically) Radio Stars, Paul Brady, Gerry Rafferty, Van Morrison, Dexys Midnight Runners, Tanita Tikaram, Ray Davies and The Waterboys.

I most certainly would not have been the agent for the 222 artists (from Blues by Five to Roy Harper, and still counting) I have had the pleasure (mostly) of representing over the years.

In truth, I have Fruupp to thank for all of that. Then again, if there had been no Blues by Five, there wouldn't have been a Fruupp. And, if we continue on that particular path, it takes us back to Goggles Anonymous. Indeed, if my mum hadn't been into Emile Ford and the Checkmates, Frank Sinatra and Tony Bennett, she would not have had her radio on listening out for their records, and I, in turn, wouldn't have enjoyed the light-bulb moment when I ran into our house and The Beatles were blasting out in magnificent style on the radio.

And so, all these adventures really started with my mum. As did everything. My mum is the character in 'Wise as Wisdom'. Mind you her wisdom was always a bit off the wall, as in, for example, "Wish in one hand and wee in the other and see which one fills first." I always loved her for each and every one of her sometimes bizarre pearls of wisdom. They've stayed with me always, and continue to bring a hint of a deeper truth to my door, while delivering a smile to my face.

Brigit Teresa Cora Charles: she was one of a kind.

"Say goodnight Paul.

"Good night."

And sweet dreams...

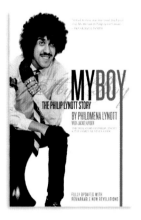